D1190412

THE RESEARCH INTERVIEW
Uses and Approaches

THE RESEARCH INTERVIEW

Uses and Approaches

Edited by

MICHAEL BRENNER
Department of Social Studies
Oxford Polytechnic
Headington, Oxford

JENNIFER BROWN
Department of Psychology
University of Surrey
Guildford, Surrey

DAVID CANTER
Department of Psychology
University of Surrey
Guildford, Surrey

1985

ACADEMIC PRESS
(Harcourt Brace Jovanovich, Publishers)
London Orlando San Diego New York
Toronto Montreal Sydney Tokyo

ACADEMIC PRESS INC. (LONDON) LTD.
24–28 Oval Road
LONDON NW1 7DX

United States Edition published by
ACADEMIC PRESS, INC.
Orlando, Florida 32887

BRITISH LIBRARY CATALOGUING IN PUBLICATION DATA
The Research interview : uses and approaches.
1. Research—-Methodology 2. Interviewing
I. Brenner, Michael II. Brown, Jennifer
III. Canter, David, Date-
001.4'222 Q180.M4

LIBRARY OF CONGRESS CATALOGING IN PUBLICATION DATA
Main entry under title:

The Research interview, use and approaches.

Includes bibliographies and index.
1. Psychology—Research—Methodology. 2. Social sciences—Research—Methodology. 3. Interviewing. 4. Interviewing in sociology. I. Brenner, Michael. II. Brown, Jennifer, Date III. Canter, David V.
BF76.5.R463 1985 300'.72 85-7453
ISBN 0-12-131580-0 (alk. paper)

PRINTED IN THE UNITED STATES OF AMERICA

85 86 87 88 9 8 7 6 5 4 3 2 1

The present book was developed with the inspiration and guidance of Michael Brenner. It was with great sadness that we learnt of his sudden death shortly after he had completed his contribution to the book. Michael was always a staunch advocate of the uses of the scientific interview, and in his numerous writings on the topic, he encouraged us and many others to see the values inherent in effective interviewing. His enthusiasm was first shared with us when he approached us to join him in the preparation of a symposium on the uses of the research interview. It was out of that symposium that the present volume grew.

His early death was a severe, untimely loss to the scientific community, and it took from us a valued and entertaining friend. This book is a token of our esteem for Michael Brenner and his work. We also owe a debt of gratitude to Marylin Brenner, who assisted us in the completion of the present volume during the time of her own great personal grief.

Contents

Contributors

Numbers in parentheses indicate the pages on which the authors' contributions begin.

LISANNE BAINBRIDGE (201), Department of Psychology, University College, London WC1E 6BT, England

MICHAEL BRENNER[1] (1, 9, 147), Department of Social Studies, Oxford Polytechnic, Headington, Oxford OX3 0BP, England

JENNIFER BROWN (1, 79, 217), Department of Psychology, University of Surrey, Guildford, Surrey GU2 5XH, England

DAVID CANTER (1, 79, 217), Department of Psychology, University of Surrey, Guildford, Surrey GU2 5XH, England

WIL DIJKSTRA (37), Vrije Universiteit, Subfaculteit der Sociaal-Culturele Wetenschappen, Afdeling Methoden en Technieken, 1075 BH Amsterdam, The Netherlands

LINDA GROAT (79), Department of Architecture, The School of Architecture and Urban Planning, The University of Wisconsin Milwaukee, Milwaukee, Wisconsin 53201

BARBARA MOSTYN (115), Applied Social Psychologist, London N.6, England

MICHAEL MULKAY (247), Department of Sociology, University of York, Heslington, York YO1 5DD, England

JONATHAN POTTER (247), Psychological Laboratory, University of St. Andrews, St. Andrews, Fife KY16 9JU, Scotland

STEPHEN K. TAGG (163), University of Strathclyde, Social Statistics Laboratory, Glasgow G1 1XQ, Scotland

T. D. WILSON (65), Department of Information Studies, University of Sheffield, Sheffield S10 2TN, England

LIENEKE VAN DER VEEN (37), Vrije Universiteit, Subfaculteit der Sociaal-Culturele Wetenschappen, Afdeling Methoden en Technieken, 1075 BH Amsterdam, The Netherlands

JOHANNES VAN DER ZOUWEN (37), Vrije Universiteit, Subfaculteit der Sociaal-Culturele Wetenschappen, Afdeling Methoden en Technieken, 1075 BH Amsterdam, The Netherlands

[1]Deceased.

Preface

The interview is one of the most widely used procedures in research, yet the changes and developments in its use over the past few years have not been widely reported. In the present book, David Canter, Professor of Applied Psychology at the University of Surrey, Jennifer Brown, a senior research fellow at the University of Surrey, and the late Michael Brenner, formerly of Oxford Polytechnic, bring together a variety of contributions dealing with many aspects of the uses of the interview in research. The structured interview, as well as more open-ended procedures, are considered, together with sorting procedures and life history analyses. Some especially innovative uses of the interview in understanding decision processes and activities in emergencies are also considered. In addition, procedures for analysing and interpreting interview data are described, such as content and thematic analyses. Problems of reliability and validity are variously discussed by the contributing authors.

The book will be of value to all people in the behavioural, social, and managerial sciences who wish to enrich their use of interviews in research.

1

Introduction

MICHAEL BRENNER
JENNIFER BROWN
DAVID CANTER

USING INTERVIEWS IN RESEARCH

Recent social science research has witnessed the development of the applications and techniques of interviewing. Many kinds of social science enquiry now use interviews as a method of serious data collection. These varied uses of research interviews have inspired the emergence of many new forms of interview, such as account-gathering, the self-confrontation interview, and open-ended multiple sorting procedures.

Parallel with the development of new kinds of research interview has been a growing awareness of the built-in limitations of interview methods. Much of this awareness stems from the study of the research interview as a social process of considerable complexity. There has thus been a coming together of the study of social interaction in interview settings and the development of uses of interviewing as a way of collecting data.

A third discernible trend is in the uses made of interview material. Through the development of procedures such as content analysis and multidimensional scaling techniques, it is now possible to produce systematic, quantitative summaries of responses that would not have been amenable to analysis in the past, when such data might have been dismissed as "too qualitative." These data can now form the basis of research activity.

This book covers all these trends by bringing together contributions describing a range of interview methodologies and analytic procedures. The subject matter, used as a vehicle to illustrate the uses of the research interview, also reflects the diversity of contexts in which the interview has been found to be of value. Industrial processes, clinical case histories, ac-

ISBN 0-12-131580-0

tion in emergencies, scientists' accounts of their activities—are all taken as examples by one contributor or another throughout the book. The areas of the social sciences from which the contributors are drawn show that interviewing is a truly interdisciplinary process.

OBJECTIVES FOR THE BOOK

The contributors' intentions are to broaden people's awareness of the ways in which interviewing procedures can be incorporated into many research strategies. In the past, the interview has been regarded as a useful adjunct to many social science procedures, but it is only in recent years that its value as a research tool in its own right has come to the fore. Until very recently, the interview has been seen as of possible value for pilot research or as a useful procedure in less systematic activities like therapy or job selection, but its integration into the researcher's tool kit, being given an equal status with other instruments, has been regarded with some scepticism.

One reason for most researchers' unwillingness to embrace the interview as a research procedure has been the doubts cast on it in the early part of the twentieth century because of biases and unreliability. With the upsurge in statistical refinements, most notable in the development of attitude scaling procedures by Thurston and Likert during the late 1920s and early 1930s, the more subtle and richer forms of interaction with respondents made possible by the research interview tended to be eschewed by academic researchers. The present book has the objectives of redressing this balance by illustrating the great variety of ways in which interviewing can play a full part in many research activities. It is, however, not meant to be a handbook, but rather an illustration of a range of possibilities so that others can learn from the examples and develop the important contributions the interview can make. We would like to present not so much a fully orchestrated symphony but rather draw out a number of themes upon which others can develop their own variations.

THE VALUE OF THE INTERVIEW

As long ago as 1942, Allport pointed out that if you wanted to know something about people's activities the best way of finding out was to ask them. Kelly (1955) reiterated this and greatly strengthened it through the development of Personal Construct Theory and Role Repertory Grids. Twenty years later, Harré and Secord (1972) made a similar point, emphasising the expertise and experience that is unique to the respondent in research and the viability of using the respondent's own accounts as scientific data. A decade later, this tradition has evolved to cover the examination of human actions and explanations of them, in all their richness (von Cranach and Harré, 1982). It is this willingness to treat individuals as the heros of their own drama, as valuable sources of particular information, which is at the base of the resurgence of interest in various interviewing procedures. For it is only when the researcher and the respondent have the possibility of communicating directly with each other that the subtleties of the mutual understanding between the two parties can be harnessed.

An interview, then, is taken as any interaction in which two or more people are brought into direct contact in order for at least one party to learn something from the other. The conversational mode this definition implies is open to many variations. Indeed, one of the difficulties of using the interview as a research procedure is that it is associated with journalistic and other forms of media interview that are usually set up in order to entertain rather than to obtain authentic, detailed accounts from an individual. Thus, for the interview procedure to be used in a research context, its particular qualities need to be identified and its weaknesses carefully stated so that they can be minimised.

Strengths of the Interview

Probably the central value of the interview as a research procedure is that it allows *both* parties to explore the meaning of the questions and answers involved. There is an implicit, or explicit sharing and/or negotiation of understanding in the interview situation which is not so central, and often not present, in other research procedures. Any misunderstandings on the part of the interviewer or the interviewee can be checked immediately in a way which is just not possible when questionnaires are being completed, or tests are being performed. Of course, many interviews are established in such a way that use is not made of this central advantage. In such cases interview material is often relegated to pilot work and not reported.

In addition to the value of the negotiation in the interview, there is the advantage that it gives rapid, immediate responses. It is no accident that public opinion surveys are built around interviews; interviews enable an on-the-spot directness to the information and a general speed of response not obtainable any other way.

Survey research based on the use of questionnaires, administered in face-to-face interviews, permits the collection of the most extensive data on each person questioned. Furthermore, all kinds of data may be collected—for example, health information, residential histories, political attitudes—within the same interview. Given that the researcher has confidence in her/his results through validity and reliability checks, then (s)he may generalise her/his findings to total populations beyond the sample surveyed.

Some Disadvantages

Surveys often depend on the employment of large numbers of interviewers. These need to be trained and supervised, to achieve a reasonably appropriate performance overall. Interviewer training, in turn, requires that the researcher invest considerable effort into the design of (1) the questionnaire suitable for use in interviewer–respondent interaction, (2) effective interviewing techniques, and (3) the totality of organizational issues in a data collection programme, as they apply to the interviewers. Although economical on time, survey interviewing can be a very costly means of collecting data: "the cost of assembling and training a field staff to do the interviewing are much greater than many people would anticipate" (Scott and Chanlett, 1973, p. 11).

Another disadvantage is that, because the contact between interviewer and respondent is face-to-face and may be intensive, there is ample opportunity for bias to occur (see Hyman et al., 1954). Clearly, there are limits to the use of surveys. For example, when respondents feel sensitive about topics raised in the interview, the answers, if provided at all, are likely to be invalid (see Phillips, 1973). Another example is memory decay, this leading to an underreporting of past events. Cannell et al. (1979), have shown, for the case of health reporting, that incidents of hospitalization are underreported. This could be demonstrated by comparing health records with the patients' answers. When the limits of survey research are recognized, it is necessary to select other research techniques, perhaps in simultaneous or sequential combination.

Other difficulties with verbal responses are the possible distortions in data transformation and/or the lack of conceptual or theoretical schemes to aid interpretation. In effective research the rationale for a particular model of data transformation is usually justified in terms of the nature of the research problem itself. Yet verbal data, by virtue of its quantity and varying degrees of structure, are particularly susceptable to error in interpretation.

ORGANISATION OF THE BOOK

An interview has three basic components: informants, interviewers, and information. The setting in which the interview takes place has dynamics of its own, as well as variations contributed by the three constituent parts, which influence reliability and validity of the information. Interviews vary on a great range of dimensions, such as

1. Scale (large or small number of informants).
2. Scope (general or focussed content areas).
3. Time (long or short interviews–retrospective, contemporary anticipatory information).
4. Interpretive schemes (univariate, multivariate statistical procedures/ content analysis).
5. Format (open or closed questions).

The book contains three types of chapters that reflect the degree of structure imposed on the interview situation. In the first three chapters, Brenner; Dijkstra, van der Veen, and van der Zowwen; and Wilson deal with the structured procedures and focus on the role of the interviewer with respect to question framing, interviewer style, and training. The next four chapters (Canter, Brown & Groat; Mostyn; Brenner; and Tagg), describe the open-ended procedures, and tend to focus on the role of the informants and on finding data collection procedures that facilitate public discussion of their personal experiences. The final three chapters, by Bainbridge; Potter and Mulkay; and Brown and Canter, examine the characteristics of some innovative information and interpretative schemes.

SOME RECURRING THEMES

The suggestion that each group of contributions has a particular emphasis does not mean that chapters do not address issues related to the other components of interviews. There are common threads running through all the chapters, with the authors proposing their own particular solutions to problems involved in using interviews as a research instrument. For example, as to the use of categories in forming, answering, and interpreting information, Wilson looks at the importance of categories in interview schedules; Canter, Brown, and Groat show how multiple sorting tasks can be used to elicit people's own implicit conceptual schemes, and Bainbridge uses categories as the basis for an analytic scheme for interpreting verbal reports.

A consistent theme reiterated by all the authors is the importance of clearly defined research goals and the choice of appropriate methods of data collection and analysis to suit the research question. The point is made several times that methods are sometimes chosen for the researcher's convenience rather than out of consideration for the informant or the quality of the information. This can be appropriate when the cost-effectiveness of data collection is being emphasised, but inappropriate when the respondent is sacrificed to the researcher's whims. Mostyn and Bainbridge both discuss the difficulties of handling verbal responses but remain optimistic that content analyses provide a firm and rich basis for understanding human experience. Brenner and Dijkstra et al. devote some discussion to outlining rules for interviewing, the importance of training interviewers, and the possible confounding effects of different interviewer styles.

All authors address the problems of reliability and validity and offer their own particular solutions. The most divergent views are illustrated by the first and last chapters. On the one hand, Brenner suggests, for quantitative survey interviewing, the adoption of a set of rules that govern the question–answer sequence. These rules enable the accomplishment of adequate answers within the framework of the designed questionnaire and maximize comparisons between informants.

Potter and Mulkay, on the other hand, suggest that it is not so much a reconstruction of consistent responses that they are after in their interviews with scientists, but rather the discovery of the variability of interpretative repertories used by their informants within any given interview situation. Whereas Brenner is trying to minimize inconsistency, Potter and Mulkay draw attention to the possibility of its importance as data in its own right.

The remaining authors occupy intermediate positions, providing particular techniques for establishing the reliability and validity of responses. These have to do variously with the roles of the interviewer, interviewee, and the eliciting situation. A conceptual framework within which these techniques may be applied is offered by Brown and Canter, who review a legal model for psychological enquiry, wherein psychological data may be treated like evidence presented in a court of law and subjected to corroborative checks.

Another theme reiterated throughout the book is the different methods for the analysis of interview data. Tagg discusses computer-based content and statistical analyses; other chapters provide detailed examples—Mostyn describes a method of descriptive content analysis, and Canter et al., methods of multidimensional scaling from the Guttman-Lingoes series of statistical programmes.

Analysis may reflect sequential components of behaviour or time perspective. Tagg discusses the use of transformation matrices, that is, the frequencies with which actions follow or precede each other. Bainbridge describes a method for identifying sequences of actions and infering the particular cognitive processes underlying them.

Tagg also draws attention to three attributes of reconstructing interview data: (1) the description of events, actions, and places; (2) the respondents involvement in or with events, actions, or places; (3) evaluation of these events, actions, or places. His analytical approach gives examples of procedures through which reconstruction can be undertaken.

In a later chapter, Brown and Canter use the same attributes in their discussion of the conceptual status of types of explanations. Tagg's attributes of description, involvement, and evaluation correspond to their elaboration of descriptive, agency, and moral types of explanation.

Another important issue raised by Tagg is that reconstruction of a personal experience can be teased out not only in the interview itself but also during analysis. The contributors in the early part of the book concentrate on the procedures for effective communication between researcher and informant in order to obtain a complete account of the events being investigated. Brown and Canter and Potter and Mulkay, whose chapters appear in the latter part of the book, provide examples of how to cull the verbal reports obtained from interviews to gain further details of people's experience of which they may not be consciously aware. For example, Brown and Canter illustrate how sequential measures of the distance people have moved through a building on fire are more accurate when derived from their accounts than when the informants are asked more directly to estimate distance.

CONCLUSION

The assumptions underlying the use of interviews are that people not only can comment on their experiences and feelings, but also that they do this in everyday life. The interview is attempting to harness the daily occurring activity of talk. The research situation, however, is a rather special conversational interaction in that it has its own particular dynamics, such as interview style and setting, that have to be taken into account.

Yet, because the interview as a research tool is very flexible, it can deal with a variety of subject matter at different levels of detail or complexity. It can cope with the general public or specialist groups as informants. Reports of the data can reflect sequences of actions and their content or propriety. Information may deal with past, present, or future happenings, with the informants' own behaviour, or with commentary on others. It is a happy circumstance that human behaviour includes speech, which allows social scientists access to techniques denied other disciplines. Not only can the social scientist ask questions about her/his informants' behaviour and experience, but the informants themselves can give answers.

REFERENCES

Allport, G. W. (1942). *The use of personal documents in psychological science.* New York: Social Sciences Research Council.

Cannell, Ch. F., Oksenberg, L., and Converse, J. M. (1979). *Experiments in interviewing technique.* Ann Arbor, MI: Institute for Social Research.
Hyman, H. (1954). *Interviewing in social research.* Chicago, IL: University of Chicago Press.
Harré, R., and Secord, P. F. (1972). *The explanation of social behaviour.* Oxford: Blackwell.
Kelly, G. (1955). *The psychology of personal constructs.* New York: Norton.
Phillips, D. L. (1971). *Knowledge from what?* Chicago, IL: Rand McNally.
Phillips, D. L. (1973). *Abandoning method.* San Francisco, CA: Jossey-Bass.
Scott, J., and Chanlett, E. (1973). *Planning the research interview.* Chapel Hill, NC: University of North Carolina.
Von Cranach, M., and Harré, R. (1982), (Eds.). *The analysis of action: Recent theoretical and empirical advances.* Cambridge: Cambridge University Press.

2

Survey Interviewing

MICHAEL BRENNER

SURVEY RESEARCH AS GOAL-DIRECTED ACTION

In essence, scientific survey research is aimed at the provision of evidence for particular hypotheses or theories by means of the maximally valid, reliable, and precise measurement of phenomena covered by the hypotheses or theories concerned. It is the fundamental goal of survey research to attempt a rigorous context of "explanation and understanding in the social sciences" (Nagel, 1961, Chapter 14). This context is regulated by a particular structure of action, directed towards the maximal attainment of adequate measurement (see Hyman, 1955).

Measurement requires units of measurement, which are, in the case of survey research, the respondents. The units must possess properties capable of classification or quantitative gradation; otherwise, measures of phenomena would be unobtainable. The properties of respondents, such as their demographic characteristics, aspects of their social and physical environment, their activities in areas such as work and leisure, their opinions, sentiments, and attitudes, among others, are typically referred to as attributes. "Attributes can be thought of as abstractions imposed by the investigator on the flux constituting the behavior being studied" (Sonquist and Dunkelberg, 1977, p. 234). The amount of an attribute present at the time of measurement is its magnitude, which enables the comparability of units of measurement—the respondents—with regard to a particular attribute. Measurement pertains to an attribute; it is the assignment of numbers to represent the magnitudes of each of the attributes of respondents.

In practical terms, the magnitudes of respondent attributes are determined by the interviewer presenting each respondent with a set of stimuli—questions and questioning procedures—common to all respondents.

ISBN 0-12-131580-0

The response—the answer by the respondent—to each stimulus is taken to represent a particular magnitude of an attribute. Measurement is straightforward when questions have been designed as variables. That is, the question involves a set of categories and a procedure for the respondent to answer. As the respondent should select only one answer from the set, such questions are forced-choice, or "closed," questions. The assignment of numbers to categories is usually done by printing them beside the categories in the questionnaire. When "open" questions are used, that is, questions that do not prescribe a particular form of response, and, therefore, require the respondents to answer in their own words, the measurement—the assignment of numbers to the magnitudes of particular attributes—is delayed until the coding stage of the research.

Given the stimulus–response character of measurement in survey research, it is clear that the data collection, frequently involving a multitude of interviewer–respondent interactions, must be maximally standardized; "questions are presented with exactly the same wording, and in the same order, to all respondents" (Selltiz et al., 1976, p. 306). Assuming that only "closed" questions were used in this manner, the simplest data structure generated by a survey is one answer for each respondent to each of a set of questions. "The answers are represented by single values of a set of variables purporting to measure relevant attributes of that respondent at that point in time" (Sonquist and Dunkelberg, 1977, p. 21). This structure can be represented as a data matrix with N rows and M columns, where the row subscript, i, varies over the units of measurement, the respondents, R_1, $R_2, \ldots, R_n$, and the column subscript j varies over the variables, V_1, V_2, $\ldots$, V_m. Each element, c_{ij}, is the value of the jth variable for the ith respondent (see Table 1). This is exactly the form in which survey data are usually organized for computer storage and data analysis.

Galtung (1970) has suggested that the grouping of measurement results in

Table 1
HYPOTHETICAL SIMPLEST DATA MATRIX

	Variables			
Respondents	V_1	V_2	V_j	V_m
R_1	4	7	46	1
R_2	1	3	27	5
$\vdots$				
R_i			c_{ij}	
$\vdots$				
R_n	5	1	64	7

the form of a data matrix can be performed with confidence when three principles—comparability, classification and completeness—can be fulfilled. The principle of comparability entails that each "combination of a given stimulus with a unit of analysis shall be *meaningful.*" That is, answers can be regarded as commensurate only if the same question is asked of all respondents. "The emphasis is on 'same': the stimulus shall not be changed from one object to the other." The principle of classification says that for each respondent–question combination, "there shall be *one* (exhaustiveness) *and only one* (mutual exclusiveness or single-valuedness)" answer. "When this condition is fulfilled, we are guaranteed a response for each possible combination of unit and stimulus, and a *single* response." The third principle of completeness means "*leave no cell open.* This *desideratum* is easily pronounced but not easily fulfilled, so all we have is a norm that the amount of cells with 'no information', 'no answer', etc. shall be kept 'as low as possible' " (Galtung 1970, pp. 11–13).

Clearly, Galtung's principles, although required by the "logic of the matrix," are essentially normative; they project goals that we must seek to obtain when conducting survey research for scientific ends. This is a difficult task, as research into the numerous sources of bias operating in survey research data collection has demonstrated (see Sudman and Bradburn, 1974) that it would be naive "to assume 'identical' interviews with 'identical' questions and responses" (Cicourel, 1964, pp. 100–101). Avoidance of bias, together with a realistic acceptance of the ultimate limits of data collection by means of interviewer–respondent interaction, are, therefore, primary concerns when preparing, and finally conducting, a particular measurement programme.

Consider as an illustration the problem of language and meaning in survey research measurement. Galtung's principle of comparability implies that questions and answers should be equivalently meaningful to the researcher, all interviewers, and all respondents; otherwise, the values entered in one row of the data matrix would, in reality, mean something more or less or different than the values of another. Total equivalence of meaning can only be assumed when it can be shown, for a particular survey, that the researcher, all interviewers, and all respondents have used the same linguistic "code," in the researcher's wording of the questions, in the interviewers' and respondents' understandings of the questions, in the interviewers' understandings of the respondents' answers and in the researcher's understanding of the interviewers' understandings of the respondents' answers, so that we can be sure that in the transmission of meaning, distortion or loss of information did not occur.

The quest for total equivalence of meaning is certainly unrealistic, if only for sociolinguistic reasons: participants in a typical cross-sectional survey will not share the same linguistic "code" (see Edwards, 1976). Or as Mitchell (1965, pp. 678–679) has put it: "Since those who prepare questionnaires are typically from the middle and upper classes, the instruments they produce are likely to be somewhat inappropriate for large segments of the population." The issue becomes most serious in intercultural surveys, as we cannot assume that different languages are just alternative "codes" comprising identical sets of referents (see Brown, 1958, Chapter 7). Notice, however, that the goal of "equivalence of meaning" can be pursued, by taking into account the real communication problems that are likely to arise in a data collection programme, for example, by taking care in intercultural research that questions appear in appropriate translations (see Galtung, 1970, p. 12).

Similar lines of argument can be developed for the avoidance, or, minimally, partial control, of all known sources of bias in survey research data collection, as we can attempt to make our measurement practices "transparent," using intensive pretesting of the questionnaire and the interviewing techniques to be employed, and also careful *post festum* assessment methods, to determine the extent of the likely measurement inadequacy, among other possible procedures (see Andersen et al., 1979; Cannell et al., 1979). (The chapters by Wilson and Dijkstra et al. in Part I provide good examples of strategies useful for the avoidance and control of sources of bias, at least in part.) Next, I will consider just one aspect of survey research data collection—the most crucial one—interviewing.

SURVEY INTERVIEWING AS A PROBLEM IN THE PSYCHOLOGY OF ACTION

As noted above, data collection in survey research is typically conceptualized in stimulus–response terms. This is useful, if only as a goal, as there is only one objective of survey interviewing, namely, to obtain from respondents valid answers in response to the questions put to them. These should also meet the particular response requirements posed by questions, for example, questions involving the use of a response card or some other predetermined answering procedure. How can we attempt to accomplish this objective in interviewer–respondent interaction?

One of the ways, first suggested by Kahn and Cannell (1957, Chapter 2), is to think of interviewing as a problem in the psychology of action, as measurement in the interview happens as a social interactional process in the form of interviewer–respondent interaction. There are a number of action psychological concepts that I first introduce in general terms before turning more specifically to a consideration of the roles of interviewer and respondent.

Action is Goal-Directed

People act in keeping with their goals. Goals are developed actively or reactively, that is, freely by people, or in response to internal or external influences or pressures. Active goal development is captured in statements such as "he acts because he wants to do it," "he has chosen to do it." Reactive goal development is expressed in statements such as "he wants to do it because he is angry," "he does it because he knows circumstances will not permit another line of action."

Whatever the origin of goals, once a goal is noticed, it directs action towards outcomes anticipated when the goal has been recognized. This is the reason for the equifinality of action (Heider, 1958, p. 108); as long as the cognition of the goal is predominant, people will select and try (perhaps variable) lines of action until the goal is attained. This implies that goals, besides directing action, also energise action through "the arousal of tension upon the activation of the goal, which continues to exist until either the goal has been reached or it has been deactivated in some manner" (Staub, 1978, p. 91). The concept of goal is, therefore, close to the more familiar concept of motivation, as goal-directed action implies not only a definite preference for the attainment of particular outcomes of action, or, more often, social interaction, but also a striving towards particular outcomes.

Action Requires Knowledge

Effective action is impossible when people are unable to select a line of action that is likely to be appropriate for the particular situation within which a goal is pursued. Furthermore, situational knowledge is also required for the effective selection of goals here-and-now. In survey interviewing, for example, it is important that the interviewer know the powers for action that respondents can express. He[1] has to be prepared, by developing *ad hoc* reactive goals, to meet adequately requests for clarification, the occurrence of inadequate answers, and refusals to answer, among other respondent actions, in keeping with the ultimate goal of each particular question-answer sequence—which is to obtain, whenever possible, an adequate answer. The concept of knowledge, as used here, is equivalent to the concept of competence, commonly used in linguistics to account for the possibility of speech performances in tune with definitions of social situations (see Edwards, 1976, pp. 141–142).

[1]I refer to interviewer and respondent as "he"; "she" would be just as appropriate, of course.

Action Requires Skill

Given goals and knowledge, effective action relies, first and foremost, on adequate motor performance. That is, people must have the behavioural, verbal and nonverbal, capacity to express actions as intended. The relevance of motor skills for effective action is most apparent when considering examples from the psychology of work (see Hacker, 1978), such as operating complex machines. However, the adequate motor performance of social behaviour is similarly important. Argyle and Trower (1979, p. 116) give an example of skilled goal-directed action, unrelated to survey interviewing:

> He sizes up the situation, reads the social signals, and decides on a line of action. From his repertoire of skills he chooses one which he thinks will have the desired effect; to dominate, persuade, seduce or provoke. Having acted, he will watch the effect, and act accordingly, perhaps changing his tactic, deploying another skill.

It is clear from this example that it is not only skilled motor performance which makes action effective; people have also to be good at perceptual skill, that is, "the coding of, and giving coherence to, the multitudinous sensory data that pour in through the sense organs, and in linking these data to material stored in memory to give them context in both space and time" (Welford, 1976, p. 12). Furthermore, people need to employ intellectual skills, that is, the "ability to decide what should be done in particular circumstances" (Welford, 1976, p. 12). Notice that it is through the use of adequate intellectual skills that we are able to arrive at situationally appropriate decisions for action.

Action is Often Social

Action is social action when people orient their actions to others. Action is social in the sense that we act, to a great extent, for others as well as for ourselves. Others make a difference to us when we act; we are influenced by their actions, as they are by ours. Social interaction is, therefore, invariably a mutual social influence process, as captured so well in Lewin's Field Theory (for a summary see Shaw and Costanzo, 1970, Chapter 5). As Blumer (1953, p. 194) has pointed out:

> Taking another person into account means being aware of him, identifying him in some way, making some judgement or appraisal of him, identifying the meaning of his action, trying to find out what he has on his mind or trying to figure out what he intends to do.

When action is social interaction, requiring from people mutual interpretational attention to an ongoing social influence process, they have to fit their own action to the actions of others, which are, of course, also goal-directed. Given that people do not agree about which goal to pursue jointly in interaction, as is frequently the case in survey interviewing, there is the problem of "bargaining" between them which goal should be dominant here-and-now. Interaction may thus be cooperative, but there is always the likelihood of goal conflict, this necessitating, in the case of survey interviewing, particular kinds of knowledge and skill on the part of the interviewer, useful for resolving, whenever possible, the problems at hand.

To summarize the general characteristics of action as needed for an understanding of survey interviewing in terms of interviewer–respondent interaction: these are the concepts of goal, knowledge, skill, and the social quality of action. The relationships between the concepts are depicted in Figure 1, where just one person is considered. (Notice that the concepts of goal, knowledge and skill provide the necessary and sufficient conditions for a person's action, that is, if one characteristic is absent or cannot be performed, action is impossible.)

I will now turn to a consideration of the survey interview in terms of social situation. I abstract from the physical location—and the physical properties—of interviewing, in the full knowledge, however, that these are important (see Atkinson, 1971). The emphasis will be on a discussion of interviewer and respondent roles.

Once the interview commences, a clear division of labour takes place between interviewer and respondent, involving complementary role performances. The roles of interviewer and respondent differ significantly, particularly in terms of the skills required in their performances and in terms of the degrees of freedom for action available.

The most crucial component of the social situational circumstances affecting the answering process is the interviewer (see Hyman et al., 1954), or, more precisely, interviewing technique (see Brenner, 1981a). Interviewing technique must meet, ideally, two requirements: it must not bias the

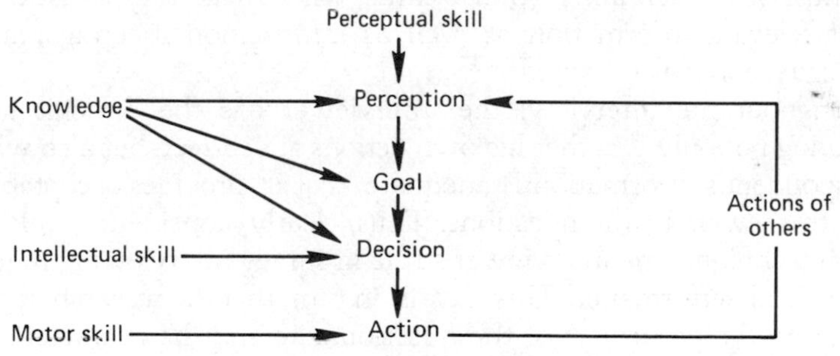

Figure 1 The person's action system.

answers, and it must ensure a socially effective interaction that helps, and motivates, the respondent to report adequately.

While, for the purposes of measurement, the interviewer must try "to direct and control the communication process to specific objectives" (Kahn and Cannell, 1957, p. 62), this must be done nondirectively, to avoid bias. That is, the interviewer, in his use of questioning techniques, must leave it entirely to the respondent to provide answers to questions. For example, questions must never be asked in a leading manner or directively, as this exerts pressure on respondents to answer in particular ways. (Consider the leading "You don't, you haven't experienced any problems in getting information from these staff," which implies the "right" answer is "No," as against the nondirective "Do you experience any problems in getting information from these staff?") In more general terms, the interviewer must maintain a neutral stance; whatever the topic of the conversation, he must not express his personal views about the issues under consideration, as this amounts to an explicit interviewer effect on the respondent, which might endanger, as in the case of leading or directive questioning, the validity of the information reported.

While intensive interviewing requires, for the avoidance of interviewer bias through questioning, the consistent use of nondirective interviewing technique (see Chapter 7), survey interviewing, based as it is on the use of a standardized questionnaire, necessitates the command of a much more comprehensive set of skills. In addition to nondirective questioning, the interviewer must take care that the questionnaire is always used in the interview situation as intended by the researcher. Most importantly, the interviewer must not alter the wording of the questions or omit them by mistake. The former mistake has the consequence that respondents are actually exposed to questions different from those printed in the questionnaire, which may lead to invalid responses; the latter means that possible answers are simply lost. Furthermore, the interviewer must use the various questioning procedures as prescribed by the questionnaire; routing instructions must be obeyed and response cards, where necessary, must be used, so that relevant information as well as information meeting particular forms of response is obtained.

Throughout the interview, the interviewer has the difficult task of monitoring not only whether his own actions are correct, but also whether the respondent's information is adequate, that is, provides acceptable and complete answers to the questions. Thus, clearly, considering only interviewing technique, the interviewer's role in survey interviewing requires a highly skilled performance. This means, in turn, that the researcher, paying attention to the particulars of the questionnaire and the characteristics of the respondent sample, must design the repertoires of action needed for adequate data collection in detail. Also, to enable the acquisition of the skills required, intensive interviewer training must be given. Notice, and this relates to interviewing technique only, that the interviewer has practically no degree of personal freedom for action. He cannot improvise decisions for actions; all decisions to be made, in the context of, perhaps, highly variable respondent actions in question–answer sequences, are literally predetermined by the repertoire of interviewing techniques as designed by the researcher. (The necessary quest for maximal control over the interviewer's performance implies, of course, that the researcher is able to provide an exhaustive repertoire, together with effective interviewer training, which eliminates *a priori* the need for improvisation when dealing with respondents, with their problems in particular.)

The interviewer's role cannot possibly be restricted to its quite rigid measurement aspects, as interviewer–respondent interaction is social interaction nevertheless. The interviewer's role extends, thus, to the management of the response process in terms of action beyond interviewing technique: the interviewer, by means of socially effective interaction with the respondent (the expression of sympathetic understanding, of attention, of interest, often performed nonverbally or paralinguistically), must try to maximize, on the part of the respondent, the motivational forces to report adequately, or, more generally, to stay involved in the interviewing encounter. This requires from the interviewer continuous efforts "to reduce or eliminate the negative forces, the barriers to communication" (Kahn and Cannell, 1957, p. 62). Thus, the interviewer's role, while necessitating the precise command of a fairly complex repertoire of interviewing techniques, does not involve impersonality of performance; quite to the contrary, as it is within the medium of, first and foremost, socially effective interaction with the respondent that the interviewing task is achieved. (Notice that I am, in my statements above, which extend beyond interviewing technique, limited by my own experience of interviewing in Britain; in other countries, other styles of interviewing may be more appropriate. In the U.S., for example, as the Interviewer's Manual (Institute for Social Research, 1976) demonstrates, a more formal style of interviewing, such as that used by Dijkstra et al., Chapter 3, Part I, seems to be more appropriate for the avoidance of interviewer bias.)

Considering now the respondent: his only role function, which is predetermined by the definition of the situation as survey interview, is that of informant. He is asked to provide information that, because of lapse of time, distance, attempts at secrecy or other reasons, is not available for direct observation. The respondent serves, as it were, as a substitute for more direct forms of measurement. He must, therefore, be competent (capable of good recall, in particular) and sufficiently motivated to perform on the lines of a "faithful" respondent role. Such a role implies not only that the respondent will do his best to answer truthfully, but also that he will follow the interviewer's guidance.

Of all sources of bias in the interview situation, the respondent constitutes the greatest threat to measurement adequacy. We cannot generally assume that all respondents will be competent; Cannell et al. (1979), in their numerous experimental surveys on health reporting, have shown, in study after study, that incidents of hospitalization, among other health events, are usually underreported, for example. As regards the biasing effects of inadequate respondent motivation, it must be noted, at least in principle, that respondents are free to use any means of action to damage, or even to destroy, the interview as a measurement situation. "If the respondent is not sufficiently motivated to perform his role, the whole enterprise falls apart" (Sudman and Bradburn, 1974, p. 16). Notice in particular that the interviewer cannot exert pressure, attempting to control the respondent's conduct, as this would amount to an explicit interviewer effect on the respondent. The interviewer can only try to resolve any apparent problems by means of the appropriate actions discussed above, most prominently nondirective interviewing techniques. Ultimately, therefore, measurement adequacy in the survey interview relies on the respondent's good will to maintain the necessary working consensus with the interviewer, which the interviewer can try to reinforce positively, but cannot entirely create, or recreate, on his own.

Leaving aside the "negativistic" respondent who seeks to damage, or to destroy, the interview as a measurement situation, the interviewer must be prepared for the respondent to raise, basically, four kinds of problem in Q–A sequences. The respondent may require the interviewer to repeat an action (a question, a probe, an instruction, for example); he may request clarification (what is meant by a question, an instruction, for example); he may give inadequate information, that is, information that does not meet the objective of a question; finally, he may refuse to answer. When such problems arise, the interviewer must try to deal with them in a way that enhances the likelihood that, in the end, adequate answers will be accomplished.

One of the ways of identifying the knowledge and the intellectual skills (see Figure 1) that the interviewer, ideally, should involve for the purposes of adequate measurement is to write them as rules of interviewer–respondent interaction. The concept of rule is used here

> to mean a general prescription guiding conduct or action in a given type of situation. A typical rule in this sense prescribes that in circumstances X, behaviour of type Y ought, or ought not to be, or may be, indulged in by persons of class Z. (Twining and Miers, 1976, p. 48)

The rules of survey interviewing are not by fiat; they are the result of extensive research into the biasing effects of inadequate interviewer performance (for a review see Brenner, 1981a). While there are no particular rules for the respondent (besides the "weak" rule that he should provide adequate answers, having agreed to the interview), the set of rules for the interviewer is comprehensive. In general, considering the task aspects of interviewer–respondent interaction only, there are rules for asking the questions, rules for dealing with the respondent's answers, rules for interacting with the respondent, and rules for dealing with respondent problems. I will now consider these sets of rules; notice, however, that rules relating to nonverbal aspects of interviewer action are omitted here (for this see Brenner, 1981b).

---

1. Rules for asking the questions.

Read the questions as they are worded in the questionnaire. This is necessary because changes in the wording of questions may result in biased answers.
Read slowly. The interviewer must give the respondent time to understand the question.
Use correct intonation and emphasis. This is to help the respondent understand the question precisely as meant by the researcher.
Ask the questions in the correct order. By obeying the routing instructions, the sequence of questions is kept as intended by the researcher.
Ask every question that applies. This prevents loss of information by mistake.
Use response cards when required. This is to obtain the kinds of answers required by the researcher.

2. Rules for dealing with the respondent's answers.

Record exactly what the respondent says. This is to avoid any distortion of the answer, by leaving out, or rephrasing, information.
Do not answer for the respondent. The interviewer's inference of the respondent's answer may be invalid.
Show an interest in the answers given by the respondent. This is to encourage the respondent's full participation in the interview.
Make sure that you have understood each answer adequately. This is to ensure that the answer is recorded as meant by the respondent.
Make sure that each answer is adequate. This is to avoid the acceptance of incomplete answers or inadequate information.
Do not show approval or disapproval of any answer. This may bias answers. The respondent may be led to believe that certain answers are more acceptable to the interviewer than others.

3. Rules for interacting with the respondent.

Probe only nondirectively. This is to avoid implying or suggesting to the respondent a particular answer or direction of answering.
Where necessary, volunteer clarification. This is to help the respondent in the provision of an adequate answer, when problems in answering are apparent.

Where necessary, repeat the question (or probe, instruction, clarification). Again, this is to help the respondent in the provision of an adequate answer, when problems in answering are apparent.
Do not give directive information about question meaning. This is to avoid suggesting to the respondent a particular answer or attitude towards the question.
Do not seek or give information unrelated to the question. This may distract the respondent from the question–answer process.
Thank the respondent from time to time for his cooperation. This is to encourage his cooperation.

4. Rules for dealing with respondent problems.

When the respondent requests the interviewer to repeat an action, he must repeat.
When the respondent seeks clarification, the interviewer must clarify nondirectively. The clarification must be given in a form that does not suggest a particular answer or direction of answering.
When the respondent gives an inadequate answer, the interviewer must try to obtain an adequate answer by means of nondirective probing, repetition of the question or instruction, or nondirective clarification. This is to avoid the acceptance of inadequate information.
When the respondent firmly refuses to answer a question, the interviewer must accept the refusal.
When the refusal is "half-hearted," that is, the respondent, although refusing to answer, still provides a basis for discussing the refusal and moving towards an answer, the interviewer must try to obtain an answer by clarifying nondirectively, probing nondirectively, or repeating the question. This is to avoid loss of information.

When the interviewer is able to follow the rules of survey interviewing, his actions, under variable conditions of respondent action, are not only predictable (which meets the requirements for reliability and precision in his performance), but are also likely to guide the respondent through question–answer sequences, as we will see, in such a way that, irrespective of particular respondent problems, a maximum of adequate answers may be obtained.

THE STRUCTURE OF ACTION IN SURVEY INTERVIEWING

In order for the interviewer to follow the rules of interviewing effectively, he must possess a repertoire of actions that enables him to perform adequately. In designing such a repertoire, we need to consider a number of issues now in more detail.

First of all, questions vary in terms of the form of answers desired. There are two main types of questions, "closed" and "open." A question is "closed" if it requires a definite response, such as "Yes" or "No"; it is "closed" when the respondent must choose a response from a range of answers given to him on a card; it is "closed" when the respondent is required to select a response from a range of answers which is read to him by the interviewer. "Open" questions can have two forms, open follow-up questions, after a closed question, and independent open questions. In contrast to closed questions, open questions require the respondent to answer in his own words and in a form not limited to a predetermined range of responses.

Second, question–answer sequences vary in terms of problems created by respondents. There are two main types of question–answer sequences: (1) those that involve an unproblematic elementary structure, where the question is followed by a set of actions by respondent and interviewer required in the communication of an adequate answer and its recording and assessment, and (2) those that entail one or more problems. That is, question–answer sequences are complicated by requests for repetition of the interviewer's actions, clarifications, inadequate answers, and refusals.

I now propose action repertoires for adequate survey interviewing, beginning with the elementary action structures of closed and open question–answer sequences, and later turning to action repertoires suitable for meeting effectively the various respondent problems. Notice that the action repertoires below offer just a general solution to the design of elementary question–answer sequences as well as problem sequences. It is likely, given a particular interview programme, that these action sequences may need refinement and alteration.

Structure of action involved in "closed" questions with definite response.

Action	Function	Example
Introductory statement	To open the question–answer sequence	I: Now.
I reads question as worded, slowly and with correct intonation and emphasis	To give R time to understand the question as meant by the researcher	I: Do you read *regularly* any journals or magazines related to your work?
(Pause)	(Where necessary I gives R time to provide a response)	
R answers adequately		R: No
I records the response	To enter the response into the questionnaire	
(I may repeat the response)	(To ensure, if in any doubt, that the answer recorded is correct)	I: No

(*continued*)

Action	Function	Example
(R may give feedback)	(To indicate whether the response is correct)	R: Mm
(I may thank R for his cooperation)	(To encourage R in his cooperation)	I: Fine

Structure of action involved in "closed" questions with cards

Action	Function	Example
Introductory statement	To open the question–answer sequence	I: Next
I hands the card over to R	To provide R with the set of response alternatives	I: Can you look at this card please and give me an answer from there
I reads question as worded, slowly and with correct intonation and emphasis	To give R time to understand the question as meant by the researcher	I: How satisfied are you with the *size* of your house?
(Pause)	(Where necessary I gives R time to provide a response)	
(I repeats the question)	(When the pause becomes too long I may repeat the question)	I: How satisfied are you with the *size* of your house?
(Pause)	(Where necessary I gives R time to provide a response)	
R answers adequately		R: Oh, satisfied.
I records the response	To enter the response into the questionnaire	
(I may repeat the response)	(To ensure, if in any doubt, that the answer recorded is correct)	I: Satisfied.
(R may give feedback)	(To indicate whether the response is correct)	R: Yes
(I may need to ask R to return the card)	(To obtain the card back)	I: Can I have the card back please?
(I may thank R for his cooperation)	(To encourage R in his cooperation)	I: Right, fine.

(continued)

Structure of action involved in "closed" questions with read range of answers.

Action	Function	Example
Introductory statement	To open the question–answer sequence	I: Here is the next question.
I reads question as worded, slowly and with correct intonation and emphasis	To give R time to understand the question as meant by the researcher	I: In *general*, do you feel you get *too much* information, *too little* information, or about the *right amount*?
(Pause)	(Where necessary I gives R time to provide a response)	
R answers adequately		R: About the right amount, I think.
I records the response	To enter the response into the questionnaire	
(I may repeat the response)	(To ensure, if there is any doubt, that the answer recorded is correct)	I: About the right amount, you say.
(R may give feedback)	(To indicate whether the response is correct)	R: Yes, about the right amount.
(I may thank R for his cooperation)	(To encourage R in his cooperation)	I: Thank you.

Structure of action involved in "open" questions

Action	Function	Example
Introductory statement	To open the question–answer sequence	I: Now
I reads question as worded, slowly and with correct intonation and emphasis	To give R time to understand the question as meant by the researcher	I: What would you say are the *disadvantages* of living in the Upper Afan?
(Pause)	(Where necessary I gives R time to provide a response)	
R answers adequately, I records the information verbatim immediately.	To enter R's information as accurately as possible into the questionnaire	R: Well, you have to catch a bus if you haven't got a car to go from the village; that's a disadvantage.

(*continued*)

Action	Function	Example
(I may give feedback)	(To indicate attention)	I: Mmhm
(R may provide more adequate information; I records the information verbatim immediately)	To enter R's information as accurately as possible into the questionnaire)	R: The other disadvantage is you've got to work outside, because the colliery is now closed
(I may request the repetition of previous information)	To become able to enter R's information as accurately as possible into the questionnaire	I: Sorry, can you repeat what you've just said?
(R repeats previously given information)		R: Yes, we've got to work outside because the colliery is now closed.
(I may probe nondirectively for further information)	To obtain more information	I: Are there any other disadvantages?
(R provides more adequate information, I records the information verbatim immediately)	To enter R's information as accurately as possible into the questionnaire	R: No I don't think so.
I repeats the full answer	To ensure that the information recorded is correct	I: I now repeat your answer to make sure that I have understood you correctly; you said that one disadvantage is that you have to catch a bus, if you haven't got a car, to go from the village; the other disadvantage is that you've got to work outside because the colliery is now closed.
(R may give feedback.)	To indicate whether the information is correct	R: Yes that's it.
(I may thank R for his cooperation.)	(To encourage R in his cooperation)	I: Fine.

While probing has no place in elementary question–answer sequences related to closed questions, probes are often necessary in the context of open questions, in order to obtain full answers from respondents. As has been pointed out, all probing must be done nondirectively, which is to avoid implying or suggesting to the respondent a particular answer or direction of answering. The importance of nondirective probing for valid reporting in the survey interview can be pointed out by briefly considering the consequences of two kinds of rule-breeching probing, leading probing and directive probing.

When the interviewer probes in a leading manner, he usually suggests a particular answer to the respondent, thus preventing him from selecting freely a response within the range of answers associated with a closed question or from forming an independent answer in response to an open question. In fact, leading probing only allows the respondent's agreement or disagreement with the answer suggested. Consider this example:

Action	Action Description
I: Now how satisfied are you with the size of your house?	I omits card by mistake.
R: Oh big enough for us.	R gives inadmissible answer.
I: Would you say very satisfied?	I uses leading probe.
R: No.	R gives inadmissible answer.

Directive probing is like leading probing, only much stronger in its effect on the respondent. The difference between leading and directive probing lies in the force ("Is it . . . ?" versus "It is . . . isn't it?", for example) in which the suggestion of an answer is made. Unlike leading probing, directive probing forces upon the respondent just one action, namely, to accept the answer suggested. Consider this example:

Action	Action Description
I: How satisfied are you with the size of your house?	I omits card by mistake.
R: It's alright.	R gives inadmissible answer.
I: So you're really quite satisfied aren't you?	I uses directive probe.
R: Yeah.	R gives feedback.

I will now list the most common nondirective probes that are available for the purposes of obtaining further information in the context of "open" questions:

Anything else?
Can you think of any other reason?
Can you tell me more about it?
In what way?
Can you explain this a little more?
Can you be more specific about this?
Why do you feel that way?

Can you tell me more about your thinking on that?
Why is this?
Are there any other issues involved?

Although it is apparent that, in the reality of survey interviewing, the action structures related to closed and open questions will be behaviourally more complex and varied than sketched out above, to think of survey interviewing as involving action structures is advantageous in a number of ways. First, it forces the researcher to conceptualize measurement in the survey interview as a problem in the psychology of action. He has to devise the actual social interactional means by which adequate measurement can be maximally accomplished. Second, once action repertoires for adequate survey interviewing exist, these may be used for detailed interviewer training. Finally, once the interviewer commands the action repertoires, he will have a clear cognitive understanding of the structure of action involved in question–answer sequences. Thus, he is able to clearly monitor and regulate the response process.

Having dealt with the elementary action organisation of question–answer sequences, I now propose action repertoires which are likely to solve the problems respondents can raise. Respondent problems typically interrupt the course of an otherwise elementary question–answer sequence. That is to say, for the interviewer, respondent problems, although they can occur in sequence, are just "islands of disturbance"; once they are solved, the course of elementary interviewing is taken up again.

Of all respondent problems, requests for repetition of an interviewer's action are most easy to meet. The interviewer simply restarts the subsequence where the respondent wishes, as in this example:

Action	Action Description
I: Does an important part of your work involve seeking information from other members of staff in your department?	I asks question as required.
R: I'm sorry could you repeat the question?	R requests repetition.
I: (the question is repeated)	

When the respondent asks for clarification, the interviewer must give it, but always nondirectively. That is, the clarification must not suggest a particular answer or direction of answering. Clarifications, therefore, simply restate the issue or task at hand, by repeating the question or instruction, for example. The interviewer may also use predetermined clarifications, printed in the questionnaire, which are designed by the researcher to explain further what is meant by a question or procedure.

There are three kinds of clarification. First, requests for clarification may just be "rhetorical"; that is, the respondent is not in any serious difficulty. "Rhetorical" clarifications are best met by the interviewer giving feedback, as in this example:

Action	Action Description
I: Do other people in the department ask you for information on matters connected with your work?	I asks question as required.
R: Other people in the department?	R requests "rhetorical" clarification.
I: Yes.	I gives feedback.

Second, the respondent may have problems in understanding the meaning of the question. This is expressed in the form of "How do you mean?" or "How do you mean, 'friends'?". Here the interviewer must repeat the question. In addition, he may emphasize the task at hand, as in the following example:

Action	Action Description
I: What would you describe as the disadvantages of living in the Upper Afan?	I asks question as required.
R: How do you mean 'disadvantages'?	R requests clarification of a word meaning.
I: Well, it says here: What would you describe as the disadvantages of living in the Upper Afan? So it's your task to tell me which disadvantages you think there are.	I repeats the question and emphasises the task at hand.

Requests for clarification related to meaning issues may also be met, where available, by predetermined clarifications, as in this example:

Action	Action Description
I: Do you have any specialised knowledge relating to your work?	I asks question as required.

R: What do you mean by 'specialised knowledge'?	R requests clarification of a word meaning.
I: By specialised knowledge we mean knowledge which you have that not everyone doing your kind of work might be expected to have.	I uses predetermined clarification.

Third, the respondent may have difficulty in following a procedure such as using a card. Here, the interviewer must repeat the instruction; he may also explain further the procedure to be followed. Consider this example:

Action	Action Description
I: On this list are some types of information that you may need in your work (pause); I'd like you to think about each type listed and indicate how important that kind of information is for your job; please tick the appropriate box for each type of information. (pause)	I hands the card over to R and explains the task at hand.
R: I'm sorry what do I do?	R requests clarification of the procedure.
I: I'd like you to tick the appropriate box for each type of information to show how important that information is for your job.	I repeats the instruction.

A common problem in survey interviewing is that respondents provide inadequate answers, that is, information which does not meet the requirements of the answering task. Inadequate answers have to be dealt with by means of nondirective probing, repetition of the question or instruction, or nondirective clarification. There are three kinds of inadequate answers: (1) answers that are incomprehensible, for semantic or other reasons, (2) answers that are irrelevant, in that they bear no relationship to the question or task at hand, and, (3) inadmissible answers—those relating to the question but do not meet the form of answering required.

As regards incomprehensible answers, the interviewer must attempt to improve the answer by nondirective probing, as in the following example:

Action	Action Description
I: What would be your most important reasons for moving?	I asks question as required.

R: Well it's the closure if the closure if the closure houses closure isn't it?	R's answer is incomprehensible.
I: You said it's the closure can you tell me more about it?	I probes adequately.

It can happen that respondents provide information in reply to a question which is irrelevant to the answering task at hand. The interviewer must deal with this by means of repetition of the question or instruction, as in this example:

Action	Action Description
I: In general, how many hours in a typical week do you spend in formal meetings with people from inside or outside the department?	I asks question as required.
R: I tell you I don't find meetings very fruitful; they're just talk shops, opportunities for showing off for some people.	R gives irrelevant information.
I: Sorry, let me repeat the question. (the question is repeated.)	I repeats the question.

On occasion, when dealing with irrelevant information, it is useful, besides the repetition, to clarify, as in the example below:

Action	Action Description
I: How often have you discussed moving from the Upper Afan recently?	I asks question as required.
R: Well, as my wife said, if there were a shopping centre near us we would like to stay.	R gives irrelevant information.
I: Sorry, this is about the number of your recent discussions about moving from the Upper Afan; how often have you discussed moving from the Upper Afan recently?	I clarifies and repeats the question.

Finally, there are inadmissible answers; these can only occur in the context of closed questions, as open questions do not require particular forms of answering. In dealing with inadmissible answers, the interviewer must repeat the question and/or instruction; he may also clarify if necessary, as in the following example:

Action	Action Description
I: Can you look at this card please (pause); In general, how useful is the information you get from outside organizations for your job?	I hands card over to R and asks question as required.
R: Well, it's alright.	R gives inadmissible answer.
I: Can you look at the card, please, and give me an answer from there; in general, how useful is the information you get from outside organizations for your job?	I repeats the instruction, clarifies, and repeats the question.

Nondirective probing is the adequate means for attempting to improve incomprehensible answers. I will now list the most common nondirective probes to be used in this context:

Sorry?
Can you tell me more about it?
Can you explain more fully what you mean?
How do you mean?
What do you mean?

The final respondent problem in survey interviewing is refusal to answer; this occurs rarely. When the respondent firmly refuses to consider the question the interviewer must accept the refusal. This is, of course, because the respondent has not only the right to refuse, but it is also impossible to force the respondent to answer. Luckily, most refusals are really "half-hearted" refusals. The respondent raises specific problems that make it impossible for him to answer, but is otherwise cooperative. Thus, the respondent provides a basis for discussing the refusal and moving towards an answer. In negotiating the refusal, the interviewer must use repetitions as well as nondirective clarification, where necessary. Consider this example:

Action	Action Description
I: How satisfied are you with the provision of shopping facilities in the Upper Afan?	I asks question as required.

R: Well, I can't answer that because there is nothing here, is there?	R gives "half-hearted" refusal.
I: Well, we are interested in your satisfaction with the provision of shopping facilities in the Upper Afan; can you look at the card and give me an answer from there please?	I clarifies and repeats the instruction.
R: Very dissatisfied because there is nothing here.	R answers adequately.

Another good means of clarification in the context of "half-hearted" refusals is to point out the confidential nature of the data collection, as in this example:

Action	Action Description
I: Do you experience any problems in getting information from your staff?	I asks question as required.
R: I don't think I should answer that because I'd be saying things about colleagues.	R gives "half-hearted" refusal.
I: Well, as I said at the start of the interview, any answers you provide will be treated in confidence and no individual will be identified in our report.	I clarifies.

Action	Action Description
R: It's in confidence then?	R requests "rhetorical" clarification.
I: Yes.	I gives feedback.
R: Well, yes, I do have problems; some people are uncooperative. (carries on answering)	R answers adequately.

It is worth noting that the interviewer's repertoire of rule-following, problem-solving techniques is rather limited: it involves only repetition, nondirective clarification, and nondirective probing. Yet, this repertoire is, or so it seems (see Wilson et al., 1978; Brenner and Wilson, 1982), effective in meeting respondent problems, so that finally, adequate answers can be obtained.

INTERVIEWER TRAINING AND THE ASSESSMENT OF INTERVIEWING PERFORMANCE

Once the researcher, by means of pretesting, has determined the action repertoires needed for adequate data collection, these will then provide the content for interviewer training. As the action repertoires are organised into action sequences, it is clear, action-by-action, what must be done in interviewing.

Interviewer training should incorporate the following objectives (see also Cannell and Kahn, 1968, p. 586):

1. To provide the trainee with an adequate cognitive representation of the structure of action required in adequate interviewing performance; this includes a consideration of the role–rule structure of interviewing.
2. To teach the techniques of interviewing effectively.
3. To provide extensive opportunity for role-playing practice and evaluative feedback, with the aim of developing an adequate level of the perceptual and motor skills required in interviewing, as well as the ability to critically monitor the adequacy of interviewing performance.
4. To offer careful evaluation of the adequacy of interviewing performance in pre-test interviewing.

As interviewer training relies on intensive role-playing practice and evaluative feedback as the main means of skills acquisition, the group of trainees must be small (four to six trainees seems to be optimal in my experience). Also, for the training to be effective, days of practice will be needed. To facilitate realism in the role-playing, the researcher must prepare a training setting that approximates the interview environment to be encountered in the field. For example, if a data collection programme involves interviewing social workers in their offices, this environment should be reproduced to some extent in the training setting.

For the purpose of building up an adequate cognitive representation of the requirements of survey interviewing, the training starts with a lecture introducing the role–rule structure of interviewing and presenting the action repertoires involved in the administration of the questionnaire. Emphasis is given to the action repertoires designed for dealing with respondent problems. The lecture is followed by a general discussion in which the trainees are encouraged to raise any concerns about the aims and methods involved.

In order to provide an effective teaching framework for the role-playing part of the training, a cumulative learning approach is favoured. This means that the trainees are required to role-play the simple tasks first, to which then, at later stages in the training, more complex action requirements are added, until a final practice level is accomplished. In practice, the trainees start to role-play, using each other as respondents, the elementary structure of action involved in closed questions. Once the trainees have acquired the ability to perform the various kinds of closed questions, the researcher moves on to practicing the elementary structure of action involved in open questions. The role-playing of closed and open questions covers first single questions and then extends to questions in succession. The elementary phase of the training is carried out until it becomes apparent that the trainees master the basic interviewing skills required in the administration of the questionnaire.

As the next stage, the action repertoires for dealing with respondent problems are introduced, starting with repetitions, then dealing with the various kinds of clarification, and finally moving to inadequate answering and refusals. In the practice of clarifications, inadequate answers, and refusals, the importance of adequate evaluation of the respondent's action is stressed in order to develop with precision the particular perceptual skills that are required in dealing with these kinds of respondent action. Towards the end of the training, the trainees are required to enact large parts of the questionnaire, involving all conditions of interviewer–respondent interaction that are anticipated in the data collection. At this final practice level, it is desirable to involve members of the population to be interviewed as respondents. Throughout the training, extensive use is made of video-filming, which is used to discuss and correct in detail the trainees' performances.

The training is completed by assessing the adequacy of the interviewing under field conditions. The trainees are required to conduct a number of pretest interviews, which are tape-recorded and later evaluated by the researcher. If necessary, further training can then be provided.

Despite careful interviewer training, it is likely that the data collection will be imperfect. Thus, it is necessary, once the data collection has been completed, to assess the degree to which the answers have been biased by the interviewing process. Technically, one of the established ways of performing action analyses of survey interviews is to tape-record a sufficiently large sample of interviews by each interviewer. The tapes are coded, using coding systems which are sensitive to the particulars of adequate survey interviewing practice.

For example, given that survey interviewing should minimally involve following the above rules, one can assess the interviewers' performances in terms of rule-following and rule-breaching. This can be done by concentrating on the interviewers' actions only (see Cannell, Lawson, and Hausser, 1967). Having conducted such an assessment, Marquis and Cannell (1969, p. 26) found, despite careful interviewer training, that of all questions asked in a survey on employment matters, 8.16% were administered inadequately, and that, of all probes used, 11.3% were directive; irrelevant conversation (1.7% of all interviewer actions) and suggesting an answer to the respondent (.2%) occurred rarely, however. Bradburn, Sudman et al. (1979, p. 27), using interviewers who were "very good," "the best available in the areas surveyed," in a survey concerned with the study of response effects to threatening questions, found that rule-breaching questioning actions happened in over half of the question-answer sequences. More than one third of the questions were altered. "This confirms many researchers' belief that the survey presents a nonstandardized stimulus to the respondent" (p. 49).

The assessment of interviewers only, excluding the overall interviewer–respondent interaction, has the disadvantage that only sources of unreliability and imprecision in measurement can be detected. In order to determine the validity of the responses obtained, as far as this is possible by means of a tape-recording analysis of interviewing interaction, it is necessary to consider the overall context of interviewer–respondent interaction. That is, instead of concentrating on interviewer performances only, the researcher must code question–answer sequences literally action-by-action. This makes it possible, by means of sequence analysis of the data obtained, to study the effects of the participants' actions on the response process. Also, the responses noted in the questionnaires can be compared with the answers actually given by respondents. In one study, assessing the performances of professional market and social research interviewers involved in a mobility survey, I found that it mattered a great deal how the questions were asked. In the case of the closed questions used in the survey, significantly altering them led to an increase in initially inadequate responses, while asking them directively gave rise to the opposite effect. Omitting the cards with the closed questions dramatically increased the likelihood for inadequate answering. In all, it was apparent that interviewing skills mattered, as adequate answers were frequently not obtained and the response process was seriously affected by biasing interviewer effects (see Brenner 1981a; Dijkstra et al., Chapter 3, Introduction, this volume).

CONCLUSION

It has been my aim in this chapter to outline some of the possible contributions of psychology to survey interviewing practice. In essence, I have been concerned with the practical aspects of increasing the degree of social control of the measurement process in the survey interview, bearing in mind that it is the goal of survey research to accomplish maximally adequate measurement. It is likely, for all we know, that total measurement adequacy is never obtainable, as interviewing, well documented since many years (see Kahn and Cannell, 1957), involves a psychological complexity that cannot possibly be regulated by interviewing technique alone. Yet, I would say, the widespread ignorance of survey practitioners of the action character of measurement in the survey interview, among other psychological, mostly cognitive, factors (see Cannell and Kahn, 1968), is unwarranted, as we are indeed able to study and to structure the majority of the social interactional conditions under which survey data should be gathered. This is a positive contribution to survey research practice: we can avoid sources of bias in interviewer–respondent interaction a priori; we can also assess their extent *post festum,* at least in part.

REFERENCES

Andersen, R., et al. (1979). Total survey error. London: Jossey-Bass.

Argyle, M., and Trower, P. (1979). Person to person. London: Harper & Row.

Atkinson, J. (1971). *A handbook for interviewers.* HMSO: London.

Blumer, H. (1953). Psychological import of the human group. In *Group Relations at the crossroads* (M. Sherif and M. O. Wilson, Eds.), pp. 185–202. New York: Harper & Row.

Bradburn, N. M., Sudman, S. et al. (1979). *Improving interview method and questionnaire design.* San Francisco: Jossey-Bass.

Brenner, M. (1981a). Patterns of social structure in the research interview. In *Social Method and Social Life* (M. Brenner, Ed.), pp. 115–158. London: Academic Press.

Brenner, M. (1981b). Skills in the research interview. In *Social skills and work* (M. Argyle, Ed.), pp. 28–58. London: Methuen.

Brenner, M., and Wilson, T. D. (1982). *The research interview, a videofilm and manual.* Sheffield: Department of Information Studies, University of Sheffield.

Brown, R. (1958). *Words and things.* New York: Free Press.

Cannell, Ch. F., and Kahn, R. L. (1968). Interviewing. In *The Handbook of Social Psychology* (Vol. 2) (G. Lindzey and E. Aronson,

Eds.), pp. 526–595. Reading, MA: Addison-Wesley.

Cannell, Ch. F., Lawson, S. A., and Hausser, D. L. (1967). *A technique for evaluating interviewer performance.* Ann Arbor, MI: Institute for Social Research.

Cannell, Ch. F., Oksenberg, L., and Converse, J. M. (1979). *Experiments in interviewing techniques.* Ann Arbor, MI: Institute for Social Research.

Cicourel, A. V. (1964). *Method and measurement in sociology.* New York: Free Press.

Edwards, A. D. (1976). *Language in culture and class.* London: Heinemann.

Galtung, J. (1970). *Theory and methods of social research.* London: George Allen & Unwin.

Hacker, W. (1978). *Allgemeine Arbeits—und Ingenieurspsychologie.* Bern: Huber.

Heider, F. (1958). *The psychology of interpersonal relations.* New York: Wiley.

Hyman, H. (1955). *Survey design and analysis.* New York: Free Press.

Hyman, H. et al. (1954). *Interviewing in social research.* Chicago, IL: University of Chicago Press.

Interviewer's Manual (1976). Ann Arbor, MI: Institute for Social Research.
Kahn, R. L., and Cannell, Ch. F. (1957). *The dynamics of interviewing.* New York: Wiley.
Marquis, K. H., and Cannell, Ch. F. (1969). *A study of interviewer–respondent interaction in the urban employment survey.* Ann Arbor, MI: Institute for Social Research.
Mitchell, R. E. (1965). *Survey materials collected in developing countries: Sampling, measurement and interviewing obstacles to intra- and international comparisons. International Social Science Journal 17,* 668–691.
Nagel, E. (1961). *The structure of science.* London: Routledge & Kegan Paul.
Selltiz, C., Wrightsman, L. S., and Cook, S. W. (1976). *Research methods in social relations.* New York: Holt, Rinehart and Winston.
Shaw, M. E., and Costanzo, P. R. (1970). *Theories of social psychology.* New York: McGraw-Hill.
Sonquist, J. A., and Dunkelberg, W. C. (1977). *Survey and opinion research: Procedures for processing and analysis.* Englewood Cliffs, NJ: Prentice-Hall.
Staub, E. (1978). Predicting prosocial behavior: A model for specifying the nature of personality–situation interaction. In *Perspectives in interactional psychology* (L. A. Pervin and M. Lewis, Eds.), pp. 87–110. New York: Plenum Press.
Sudman, S., and Bradburn, N. M. (1974). *Response effects in surveys.* Chicago, IL: Aldine.
Twining, W., and Miers, D. (1976). *How to do things with rules.* London: Weidenfels and Nicolson.
Welford, A. T. (1976). *Skilled performance.* Glenview, IL: Scott, Foresman.
Wilson, T. D., et al. (1978). Information needs and information services in local authority social services departments (Project INISS), Final report to the british library research and development department on Stages 1 and 2, October 1975–December 1977. London: British Library.

3

*A Field Experiment on Interviewer–Respondent Interaction**

WIL DIJKSTRA
LIENEKE VAN DER VEEN
JOHANNES VAN DER ZOUWEN

INTRODUCTION

Since the interview is such a straightforward data collection instrument, useful for a multitude of social science research purposes, it is not surprising that the method, of all data collection procedures, has been used most frequently (see, e.g., Brown and Gilmartin, 1969; Wahlke, 1979). Research interviews differ in structure, depending on the researcher's data-collection goals. Of all kinds of research interview, survey interviewing (for details see Brenner's chapter in Part I) is most prominent. It is this interview method with which we are concerned here.

Given the emphasis on measurement, when using survey interviewing, the validity and reliability of the information gathered are of paramount importance; considerable doubts, however, have been expressed concerning the general availability of measurement adequacy in survey interviewing (for dramatic accounts see Phillips, 1971, 1973). Despite the numerous possible pitfalls of survey interviewing, we cannot do without it: this procedure often constitutes the only access to the information we wish to obtain, given the usual cost and time constraints (for a detailed review, which we will not even attempt here, see Dijkstra and van der Zouwen, 1982).

*Our research was supported by the Netherlands' Organization for the Advancement of Pure Research (Grant 57-68). We are grateful to Mrs. A. Van Hattum for her contribution to this chapter.

ISBN 0-12-131580-0

In this chapter, we are concerned with just one particular issue, controversial for some time: the interviewer's style of behaviour while interviewing. Primarily, the interviewer's actions are task oriented: he asks questions, probes, and clarifies, among other things. But the actions of the interviewer have also a social quality, as has social behaviour in any situation. Given the social conversational character of interviewing, it is generally accepted that the interviewer must maintain, besides the task *sensu stricto,* a personal relationship with the respondent. Which kind of relationship should we favour? Here is where the controversy arises.

Some methodologists believe that the interviewer should be supportive and sympathetically understanding towards the respondent (see, e.g., Denzin, 1970, Chapter 6). That is, the interview situation should approximate maximally routine, everyday social conversation, so that the respondent realizes "I am in a personal relationship with the interviewer." Using this, as we call it, *socio–emotional style* of interviewing, it is maintained, is a prerequisite for adequate information reporting, particularly when sensitive, personal topics are involved.

Others recommend that the interviewer should act in a strictly task-oriented manner; more person-oriented actions should be minimized. The reason for this recommendation is that the stimulus conditions should be the same for all respondents, across all interviews, so that the data collection situations may be regarded as equivalent. When the stimulus conditions vary, this may lead to measurement bias (see, e.g., Hyman et al., 1954; Cannell and Kahn, 1968). We call this approach the *formal style* of interviewing.

In order to investigate the two interviewing styles in their effects on respondents, we designed and conducted a field experiment. The styles of interviewing were the main independent variables; personal information reporting and adequate responding were the main dependent variables.

DATA COLLECTION

Design

Sixteen interviewers participated in the study. They were selected from about 50 applicants. The interviewers were students affiliated with the two universities in Amsterdam. The main selection criteria were a minimum age of 21 years and some interviewing experience. Very experienced interviewers were excluded, as they could have developed idiosyncratic interviewing styles, which might have interfered with our experimental manipulation and might have been difficult to unlearn. An equal number

Table 1
THE RESEARCH DESIGN

Interviewing style	Interviewers	Male respondents	Female respondents
Formal	4 male	48	48
	4 female	48	48
Socio–emotional	4 male	48	48
	4 female	48	48
		192	192

of male and female interviewers[1] were randomly assigned to either the formal style of interviewing or the socio–emotional style. The interviewers were not informed about the real purpose of the experiment.

The respondents were randomly selected from a suburb near Amsterdam. An equal number of male and female respondents were randomly assigned to the interviewers; they were replaced in cases of refusal or inaccessibility. Each interviewer interviewed 24 respondents; in total, therefore, 384 interviews were conducted. Table 1 summarizes the research design. Like the interviewers, the respondents were not told the real purpose of their participation. All interviews were audiotaped, and were expected to last about 90 minutes.

Interviewer Training

The interviewers were trained in five sessions lasting half a day each. They were trained in four different groups: two groups in the formal style of interviewing, and two groups in the socio–emotional style. The training of each group involved two parts. The first part was directed towards the learning of task-oriented behaviour and the unlearning of inadequate task-oriented behaviour.

In Table 2, some examples of adequate and inadequate task-oriented behaviour are presented. These are the general "do's and don'ts" of interviewing, which we derived from the rules formulated by Brenner (1981b, pp. 34–36). A videofilm was prepared to illustrate adequate and inadequate task-oriented behaviour; the training of adequate behaviour was performed as role-playing, using video for behaviour control and feedback.

Our training approach is summarized in Table 3. As can be seen, all interviewers were first trained in adequate task-oriented behaviour. The

[1]Although we employed male and female interviewers, we refer to the interviewer to simplify matters in terms of "he"; "she" would have been just as appropriate, of course.

Table 2
EXAMPLES OF ADEQUATE AND INADEQUATE TASK-ORIENTED BEHAVIOUR

	Behaviour
Adequate	Questions are read as worded in the questionnaire. Questions are read in the prescribed order. Probing and clarifications are nondirective. Adequate answers of the respondent are repeated. The interviewer gives positive feedback if the respondent's answer is adequate (e.g., "Thank you").
Inadequate	The question is changed in such a way that its meaning is altered. Questions are not read in the prescribed order. Questions are omitted. Answers of the respondent are interpreted. The interviewer answers for the respondent.

second part, however, was different for the groups; it was directed specifically to the training of the appropriate interviewing style.

Interviewers allocated to the socio–emotional style were told that a good relationship with the respondent is a prerequisite for the respondent's willingness to provide adequate information. They were instructed to react in a personal, sympathetic, understanding manner, especially when the respondent conveyed emotional feelings or signs of distress. For example: the interviewer enacting the socio–emotional style might use utterances like: "I understand what your moving to this house meant to you"; "I can imagine that you had great difficulties with your neighbours then"; "That is nice for you." In addition, they were encouraged to initiate conversation independent of the interviewing, for example, to reveal something about themselves, or to allow the respondent to talk about personal matters.

Table 3
THE ORGANIZATION OF INTERVIEWER TRAINING

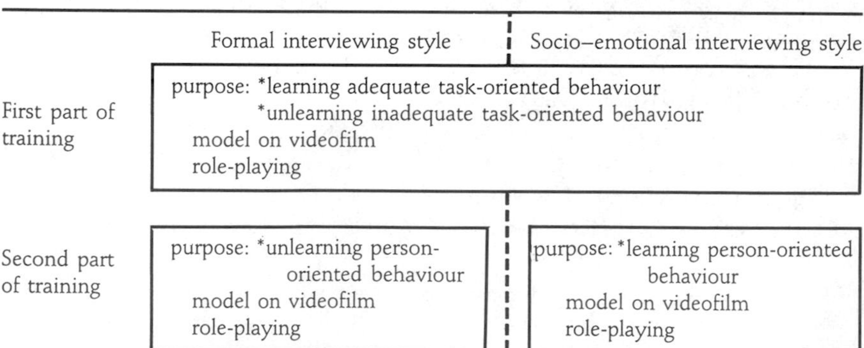

	Formal interviewing style	Socio–emotional interviewing style
First part of training	purpose: *learning adequate task-oriented behaviour *unlearning inadequate task-oriented behaviour model on videofilm role-playing	
Second part of training	purpose: *unlearning person-oriented behaviour model on videofilm role-playing	purpose: *learning person-oriented behaviour model on videofilm role-playing

Interviewers trained in the formal style were told that too much attention to personal matters would distract the respondent from the task and would lead to useless or inadequate answers. They were instructed to employ person-oriented behaviours only minimally, at a level of minimal social acceptability. Part of the training was devoted to unlearning "natural" person-oriented behaviours. All interviewers were required to emphasize, in the interview, that the information to be provided by the respondent is important, and to give positive feedback when the respondent's task-performance was appropriate. In the second part of the training (see Table 3), videofilms were also used to illustrate the style of behaviour expected from the interviewers. Interviewers allocated to the socio–emotional style were shown an interviewer acting in a very personal way; interviewers employing the formal style watched an interviewer performing strictly in accordance with the task. The various kinds of behaviour were acquired through role-playing, with the aid of video. The role-playing involved the trainees in the roles of respondent and interviewer; we also used stooge respondents, unknown to the trainees. After the initial training, each interviewer conducted a trial interview with one of the respondents sampled. These trial interviews were audiotaped and discussed later. During production interviewing, the interviewers returned to our Department having conducted about five interviews each. Some of the audiotaped interviews were taken at random and discussed individually with the interviewer.

The Questionnaire

Our questionnaire involved the following topics: (1) satisfaction with housing and neighbourhood, (2) relationships with neighbours, and (3) feelings of social deprivation.

Two questions related to satisfaction with housing, and five questions addressing neighbour relationships were used for further analysis. These questions were all designed in the same way, as "closed" questions involving the use of response alternatives and "open" follow-up questions. For example, response alternatives to the question "how satisfied are you with your house?" would be "dissatisfied," "neither dissatisfied nor satisfied," "satisfied," and "very satisfied;" and an open follow-up question might be "can you tell me what makes you feel dissatisfied with this house?"

When the interview was terminated, respondents filled in a post-interview questionnaire with items concerning their perception of the interviewer's behaviour. The information obtained from the questionnaires was not made available to the interviewers. Respondents were asked to use in their assessment Likert-type scales with seven categories, to determine the extent to which each of a number of general descriptions of interviewer behaviour applied to the interviewers.

Table 4
THE CODING SYSTEM

Code	Speaker		Category		Behavioural orientation		Qualification or specification	
IOTL	I	interviewer	O	Opening remarks before a new set of questions	T	task-oriented	L	literal
IOTA							A	adequate
IOTI							I	inadequate
IQTL			Q	asks questions	T	task-oriented	L	literal
IQTA							A	adequate
IQTI							I	inadequate
ICTR			C	gives clarification.	T	task-oriented	R	repetition of question
ICTA							A	adequate
ICTI							I	inadequate
IATL			A	presents response alternative	T	task-oriented	L	literal
IATA							A	adequate
IATI							I	inadequate
IPTA			P	probes	T	task-oriented	A	adequate
IPTI							I	inadequate
IRTA			R	repeats answer.	T	task-oriented	A	adequate
IRTI							I	inadequate
IRTC							C	selects alternative for response based on previous answer.
IITI			I	interpretation	T	task-oriented	I	inadequate
IFTA			F	gives formal reaction.	T	task-oriented	A	adequate
IFTI							I	inadequate

IEP			E	gives sympathetic understanding reaction.	P	person-oriented		
IDPO			D	deviates from interview topic.	P	person-oriented	O	expresses opinions.
IDPE							E	talks about event.
IDN					N	neutral		
RATA	R	respondent	A	gives response alternative.	T	task-oriented	A	adequate
RATI							I	inadequate
RFTA			F	gives factual information.	T	task-oriented	A	adequate
RFTI							I	inadequate
RRTA			R	asks for repetition.	T	task-oriented	A	adequate
RCTA			C	asks for clarification.	T	task-oriented	A	adequate
RXTA			X	refuses to answer.	T	task-oriented	A	adequate
RNTA			N	"Don't know" or similar.	T	task-oriented	A	adequate
RPN			P	repeats previously given information.	N	neutral		
RDPO			D	deviates from the interview topic.	P	person-oriented	O	expresses opinions.
RDPE							E	talks about event.
RTP			T	talk unrelated to interview topic.	P	person-oriented		
RTN			T	talk unrelated to interview topic.	N	neutral		
TR	T	bystander	R	answers question for R.				
TT			T	talk unrelated to interview topic				

The Coding System

We constructed a coding system for the classification of verbal actions of interviewers, respondents, and bystanders when they participated in the interview. In line with the purpose of our study, this coding system is based on the following criteria: (1) the coding system had to be useful for evaluating the interviewers' performances in total; that is, it had to be sensitive, so that person-oriented interviewer behaviour could be distinguished with accuracy from the task-oriented style; (2) the coding system had to be useful for evaluating the interviewers' task performance—it had to enable one to distinguish between adequate and inadequate task-related actions of the interviewers; (3) the coding system had to facilitate the effects of an evaluation of interviewer behaviour on respondent behaviour, and vice versa.

The coding system used in our analysis is summarized in Table 4. It is an adapted version of the coding system developed by Brenner (1981a, pp. 132–138). Each code is made up of four letters. The *first* letter designates the speaker. The *second* letter designates speech categories; for example, questions, probes. The *third* letter indicates whether the speech category is task oriented or person oriented. Sometimes, the conversation is unrelated to the interviewing, e.g., "Do you want to have a cup of tea?" This is "neutral" talk, and we devised categories accordingly. *Finally,* task-oriented actions could appear as adequate or inadequate. When the content of a particular speech action was identical with that printed on the questionnaire, it was coded as "literal." We will now detail our coding approach.

THE INTERVIEWER CODES

The first three codes were used when a set of questions was preceded by an introduction, explaining, for example, the purpose of the set. Such openings were coded as task-oriented behaviour. They were coded as literal (IOTL) when the content in the questionnaire was not altered by the interviewer. They were coded as adequate (IOTA) when the text was changed slightly, without altering the essential content or meaning of the text. Openings were inadequate (IOTI) when the interviewer altered their meanings, by changing their content signficantly. The questions (Q) were coded in the same manner (IQTL, IQTA, or IQTI).

Instances of clarification (C) also constituted task-oriented behaviour. They appeared simply as a repetition of a question (ICTR) or of restatements of questions in other words (ICTA). A clarification was coded as inadequate (ICTI) when the meaning of the question was changed, or when examples were used to elucidate the question, or if the clarification was directive in other ways.

Category A (presents response alternative) was used when the interviewer had to provide the respondent verbally with a set of fixed response alternatives. This was coded as literal (IATL) when the set was read as worded in the questionnaire in the prescribed order. This behaviour was coded as adequate (IATA) when the interviewer did not cover all alternatives, because the respondent interrupted the interviewer, or when the range of alternatives was naturally restricted by an answer already given. Consider this example.

I: How satisfied are you with your house? (IQTL)
Would you say dissatisfied, neither satisfied nor dissatisfied, satisfied, or very satisfied? (IATL)
R: Well, I'm quite satisfied. (RATI)
I: Yes, is it satisfied or very satisfied? (IATA)
R: Very satisfied. (RATA)

Probing (P) was coded as adequate (IPTA) when it was nondirective, given that the preceding question was not misunderstood by the respondent, as became apparent from his answer. The probe in the example below is inadequate (IPTI), because the respondent clearly misunderstood the preceding question (notice that the probe is nondirective; however, instead of probing, the interviewer should have clarified the answering task at hand):

I: Would you prefer to live somewhere else because of the lack of social contacts with your neighbours? (IQTL)
R: Certainly not. I have a nice house, there are shops, playground for the children. No, I like to stay here. (RFTI)
I: Are there any more things? (IPTI)

A repetition (R) was coded as adequate when the response was either repeated verbatim, or the main points were summarized (IRTA); otherwise it was coded as inadequate (IRTI). A particular kind of inadequate repetition was coded C. This was used when the interviewer answered for the respondent based on a previous inadequate response (IRTC). Consider this example:

I: How many contacts do you have with people in this neighbourhood? (IQTL)
Would you say none, a few, in between, many, or very many? (IATL)
R: I don't have many contacts here, no. (RATI)
I: A few contacts. (IRTC)
Can you say something more about it? (IPTA)
R: Well, er, it's because I'm working shifts. (RFTA)
I: I see. You have little opportunity to become acquainted with the people here. (IITI)

The example above gives also an illustration of an interpretation (IITI). Interpretations are inferences based on previous answers of the respondent. Interpreting is a means for the interviewer to obtain adequate information. Hence, it is classified as task-oriented. However, such behaviour is inadequate, because of the possibility that the information obtained is biased.

Let us now turn to formal reactions (F). These are nonprogrammed interviewer actions, for example, feedback, related to the respondent's task. Here are examples, involving the codes (IFTA) or (IFTI), that is, adequate or inadequate formal reactions:

I: You may think a moment about it. (IFTA)
I: Thank you, that's the information we need. (IFTA)
I: This will be discussed later. (IFTA)
I: This question isn't that difficult. Why don't you understand it? (IFTI)
I: That's not of interest. Please answer the question. (IFTI)

Sympathetic understanding actions (IEP) were classified as person-oriented, as in these examples:

I: I can understand how you felt then. (IEP)
I: How nice! (IEP)
I: That must have been a very unpleasant experience for you. (IEP)

Interviewers, on appropriate occasions, deviated (D) from a particular interview topic to create a more personal relationship with the respondent. We made a distinction between the interviewer talking about his experiences (IDPE), or expressing opinions (IDPO). It can happen, of course, that the interviewer gives his own opinion about the topic of a question, but this action, obviously inadequate, never occurred in our study. Hence, there was no need for a code covering such behaviour. Finally, interviewers deviated from interview topics, using actions unrelated to our two behavioural styles of interviewing. For example, the interviewer informed the respondent that he likes sugar and milk in his tea (IDN).

THE RESPONDENT CODES

Code A was used when the respondent referred to one of the response alternatives. This was adequate (RATA) when the respondent answered in terms of one of the alternatives; it was inadequate (RATI) when the respondent used synonymous expressions. (The first and third examples above provide some illustration.) Further, the respondent gave factual information (F) relating to an open question or a probe. This action was usually coded as adequate (RFTA), but not when the respondent misunderstood the question (RFTI). (See the second and third examples above.)

The next four categories (RRTA, RCTA, RXTA, and RNTA) do not require intensive explanation. Respondents asked for questions to be repeated (RRTA), or they requested clarification (RCTA). These actions are clearly adequate and task-oriented. Refusals to answer (RXTA) or answering "don't know" or similarly (RNTA) are also adequate and task oriented. There is nothing inadequate when respondents refuse to answer or "don't know." Repeating previously given factual information (RPN) is neither clearly task oriented, nor clearly person oriented, and was therefore classified as neutral. Deviations from the interview topic usually involved personal opinions (RDPO) or related to personal experiences (RDPE), such as background information in addition to answers already provided. Here is an example:

I:	Are there any people in this neighbourhood whom you dislike?	(IQTL)
R:	Yes, sure there are.	(RATA)
I:	Can you tell me something more about it?	(IPTA)
R:	Well, there are some people who are very racist. I don't like them.	(RFTA)
	Last week, we had some trouble here. Some windows were smashed. That sort of thing.	(RDPE)
	I can't understand why people are so intolerant.	(RDPO)

Such diversions were often much longer than the one presented above.

Respondents also talked about topics that were completely unrelated to the interview topic (RTP). This usually concerned personal experiences or feelings with which respondents strongly identified.

Finally, there was another kind of respondent talk which was unrelated to interview topics. This was classified as neutral. For example, "do you want something to drink?" was coded (RTN).

THE BYSTANDER CODES

The two categories (TR and TT) refer to remarks by bystanders. Occasionally, bystanders answered questions for respondents or provided other kinds of information related to the interview topic (TR). The second code was when bystanders' remarks were not related to the interview topics (TT).

The Coding Procedure

A set of coding rules was developed, also useful in dealing with irregularities such as interruptions. These rules were similar to those used by

Table 5
EXAMPLE OF A QUESTION–ANSWER SEQUENCE

Speech	Action description	Code
I: How satisfied are you with your house? Would you say dissatisfied, neither dissatisfied nor satisfied, satisfied or very satisfied?	question asked literally response alternatives presented literally	IQTL IATL
R: Well, I'm quite satisfied.	answers inadequately	RATI
I: Yes, is it satisfied or very satisfied?	presents relevant response alternatives adequately	IATA
R: Very satisfied.	answers adequately	RATA
I: What makes you satisfied with your house?	probes adequately	IPTA
R: Well, er, there is plenty of room ( )*, much comfort, ( ) insulation could be better. That's all.	gives adequate information	RFTA
I: Thank you, that's the kind of information we need.	gives adequate formal reaction	IFTA

*( ) denotes significant pause in speech.

Brenner (1981a). We produced a manual, considering rules and codes extensively. The manual was used by the coders as a guideline for coding. The questions selected were first transcribed from the tapes and then coded. This resulted in a total of 2,688 question–answer (Q-A) sequences. An example of a Q–A sequence is given in Table 5. The coding results were put on a computer file in the following form:

102115238 IQTL IATL RATI IATA RATA IPTA RFTA IFTA.

The codes, in sequential form, were preceded by identification numbers for kind of respondent, interviewer, question, etc. This file provided the raw data for a computer programme, designed to perform various kinds of analysis.

Each coder coded the same number of randomly selected interviews of each interviewer. The random selection was done to ensure that systematic differences between coders could not interact with systematic differences between interviewers.

Reliability of the Codes

Sixteen interviews, one interview of each interviewer, were independently coded twice. The percentage of agreement, corrected for the percentage of agreement by chance, was about 80%. This is satisfactory, given also that the actual reliability was probably underestimated, as the recoding was done from the transcripts and not from the tapes. Paralinguistic information (pauses, hesitations, intonation) would have been more helpful in deciding which code to assign. The most troublesome codes appeared to be interpretations by the interviewer (IITI), and deviations from the interview topic by the respondent (RDPO and RDPE). Interpretations were typically confounded with inadequate clarifications by the interviewer, while both kinds of deviations were typically confused with each other and with adequate factual information (RFTA). For the sake of simplicity in the data analysis, literal and adequate speech categories are usually taken together, and treated as adequate, for example, IQTL and IQTA. Similarly, both kinds of inadequate repetitions of answers (IRTI and IRTC) were grouped together.

RESULTS

The Behaviour of Interviewers in Both Interviewing Styles

In Table 6, the frequencies of the codes that applied to the interviewers are presented for both styles of interviewing. From this table, we can derive the following conclusions:

1. The interviewers using the socio–emotional style of interviewing talked more than the interviewers allocated to the formal style.
2. The codes are very unevenly distributed. For example, adequate questions, adequate probes, and adequate repetitions account for about 53% of all coded events.
3. The majority of the speech acts were adequate.
4. There seem to be systematic differences between both interviewing styles.

We will now turn to these differences between interviewing styles.

STYLE-ORIENTED BEHAVIOURS OF INTERVIEWERS CONSIDERING BOTH STYLES

We expected that interviewers using a socio–emotional style of interviewing would employ more person-oriented behaviours than interviewers enacting the formal style. As can be seen from Table 7, this expectation was confirmed: interviewers trained in the socio-emotional style used considerably more person-oriented behaviours than the formal style interviewers. But notice that the majority of codes is task-oriented in

Table 6

DISTRIBUTION OF INTERVIEWER CODES IN BOTH INTERVIEWING STYLES

Code	Description	Style of interviewing: Formal	Socio–emotional
IOTA	adequate opening remarks	197 (3.2%)	166 (2.5%)
IOTI	inadequate opening remarks	9 (.1%)	26 (.4%)
IQTA	questions asked adequately	1324 (21.5%)	1314 (20.0%)
IQTI	questions asked inadequately	8 (.1%)	23 (.4%)
ICTR	repetition of question	44 (.7%)	32 (.5%)
ICTA	adequate clarification	314 (5.1%)	255 (3.9%)
ICTI	inadequate clarification	179 (2.9%)	328 (5.0%)
IATA	response alternatives presented adequately	543 (8.8%)	587 (8.9%)
IATI	response alternatives presented inadequately	32 (.5%)	33 (.5%)
IPTA	adequate probes	1051 (17.1%)	958 (14.6%)
IPTI	inadequate probes	19 (.3%)	11 (.2%)
IRTA	adequate repetition of answer	1276 (20.7%)	764 (11.6%)
IRTI	inadequate repetition	158 (2.6%)	105 (1.6%)
IITI	interpretation	411 (6.7%)	581 (8.8%)
IFTA	adequate formal reaction	392 (6.4%)	249 (3.8%)
IFTI	inadequate formal reaction	2 (.0%)	10 (.2%)
IEP	sympathetic understanding action	48 (.8%)	375 (5.7%)
IDPO	deviates from interview topic giving opinions	28 (.5%)	186 (2.8%)
IDPE	deviates from interview topic referring to events	69 (1.1%)	473 (7.2%)
IDN	neutral deviations from interview topic	59 (1.0%)	95 (1.4%)
		6163 (99.1%)	6571 (100%)

both styles. An analysis of person-oriented interviewer behaviours shows that these are equally distributed in both styles (see Table 8). However, interviewers using the socio–emotional style employ more person-oriented behaviours, as noted already.

Table 7

TASK-ORIENTED, PERSON-ORIENTED, AND NEUTRAL BEHAVIOURS OF INTERVIEWERS IN BOTH INTERVIEWING STYLES[a]

Interviewer behaviours	Style of interviewing: Formal	Socio–emotional
Task-oriented	5959 (96.7%)	5442 (82.8%)
Person-oriented	145 (2.4%)	1034 (15.7%)
Neutral	59 (1.0%)	95 (1.4%)
	6163 (100.1%)	6571 (99.9%)

[a] $\chi^2 = 720.1$; $df = 2$; $p \ll .0001$.

Table 8
PERSON-ORIENTED INTERVIEWER BEHAVIOUR IN BOTH INTERVIEWING STYLES[a]

Person-oriented interviewer behaviours		Style of interviewing	
		Formal	Socio–emotional
IEP	sympathetic understanding actions	48 (33.1%)	375 (36.3%)
IDPO	deviates from interview topic giving opinions	28 (19.3%)	186 (18.0%)
IDPE	deviates from interview topic referring to events	69 (47.6%)	473 (45.7%)
		145 (100.0%)	1034 (100.0%)

[a] $\chi^2 = .57$; $df = 2$; p not significant.

ADEQUATE AND INADEQUATE TASK-ORIENTED BEHAVIOURS OF INTERVIEWERS

Let us now ask whether the interviewers employing the two styles differ with respect to the degree of adequacy or inadequacy of task-oriented behaviour. As can be seen from Table 9, interviewers trained in the socio–emotional style showed relatively, as well as absolutely, less adequate and more inadequate task-oriented behaviours than the other interviewers. The distribution of inadequate task-oriented behaviours differs clearly between the styles (see Table 10). Notice in particular that interviewers trained in the socio–emotional style use less inadequate repetitions and more inadequate clarifications and interpretations than interviewers employing the formal style.

That the formal-style interviewers used more often inadequate repetitions is due to their using repetitions more frequently than interviewers

Table 9
ADEQUATE AND INADEQUATE TASK-ORIENTED BEHAVIOURS OF INTERVIEWERS IN BOTH INTERVIEWING STYLES[a]

Task-oriented interviewer behaviours	Style of interviewing	
	Formal	Socio–emotional
Adequate	5141 (86.3%)	4325 (79.5%)
Inadequate	818 (13.7%)	1117 (20.5%)
	5959 (100.0%)	5442 (100.0%)

[a] $\chi^2 = 93.3$; $df = 1$; $p \ll .0001$.

Table 10

INADEQUATE TASK-ORIENTED BEHAVIOURS OF INTERVIEWERS IN BOTH INTERVIEWING STYLES[a]

Task-oriented interviewer behaviours	Style of interviewing: Formal	Socio–emotional
IOTI inadequate opening remarks	9 (1.1%)	26 (2.3%)
IQTI inadequate questions	8 (1.0%)	23 (2.1%)
ICTI inadequate clarifications	179 (21.9%)	328 (29.4%)
IATI inadequately presented response alternatives	32 (3.9%)	33 (3.0%)
IPTI inadequate probes	19 (2.3%)	11 (1.0%)
IRTI inadequate repetitions	158 (19.3%)	105 (9.4%)
IITI interpretations	411 (50.2%)	581 (52.0%)
IFTI inadequate formal reactions	2 (0.2%)	10 (0.9%)
	818 (99.9%)	1117 (100.1%)

[a]$\chi^2 = 61.9$; $df = 7$; $p \ll .0001$.

trained in the other style (see Table 11). Clarifications, however, were relatively more often inadequate in the socio-emotional style group, and more adequate in the formal style (see Table 12).

The differences in adequacy, or inadequacy, of performance between both style groups may be explained thus: inadequate clarifications and interpretations are typically directive interviewer actions, which makes easier the task for the respondent in providing adequate information. Such "helping" behaviour seems to be more in line with a socio-emotional style of interviewing, than with a formal style. This implies that the information obtained using the socio–emotional style may be more biased.

Table 11

ADEQUATE AND INADEQUATE REPETITIONS OF INTERVIEWERS IN BOTH INTERVIEWING STYLES[a]

Repetitions	Style of interviewing: Formal	Socio–emotional
Adequate	1276 (89.0%)	764 (87.9%)
Inadequate	158 (11.0%)	105 (12.1%)
	1434 (100.0%)	869 (100.0%)

[a]$\chi^2 = .61$; $df = 1$; p not significant.

Table 12
ADEQUATE AND INADEQUATE CLARIFICATIONS OF INTERVIEWERS IN BOTH INTERVIEWING STYLES[a]

	Style of interviewing	
Clarifications	Formal	Socio–emotional
Adequate	314 (63.7%)	255 (43.7%)
Inadequate	179 (36.3%)	328 (56.3%)
	493 (100.0%)	583 (100.0%)

[a] $\chi^2 = 42.7$; $df = 1$; $p \ll .0001$.

RESPONDENTS' PERCEPTIONS OF INTERVIEWING STYLES

For an interviewer's style of behaviour to have some effect, it is necessary that his behaviour be perceived in some particular way by respondents. In Table 13, findings concerning four typical items from the post-interview questionnaire are presented. The higher the score, the more the description applied to a particular interviewer behaviour. As all differences were significant, the interviewing styles were perceived by the respondents as intended. (We used more items than presented in Table 13, but the results for these were essentially the same.)

The Behaviour of Respondents in both Interviewing Styles

Considering now respondents' behaviour, in Table 14 the frequencies of the codes used for the respondents participating in both interviewing styles

Table 13
PERCEPTIONS OF INTERVIEWING STYLES BY RESPONDENTS[a]

	Style of interviewing		
Interviewer behaviour	Formal	Socio–emotional	Level of significance of difference
Personal	4.52	5.16	$p < .001$
Sympathetic and understanding	3.64	4.41	$p < .001$
Formal	3.16	2.60	$p < .001$
Reserved	2.48	1.91	$p < .001$

[a] Mean scores, using a 7-point scale.

Table 14
DISTRIBUTION OF RESPONDENT CODES IN BOTH INTERVIEWING STYLES

Code	Description	Style of interviewing: Formal	Style of interviewing: Socio–emotional
RATA	gives adequate response alternative	1271 (19.6%)	1162 (16.8%)
RATI	gives inadequate response alternative	448 (6.9%)	445 (6.5%)
RFTA	gives adequate factual information	2116 (32.7%)	2188 (31.7%)
RFTI	gives inadequate factual information	323 (5.0%)	275 (4.0%)
RRTA	asks for repetition	19 (0.3%)	24 (0.3%)
RCTA	asks for clarification	185 (2.9%)	174 (2.5%)
RXTA	refuses to answer	6 (0.1%)	4 (0.1%)
RNTA	answers "don't know" or similar	59 (0.9%)	58 (0.8%)
RPN	repeats previously given factual information	355 (5.5%)	237 (3.4%)
RDPO	deviates from interview topic giving opinions	528 (8.2%)	625 (9.1%)
RDPE	deviates from interview topic referring to events	1029 (15.9%)	1300 (18.8%)
RTP	personal talk unrelated to interview topic	51 (0.8%)	294 (4.2%)
RTN	neutral talk unrelated to interview topic	80 (1.2%)	114 (1.7%)
		6470 (100.0%)	6899 (99.9%)

are given. The findings in Table 14 allow a number of conclusions. These are similar to those arrived at when we discussed the interviewer codes:

1. Respondents interviewed in the socio–emotional style talked more than respondents interviewed in the formal style.
2. The distribution of the codes is very uneven. Three codes, giving adequate response alternatives, adequate factual information, and deviations from the interview topic by the discussion of personal events, account for about 68% of all observations.
3. Most behaviours were adequate.
4. Here too, there appear to be systematic differences between both styles of interviewing.

Table 15
RESPONDENTS' BEHAVIOUR IN BOTH INTERVIEWING STYLES[a]

Respondent behaviour	Style of interviewing: Formal	Style of interviewing: Socio–emotional
Task-oriented information	4158 (64.3%)	4070 (59.0%)
Other task-oriented behaviours (requests, etc.)	269 (4.2%)	260 (3.8%)
Personal information	1608 (24.9%)	2218 (32.1%)
Neutral behaviour	435 (6.7%)	351 (5.1%)
	6470 (100.2%)	6899 (100.0%)

[a] $\chi^2 = 93.7$; $df = 3$; $p \ll .0001$.

Table 16
KINDS OF PERSONAL INFORMATION BY RESPONDENTS IN BOTH INTERVIEWING STYLES[a]

	Respondents' personal information	Style of interviewing	
		Formal	Socio–emotional
RDPE	deviations from interview topic giving opinions	1029 (64.0%)	1300 (58.6%)
RDPO	deviations from interview topic referring to events	528 (32.8%)	625 (28.2%)
RTP	personal talk unrelated to interview topic	51 (3.2%)	293 (13.2%)
		1608 (100.0%)	2218 (100.0%)

[a] $\chi^2 = 115.6$; $df = 2$; $p \ll .0001$.

STYLE-ORIENTED BEHAVIOURS OF RESPONDENTS CONSIDERING BOTH STYLES

We expected that respondents interviewed in the socio–emotional style would reveal more personal information than respondents interviewed by formal style interviewers.

To test this expectation, we combined several respondent codes. The codes RATA to RFTI indicate "task-oriented information giving." Requests for repetition or clarification, refusals to answer, and answering "don't know" were classified as "other task-oriented behaviour." The codes RDPO, RDPE, and RTP represent "giving personal information," while the codes RPN and RTN were summarized as "neutral respondent behaviour." The results of this grouping of codes appear in Table 15.

From these results, it seems that the greater number of behaviours of respondents interviewed in the socio–emotional style is attributable to the provision of more personal information in this style. The analysis of the *kinds* of personal information provided by respondents exposed to the two styles revealed that the distributions are quite different (see Table 16).

To summarize, respondents interviewed in the socio–emotional style provided more personal information of all three kinds. The greatest difference between the styles concerned personal talk unrelated to the interview topic.

ADEQUATE AND INADEQUATE BEHAVIOURS OF RESPONDENTS IN BOTH STYLES

As to task-oriented behaviours, respondents interviewed in one style did not produce more inadequate behaviours when exposed to the other style (see Table 17). In other words, the differences in interviewing styles did not affect the degree of adequate or inadequate respondent behaviours.

Table 17
ADEQUATE AND INADEQUATE TASK-ORIENTED RESPONDENT BEHAVIOURS IN BOTH INTERVIEWING STYLES[a]

Task-oriented respondent behaviours	Style of interviewing	
	Formal	Socio–emotional
Adequate	3656 (82.6%)	3610 (83.4%)
Inadequate	771 (17.4%)	720 (16.6%)

[a] $\chi^2 = 96$; $df = 1$; p not significant.

Summary of the Frequency Analysis Findings

1. Interviewers trained in the socio–emotional style of interviewing employed more person-oriented behaviours than interviewers trained in the formal style of interviewing. This means that our experimental manipulation was successful.
2. Interviewers trained in the socio–emotional style of interviewing behaved more inadequately, particularly by using directive actions, than the interviewers assigned to the formal style of interviewing. This means that the information obtained may be more biased when selecting a socio–emotional style of interviewing, rather than a formal style.
3. Respondents exposed to the socio–emotional style perceived the interviewers as behaving more personally than respondents interviewed in the formal style.
4. Respondents who experienced the socio–emotional style of interviewing provided the same (high) amount of adequate information in direct response to the questions as respondents interviewed in the formal style.
5. Respondents interviewed in the socio–emotional style revealed more personal information; frequently, however, information that was not related to the interview topic. This means that this style of interviewing is somewhat inefficient.

ACTION-BY-ACTION ANALYSIS

The interaction between interviewer and respondent appears in the form of question–answer sequences. Any particular question–answer sequence is a string of codes, representing the behaviour of respondent and interviewer over time and in mutual reciprocity. Any set of sequences can be represented in the form of a tree where the branches depict particular strings (see Figure 1). The numbers in Figure 1 indicate the frequencies of transition from one code to another. For the sake of simplicity, transitions < 15 are omitted. Notice that the tree in Figure 1 starts with questions asked literally (IQTL); trees may, however, begin with any code, depend-

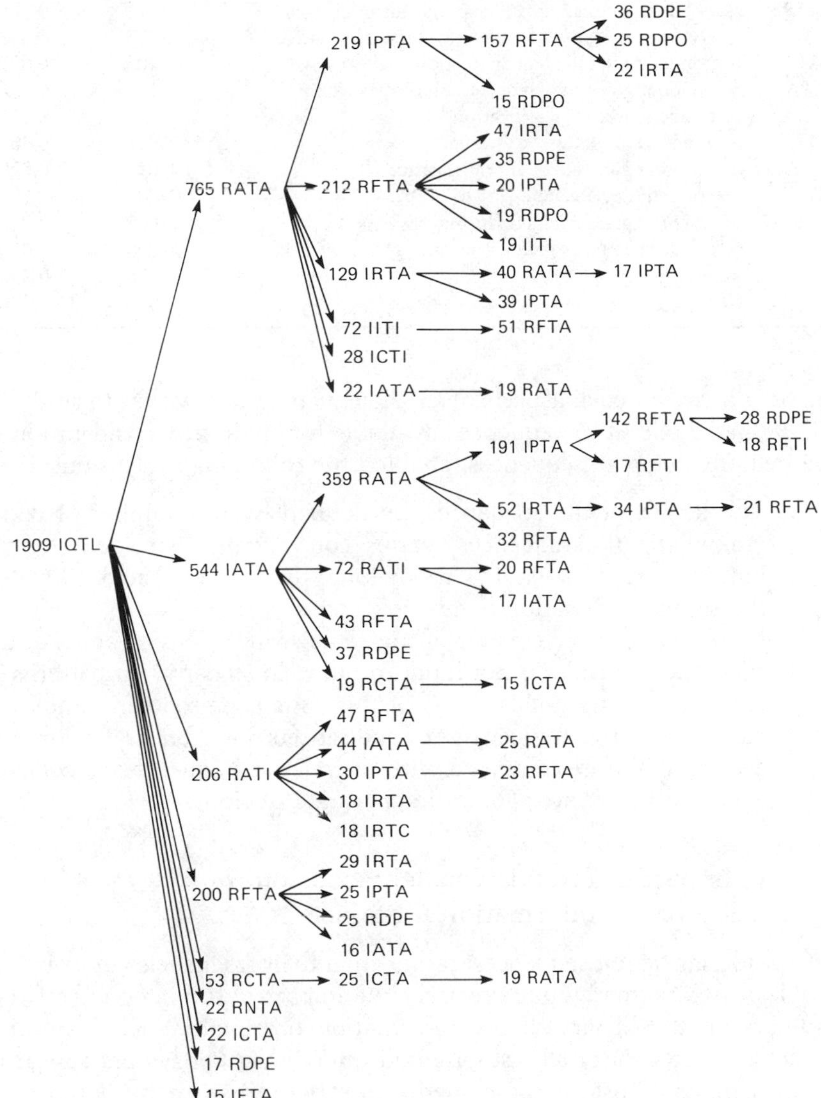

Figure 1 Tree representation of Q–A sequences beginning with questions asked literally (transitions less than 15 omitted).

Table 18
OBSERVED AND EXPECTED RELATIVE FREQUENCIES OF CODES OCCURRING AFTER QUESTIONS ASKED LITERALLY

Code	Description	Observed	Expected
RATA	respondent gives adequate response alternative	0.401	0.105
IATA	interviewer presents adequate response alternatives	0.285	0.049
RATI	respondent gives inadequate response alternative	0.108	0.039
RFTA	respondent gives adequate factual information	0.105	0.187
RCTA	respondent asks for clarification	0.028	0.016
RNTA	answers "don't know" or similar	0.012	0.005
ICTA	interviewer gives adequate clarification	0.012	0.025
RDPE	respondent deviates referring to events	0.009	0.101
IFTA	interviewer gives adequate formal reaction	0.008	0.028
RDPO	respondent deviates giving opinion	0.006	0.050
	other codes	0.026	0.395
		1.000	1.000

ing on which particular aspects of Q–A sequences one wishes to study. In all, we had 2,688 Q–A sequences available for analysis. Consideration of the tree, involving all sequences, enabled the following conclusions:

1. The length of the sequences, as defined by the number of codes making up the sequences, varies considerably. For example, the longest sequence was 111 codes long; the mean is about 10 codes: the standard deviation is nearly 7 codes.
2. Many sequences were part of the same strings. This means that the succession of codes is not random but follows particular patterns or configurations. An illustration of this issue is presented in Table 18. Here the relative frequencies of codes occurring after a question was asked literally are compared with the relative frequencies of codes as expected by chance. The differences are obvious.

The Impact of Interviewer Behaviour on the Quality of the Information Obtained

Considering action sequences, rather than their frequencies in isolation, enables us to estimate quite precisely the impact of the interviewers' behaviours on the quality of the information obtained. When inspecting Table 9, about 17% of all task-oriented interviewer behaviours appear to be inadequate. Most of these inadequate performances cannot be improved by the interviewer. For example, clarifying a question directively,

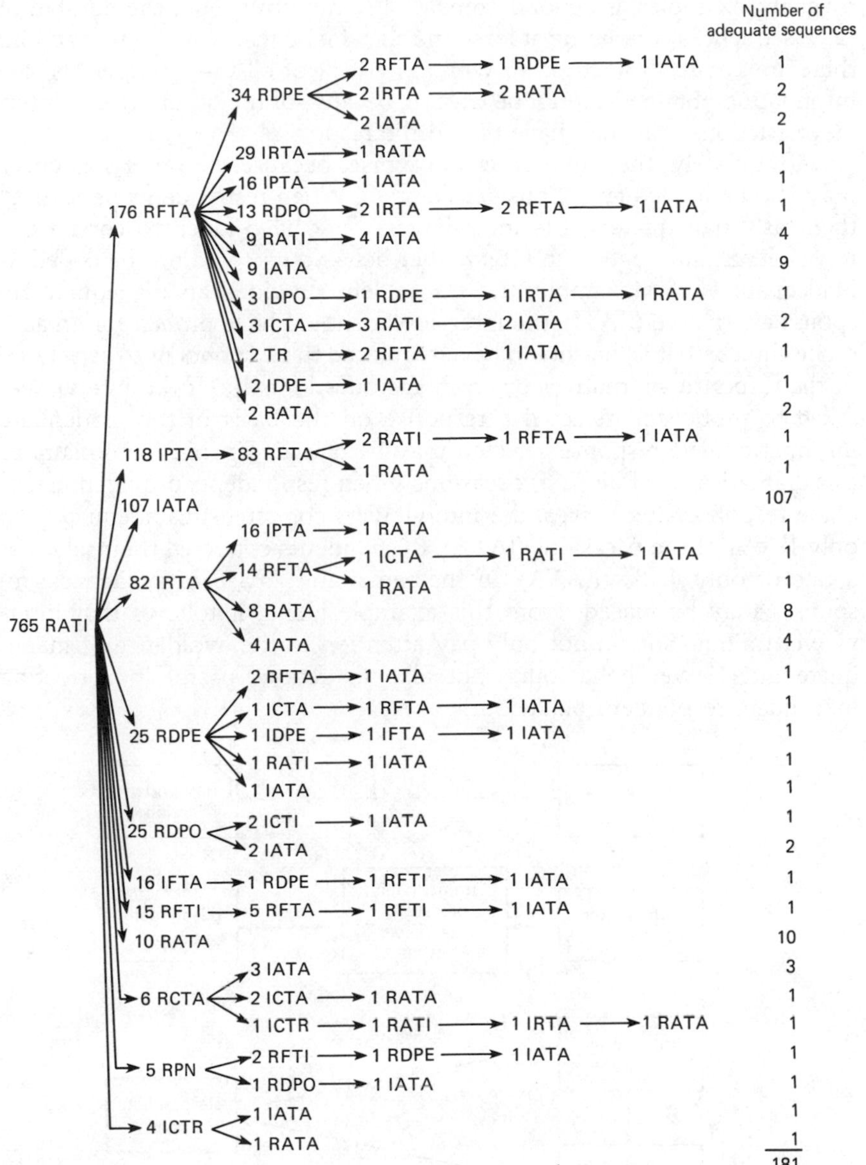

Figure 2 Inadequate Q–A sequences after respondents provided an inadequate response alternative.

by giving examples, is beyond "repair." We can now count the number of Q–A sequences containing at least one such inadequate interviewer action; there are about 40%. In other words, in 40% of all Q–A sequences, the information obtained cannot be trusted, because of the occurrence of interviewer actions that may have biased the responses.

Unfortunately, the situation is still worse, because the other sequences may also be inadequate. Consider Figure 2. When respondents performed their task inadequately, the interviewers may have failed to correct the respondents, although such interviewer behaviours could not be coded as inadequate. If, for example, the respondent provided an inadequate response alternative (RATI), the interviewer should have probed for an adequate choice; that is, he should have requested the respondent to select one of the response alternatives given in the questionnaire. If the interviewer failed to probe and selected a response on the basis of the inadequate information, the response selected may be biased. Figure 2 demonstrates this dramatically: of all (765) occasions when respondents provided inadequate response alternatives, the interviewers corrected this adequately in only 19.6% of the occasions (IATA). Respondents corrected themselves at a rate of only 4.1% (RATA). In the remaining 76.3% of sequences, responses may be biased. From this example alone, it follows that interviewer training should not only pay attention to the avoidance of inadequate interviewer behaviours, but also to actions useful in correcting inadequate respondent behaviour.

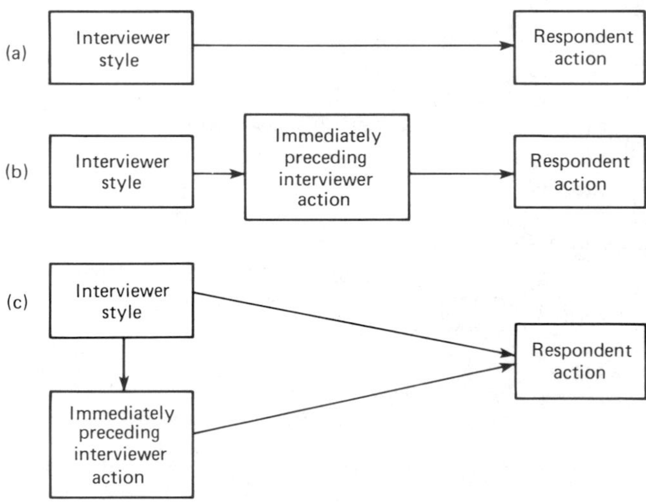

Figure 3 The possible effects of interviewer style and immediately preceding interviewer action on respondent actions.

Table 19
TASK-ORIENTED AND PERSON-ORIENTED RESPONDENT BEHAVIOURS IMMEDIATELY PRECEDED BY TASK-ORIENTED AND PERSON-ORIENTED INTERVIEWER BEHAVIOURS[a]

	Immediately preceding interviewer behaviours	
Respondent behaviours	Task-oriented	Person-oriented
Task-oriented	6691 (83.2%)	89 (11.0%)
Person-oriented	1352 (16.8%)	722 (89.0%)
	8043 (100.0%)	811 (100.0%)

[a] $\chi^2 = 2141$; $df = 1$; $p \ll .0001$.

Respondent Behaviour as Determined by either Interviewer Style or Immediately Preceding Interviewer Action

As we have seen above, respondents interviewed in the socio–emotional style provided more personal information than respondents interviewed in the formal style. Action-by-action analysis allows us to investigate the causes for this difference in more detail. Put more specifically, the respondent might have reacted vis-à-vis the general style of the interviewer, or the respondent might have acted considering only the one immediately preceding action of the interviewer.

The various possibilities are presented in Figure 3: (a) indicates that the respondent reacts only with respect to the general style of the interviewer, (b) shows that the effect of interviewer style on the respondent's actions is mediated by the immediately preceding interviewer action, and (c) takes both effects into account.

Table 20
TASK-ORIENTED AND PERSON-ORIENTED RESPONDENT BEHAVIOURS IN BOTH INTERVIEWING STYLES, AS IMMEDIATELY PRECEDED BY EITHER A TASK-ORIENTED OR A PERSON-ORIENTED INTERVIEWER BEHAVIOUR

	Preceding interviewer behaviours			
	Task-oriented		Person-oriented	
Respondent behaviour	Formal style	Socio–emotional style	Formal style	Socio–emotional style
Task-oriented	3385 (82.9%)	3306 (83.5%)	10 (25.0%)	79 (10.2%)
Person-oriented	699 (17.1%)	653 (16.5%)	30 (75.0%)	692 (89.9%)
	4084 (100.0%)	3959 (100.0%)	40 (100.0%)	771 (100.1%)

Table 21
EFFECTS OF INTERVIEWER STYLE AND IMMEDIATELY PRECEDING INTERVIEWER BEHAVIOURS ON RESPONDENT BEHAVIOUR

	z-value	p-value
Interviewer style	2.64	$< .005$
Immediately preceding interviewer behaviour	16.65	$\ll .001$

From Table 19 it appears that the immediately preceding interviewer action does affect the respondent's actions considerably. The relative effects of interviewer style and the immediately preceding interviewer action were estimated with the aid of Goodman's multivariate contingency table analysis (see Tables 20 and 21).

The effect of interviewer style and the immediately preceding interviewer action on the respondent's action are expressed as z values. It can be seen that the effect of the immediately preceding interviewer action, with the effect of interviewer style eliminated, is much greater than the effect of interviewer style, with the effect of the immediately preceding interviewer action eliminated.

It must be concluded that the effect of interviewer style on the extent of personal information that the respondent gives is mediated mostly by the interviewer's immediately preceding behaviour.

SUMMARY

In this chapter we have presented the design and the preliminary results of a research project concerning the interaction between interviewer and respondent in the setting of a typical survey interview. To investigate the effects of the (style of) behaviour of the interviewer on the behaviour of the respondent, and to avoid the methodological drawbacks of earlier research in this field, we designed an experiment in which interviewer style is the main independent variable. Analysis of the speech acts of interviewer and respondent has brought us to the following conclusions:

1. In comparison with interviewers trained in the formal interview style, interviewers in the socio–emotional interviewer style (a) perform more person-oriented behaviours (which means that the experimental manipulation was successful); and (b) perform more inadequate speech acts, for example, inadequate clarifications (with the consequence that the information obtained may be more biased).
2. In comparison with respondents interviewed by formal-style inter-

viewers, respondents interviewed by interviewers trained in the "socio-emotional" style (a) give more personal information; however mostly information that is unrelated to the interview-topic; and (b) give the same high amount (83%) of adequate information in direct response to the questions.

An analysis of question–answer sequences has led us to the following conclusions:

3. In about 40% of all question–answer sequences, the interviewer, somewhere in the sequence, acts inadequately without correcting this mistake later. The information obtained as the result of such sequence is probably biased.

4. From the finding that our well-trained interviewers usually did not correct inadequate respondent behaviours, we formulated the rule that interviewer training should also pay attention to reacting to inadequate respondent performance in the correct manner.

5. The behaviour of the respondent is strongly affected by the immediately preceding behaviour of the interviewer. Compared with this effect, the effect of interviewer style in general is rather small.

REFERENCES

Brenner, M. (1981a). Patterns of social structure in the research interview. In *Social method and social life* (M. Brenner, Ed.), pp. 115–158. London: Academic Press.

Brenner, M. (1981b). Skills in the research interview. In *Social skills and work* (M. Argyle, Ed.), pp. 28–58. London: Methuen.

Brown, J. S., and Gilmartin, B. G. (1969). Sociology today: Lacunae, emphases and surfeits. *American Sociologist, 4,* 283–291.

Cannell, Ch. F., and Kahn, R. L. (1968). Interviewing. In *The Handbook of social psychology* (Vol. 2) (G. Lindzey and E. Aronson, Eds.), pp. 526–595. Reading, MA: Addison-Wesley.

Denzin, N. V. (1970). *The research act.* Chicago, IL: Aldine.

Dijkstra, W., and van der Zouwen, J. (Eds.) (1982). *Response Behaviour in the survey–interview.* London: Academic Press.

Hyman, H. H. et al. (1954). *Interviewing in social research.* Chicago, IL: University of Chicago Press.

Phillips, D. L. (1971). *Knowledge from what?* Chicago, IL: Rand McNally.

Phillips, D. L. (1973). *Abandoning method.* San Francisco: Jossey-Bass.

Wahlke, J. C. (1979). Pre-behavioralism in political science. *American Political Science Review 73,* 9–30.

4

Questionnaire Design in the Context of Information Research

T. D. WILSON

PROJECT INISS:[1] A STUDY OF INFORMATION-SEEKING BEHAVIOUR IN SOCIAL SERVICES DEPARTMENTS

The work reported here was part of a 5-year action research project to identify the information needs and information-seeking behaviours of social workers and their managers, with a view to introducing evaluated innovations in organizational information systems.

The project had three phases:

1. An observational study of staffs of social services departments, covering all aspects of information transfer and communication. Twenty-two members of staff, ranging from Basic Grade Social Worker to Director of Social Services, were each observed for 1 working week.
2. Interviews of 151 members of staff, stratified by work role and randomly sampled from staff lists using random number tables. The work-role categories used were: Directorate, for the Assistant Director level and above; Middle Management, for managerial levels down to Area Director; Specialist, for Advisors, Training Officers, and Research Officers; Field-workers, for Senior Social Workers and Social Workers; and Administrative Support Staff, for Clerks, etc.
3. An innovation phase in which a number of ideas for improving information transfer were tested in seven departments. The innovations were the direct result of the field-work experience, and were introduced in

[1]Project on information needs and information services in local authority social services departments (Wilson et al., 1978).

ISBN 0-12-131580-0

the departments through negotiation, not only at the top of the organization, but also with the levels of staff most directly affected. Consequently, the innovations adopted were those perceived by the staff to be the most likely to make a contribution to their daily work.

The project as a whole has been widely discussed in the professional social-work press and in the information-science literature, and has led to occasional short courses in information handling and communication under the auspices of the National Institute for Social Work. The results are readily accessible through a number of publications (see Wilson and Streatfield, 1977, 1980, 1981; Streatfield and Wilson, 1980; Wilson et al., 1978). In this chapter, I am concerned with an aspect of the project not previously discussed in detail: the design of our study questionnaire and its employment in the interviews.

PRINCIPLES OF QUESTIONNAIRE DESIGN

The design of questionnaires involves a process with several general stages:

1. Preliminary design work on the areas to be explored in the interview.
2. Question wording and sequencing.
3. Physical design or layout.

Pilot testing may be part of any, or all, of these stages of design.

In the standard texts on survey research methods, most attention is given to problems of question wording and sequencing and to physical design (see Hoinville, Jowell, et al., 1978; Hughes, 1976; Madge, 1953; Mayntz et al., 1969; Moser and Kalton, 1971; Oppenheim, 1966). In only two of these texts is preliminary design work given any attention: Hoinville, Jowell et al. (1978, p. 9) note: "The soundest basis for developing structured questionnaires is preliminary small-scale qualitative work to identify ranges of behaviour, attitudes and issues." They then proceed to discuss in-depth interviewing and group interviews as the appropriate kinds of "qualitative work." Oppenheim (1966, p. 25) comments: "The earliest stages of pilot work are likely to be exploratory. They might involve lengthy, unstructured interviews; talks with key informants; or the accumulation of essays written around the subject of the inquiry." In none of the texts mentioned, however, is there any detailed discussion of the relationships between pilot work, or "qualitative work," and the more specific aspects of questionnaire design. By presenting a case study, I intend to address these relationships.

THE OBSERVATIONAL PHASE OF PROJECT INISS

As noted above, the first phase of Project INISS involved 22 person-weeks of observation in five social services departments. The form of observation used was "structured observation," as defined by Mintzberg (1973, p. 231):

> a method that couples the flexibility of open-ended observation with the discipline of seeking certain types of structured data. The researcher observes the manager as he performs his work. Each observed event . . . is categorized by the researcher in a number of ways . . . as in the diary method, but with one important difference. *The categories are developed during the observation and after it takes place.*

The one amendment we made to this definition, in the case of Project INISS, is that the explanatory categories were developed *before,* during, and after the observation, relying for the precategorization, in part, upon Mintzberg's work.

All observed communication events (a change of event being signalled by a change in the subject of communication) were recorded on edge-notched cards (see Figure 1) and, in total, 5,839 such cards were produced for the 22 participants. Manual analysis was performed on the predetermined variables, such as duration of event, location of the event, and channel of communication used. Further definition of events in terms of the activity engaged in while communicating and the subject of the com-

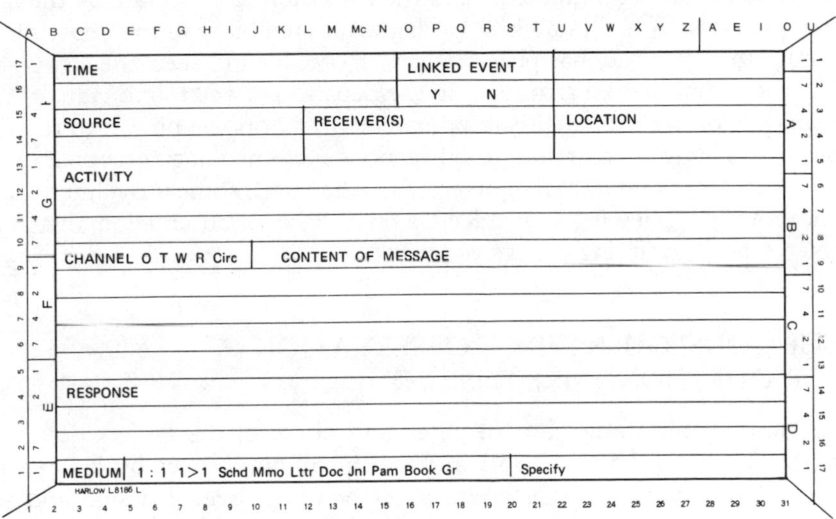

Figure 1 Card for structured observation.

munication was carried out after observation. The categorization of activity was performed using Mintzberg's analysis of managerial behaviour into interpersonal, informational, and decisional roles, slightly expanded by the inclusion of a "social work practitioner" role, a "decision-seeker" role, and a "negotiation-prompter" role, to account for observed non-managerial roles. A simple classification scheme employing two facets, "client or organization focus" and "service focus," was used to categorize the subject of communication events.

Structured observation, therefore, served primarily the purpose of collecting quantitative data. However, it also had an important *qualitative* significance, in that the observers developed an understanding of the nature of social services work and of the relationships between information channels and information types and the work carried out by different categories of staff in the departments.

This understanding extended to the political, cultural, and interpersonal relationships among individuals and groups of staff in the departments and was of a kind not reducible to statistical analysis, but was of great relevance to the interview phase of the project. The observational experience informed not only the design of the questionnaire but, most importantly, interpersonal relations between interviewers and respondents and organizational relationships between the Project and the departments. For example, interviews were carried out in departments in which observation had been done, and it was obvious, from comments made in passing, that respondents had been influenced in their decision to cooperate by the fact that project staff had established a degree of credibility in the department during the observational phase. Furthermore, having seen the extent of feedback from the research team to the department and to individuals, the managers of departments were prepared to support the project to the extent of sending memoranda to all respondents encouraging cooperation. Given that, at the start of the project, there had been some unwillingness to encourage interviewing and, indeed, a preference for observation, this indicated a very gratifying change of attitude.

THE CONSEQUENCES OF OBSERVATION FOR QUESTIONNAIRE DESIGN

Questionnaire design for the interview phase of the Project occupied some 200 person-hours of work and was greatly influenced by the experience of observation, so far as question wording, overall design and sequencing, design of response cards, and categories of questions were concerned.

The questionnaire that emerged from the design process had seven categories of questions:

1. *Work and work role.* Before observation, analysis of the literature had suggested that the chief explanatory variable for differences in information-seeking behavior would be the work done by the respondent. Observation had produced support for this proposition, in that differences were discernible among the five broad categories of staff identified above: directorate level; line managers; specialists and advisers; fieldworkers; and administrative support staff. For example, there were differences in relation to time spent in meetings, as noted below. Questions were directed, therefore, to identifying the category into which respondents could be fitted, and to discovering what specialized knowledge any respondent possessed and to what extent this knowledge was communicated to others.

2. *Contacts,* that is, personal contacts and time spent in formally scheduled meetings. Observation had shown that the dominant mode of information transfer was by word-of-mouth, either face-to-face or over the telephone. These two categories accounted for 60.4% of all observed events. Figure 2 shows a page of the contacts section of the questionnaire and also illustrates the physical layout, with its use of arrows, directing the interviewer to the correct follow-up questions.

Observation had also shown the significance of meetings in social services work, with directorate-level staff spending an average of 16.8 hours a week and line managers 13 hours a week in meetings. As a proportion of the time available in a working week, this could be very demanding: for example, two line managers spent 32% and 33%, respectively, of their working week attending meetings, one social worker 25% of her time, excluding meetings with clients, and a director of social services 70% of his time. As Figure 2 shows, the questions also covered the problems experienced in communicating with the hierarchical levels of the organization.

3. *Information use.* Figure 3 shows the response sheet used as the lead-in to this set of questions. The categories of information types differed from those usually employed in information science investigations, in that they were based on an analysis of the categories of information used by the subjects observed. Previous information needs studies have mostly used categories of information derived from a librarian's concept of information as journal, monograph, government publication, map, and so forth; that is, the categories were based generally on notions of "form of information."

Observation had shown that various difficulties were experienced in getting various kinds of information and, therefore, follow-up questions sought information on the problems and on access to more general documentary materials. These questions proved useful, as 80% of respondents

B. Contacts

In order to do their jobs, people need to communicate with sections, groups, or other individuals in the department, and outside it, for information and advice. I'd like to ask you about these contacts, and the extent to which they enter into your work

IN A 3-TIER AUTHORITY ASK QUESTIONS 4 & 5, 6 & 7, OR 8 & 9
FOR HQ STAFF, ASK QUESTIONS 4 & 5

4. Does a major part of your work involve exchanging information with staff in *[Zone—use local terminology]* offices?

N □ Y □

4.1 Do you experience any problems exchanging information with staff in *[Zone—use local terminology]* offices?

N □ Y □

4.2 What are these problems?

Response:—

5. Does a major part of your work involve exchanging information with staff in *[sector—use local terminology]* offices?

N □ Y □

5.1 Do you experience any problems exchanging information with staff in *[sector—use local terminology]* offices?

N □ Y □

5.2 What are these problems?

Response:—

Go to Q. 10

Figure 2 Part of the questionnaire.

perceived a daily need for names, addresses and telephone numbers, and as 13% experienced difficulty in getting such information; 53% needed access to client records daily and 21% experienced difficulty in getting access. In other words, two kinds of information of a common nature presented problems for significant minorities of those who needed access.

4. *Formal communication systems.* In this section, information was sought on the use of various specialized stores and files of information, such as correspondence files, financial records, case record indexes, and departmental or team libraries. The interviews confirmed the experience of observation, that is, that files of information relating to clients and to the availability of foster parents and adopters, as well as "message" books

		Frequency of Need				
		Not at all	Less than once a month	Monthly	Weekly	Daily
Information Type	Code	1	2	3	4	5
1. Legal, e.g. act of Parliament, DHSS circular		1	2	3	4	5
2. Procedural, e.g. departmental procedure note/manual		1	2	3	4	5
3. Names, addresses, telephone numbers, i.e. 'directory information'		1	2	3	4	5
4. Training, e.g. courses, information syllabuses, course materials		1	2	3	4	5
5. Central Government statistical information, e.g. DHSS statistics		1	2	3	4	5
6. Internal statistical information.		1	2	3	4	5
7. Records relating to clients, foster parents, adopters		1	2	3	4	5
8. Internal personnel and/or financial records, e.g. staff lists, budgets		1	2	3	4	5
9. News of developments in social work, including internal changes, whether written or oral		1	2	3	4	5
10. Research in social work		1	2	3	4	5
11. Evaluations of experience or ideas in social work		1	2	3	4	5
12. Other—please specify:		1	2	3	4	5
________________						
________________						
________________						
________________						
________________						
________________						
________________						

Figure 3 The initial response sheet for information use.

were highly used, whereas the use of team and departmental libraries was more sporadic. Given the nature of social work, this was to be expected.

5. *Personal information habits.* Observation had shown that social services staff maintained various personal files of information and other information aids, such as diaries and address books. The interview results showed that the most frequently used of these sources was the diary, used daily by 95% of respondents. Address books and notebooks were used

daily by 72% and 58%, respectively, of respondents. Again, observation suggested that some personal information files were maintained because of shortcomings in officially provided systems, and 32% of respondents claimed that this was indeed the case.

6. *Organizational climate and the structure of the department.* Previous work (see Olson, 1977) had suggested that information-seeking behaviour would be related to respondents' perceptions of the "climate" of the organization. Accordingly, a short form of the Litwin and Stringer (1968) climate questionnaire was devised, selecting those items which observation had suggested would be most relevant to information use. Table 1 lists the items selected. However, the only significant relationship was that between climate and work role: fieldwork staff had more negative attitudes towards management than other levels and no relationship was found between climate and any of the information-use variables.

7. *Experience and training.* These were questions covering years of experience in social services departments, in the present job, and professional qualifications.

In addition to the direct relationships between observation and questionnaire development noted above, there were two further relationships resulting from observational experience.

First, scenarios were prepared for the five work-role categories on the basis of the narrative accounts prepared following the observation. An example of a scenario is shown in Figure 4. These were sent out to re-

Table 1
LITWIN/STRINGER ITEMS USED

1. The jobs in this Department are clearly defined and logically structured.
2. Our management is not so concerned about formal organization and authority, but concentrates instead on getting the right people together to do the job.
3. Supervision in this department is mainly a matter of setting guidelines for subordinates; they then take responsibility for the job.
4. People in this department don't really trust each other enough.
5. In this department it is sometimes unclear who has the formal authority to make a decision.
6. This department is characterised by a relaxed, easy-going working climate.
7. When I am on a difficult assignment I can usually count on getting assistance from my colleagues.
8. In this department people are encouraged to speak their minds, even if it means disagreeing with their superiors.
9. The policies and structure of the department have been clearly explained.
10. One of the problems in this department is that individuals won't take responsibility.
11. It's hard to get to know people in this department.
12. I feel that I am a member of a well-functioning team.

SCENARIO (13 Information behaviour and contacts)

Social Worker
1) Please tick the appropriate box below:

This description is	Very close	Close	Not at all close

to my normal working week.
2) Please modify the account to make it a closer fit by changing various words or figures.

James Joyce's main source of information about his work is his supervisor (often during team meetings), but he also obtains information from colleagues in the department (including other social workers) and, to a lesser extent, from external contacts. Mr. Joyce never uses the department library, seldom reads journals (apart from glancing at the department's newsletter) and rarely reads other publications. Files on matters of current importance to Mr. Joyce are usually kept in his office filing cabinet, but most other records are held in the section filing system. He is a member of a department working party and occasionally attends external conferences or courses on professional topics.

Figure 4 An example of scenario.

spondents prior to the interviews, and respondents were asked to show whether the account was "very close," "close," or "not at all close" to their "information behaviour" in a particular week. They were also asked to modify the accounts to make them more representative of their experience. Analysis of these accounts was rather difficult and time consuming, but enabled the production of accurate portraits of the relevant categories of staff.

Second, the whole process of design was informed by the team's experience of observation. Individual team members assumed responsibility for particular sections of the questionnaire and prepared draft questions. These were discussed in team meetings in the course of which the researchers played the role of the people they had observed in order to test the propriety, the wording, and the sequencing of questions. The process was quite straightforward: the draft questionnaire was worked through, question by question, while each member of the team tried to respond in terms of the work roles and information-seeking behaviour of the people they had observed. As a consequence, differing perceptions of the meanings of questions emerged, and the influence of differing organizational structures was revealed. In a sense, therefore, the piloting of the questionnaire was done "in house," with the researchers representing respondents. In this way, questions were altered in their wording, resequenced, or dropped from the draft schedule. The final draft version of the questionnaire was then sent to members of the Project's advisory committee and further changes were made as a consequence. The final version of the questionnaire (by then, its sixth incarnation) was used in an interviewer training session before being used in the field. It may have been preferable to pilot the questionnaire in the field but, given the available resources, this was not possible, and the results obtained using the questionnaire suggest that role-playing on the basis of observation, coupled with informed comment from outside, was a satisfactory alternative.

In summary, therefore, the advantages of basing our questionnaire design on observation in the work settings of the respondents were considerable; the observation period was also essential, since without it the relevance of the questions to the respondents would have been problematic.

THE QUESTIONNAIRE IN USE

As noted previously, 151 interviews were carried out in the interview phase of the Project. The five interviewers (that is, the four research workers and the Project Head) all received interviewer training, conducted by Michael Brenner (an outline of the training procedure is given in his chapter in Part I). Training is often neglected in academic research interviewing (judging from the paucity of references to the subject in published research), but in the case of Project INISS, its worth was proved time and again.

One researcher, for example, was faced with a particularly "difficult" respondent on her first interview. The difficulty in the respondent's behaviour was not related to the questions, but to the interviewing relationship, as from time to time he would switch off the tape recorder, leap from his chair, and begin to hurl abuse against his section head and various other colleagues. He would then sit down again, switch on the recorder, and carry on with the interview as though nothing had happened. Without the training she had received, the interviewer might have been unable to cope with a situation such as this. As it happened, she carried on skillfully with the interview: the resulting tape recording gives no indication whatsoever that the respondent was behaving in a curious manner and no indication that the interviewer was disturbed by his activities.

Most of the problems encountered in the interviewing phase were anticipated and none proved insuperable. In fact, the main difficulty was in making contact with busy people (in some cases more than 250 miles away from Sheffield, where the research team was based) to set up the interviews. In 53 cases out of the 151, more than two attempts were needed before contact was made, and in 31 cases, four or more attempts were needed.

A very high level of cooperation was obtained from all respondents. Based on comments made to the interviewers, it is known that the cooperation was at least partly due to the team's having been observing in all four of the departments in which the interviewing was carried out. In other words, the staff in departments had gained the impression that the Project was nonthreatening and seriously intentioned and that its work was worth supporting.

As might be expected, in spite of careful design and pretesting, difficulties were experienced with some of the questions. Questions that sought generalizations about the frequency of behaviour or specific statements about the amount of time spent in particular activities presented some problems. For example, some respondents were reluctant to specify a particular frequency in answer to the question, "in general, how often do other people *in the department* ask you for advice or information about these areas?" (areas of personal expertise). Also, the question: "can you estimate about what proportion of your time is spent on these activities?" (referring to a response card), caused considerable difficulty, particularly with fieldwork staff, and frequently disrupted the flow of the interview. The main problems with this question seemed to result from difficulty on the part of the respondents in being able to describe a typical week because of the unpredictable nature of client-oriented work, or being able to generalize about the use of time spent in particular activities, possibly because the separate components of work were not usually identified as such.

The work-role scenarios for social workers, senior social workers, and specialists also caused problems. For social workers, the different demands of work on long-term care teams and intake teams, as well as demands connected with differences between urban and rural social service problems appeared to be at the root of the difficulties. For specialists, two categories of problems arose: First, the scenarios had been prepared with the work of specialists responsible for advisory work in relation to particular client groups (for example, the blind, the mentally handicapped, and the elderly) in mind. Naturally enough, specialists of a different kind, namely training officers, research officers, and information officers, found the scenario less satisfactory. Second, several advisers who appeared in the sample were concerned with residential services, whereas the observational phase had been concerned with fieldwork services only.

Two rather unusual instances of failure to complete response sheets relating to types of information or relevance to the respondents occurred: one respondent was partially sighted and the other chose to breast-feed her child during the interview leaving only one hand free to hold the sheet. In the first case the interviewer read out the categories and recorded the responses; in the second, the interviewer passed the sheets to the respondent in such a way that she did not have to move in accepting them. He then recorded the responses. (The fact that the mother was feeding her child provides unusual evidence of the relaxed manner in which the interview was carried out!)

Finally, the items related to organizational climate caused some problems: frequent hesitation was encountered with some statements containing two elements that were not always seen as naturally associated. For example: "The jobs in this Department are clearly defined and logically structured." Also, some of the apparent underlying assumptions, such as that staff should "take responsibility for the job," were challenged, and items that referred to a "team" almost certainly were understood to refer to the local, social-worker team rather than to staff more generally in the department.

These latter points are all the more disturbing when it is recalled that the Litwin–Stringer list is usually employed in self-administered questionnaire studies, without the presence of an interviewer.

CONCLUSIONS

Effective interviewing demands (for details, see Brenner's chapter in Part I):

1. Trained interviewers.
2. A questionnaire designed to meet the research objectives of a study as well as the requirements of the interview situation.
3. Respondents who are cooperative.

The observational phase of Project INISS contributed to all of these aspects:

1. The interviewers were able to employ their training effectively in the context of the organizations and staff of the departments that constituted the research setting.
2. The questionnaire was relevant; that is, it enabled the gathering of the perceptions of information use and communication held by the respondents.
3. We obtained the cooperation of respondents, at least in part, because they were acquainted with the team's earlier work in the departments.

I do not intend to emphasize that prior observation of a research setting is necessarily the best prerequisite for questionnaire design. Clearly, methods suggested by other authors, such as informal, intensive interviews (see

Part II), have their advantages, given that prolonged observation is certainly more expensive and time-consuming than interviewing. However, in a field like information science, where there is relatively little experience of complex, multimethod, social science research, we obtained intimate familiarity with the social life under study, which, in turn, provided an adequate foundation for questionnaire design.

REFERENCES

Allen, T. J. (1977). *Managing the flow of technology.* Cambridge, MA: M.I.T. Press.

Bybee, C. R. (1981). Fitting information presentation formats to decision-making. *Communication Research, 8,* 343–370.

Crane, D. (1972). *Invisible colleges.* Chicago, IL: University of Chicago Press.

Havelock, R. G. (1973). *Planning for innovation through dissemination and utilization of knowledge.* University of Michigan, Center for Research on the Utilization of Scientific Knowledge, Ann Arbor, MI.

Hoinville, G., Jowell, R., et al. (1978). *Survey research practicey.* London: Heinemann.

Hughes, J. A. (1976). *Sociological analysis: Methods of discovery.* London: Nelson.

Litwin, G. H., and Stringer, R. A. (1968) *Motivation and organizational climate.* Boston: Harvard University Press.

Madge, J. (1953). *The tools of social science.* London: Longmans.

Mayntz, R., Holm, K., and Hübner, P. (1969). *Introduction to empirical sociology.* Harmondsworth, Middlesex: Penguin.

Mintzberg, H. (1973). *The nature of managerial work.* New York: Harper and Row.

Moser, C. A., and Kalton, G. (1971). *Survey methods in social investigation.* London: Heinemann.

Olson, E. E. (1977) Organizational factors affecting information flow in industry. *Ashib Proceedings, 29,* 2–11.

Oppenheim, A. N. (1966). *Questionnaire design and attitude measurement.* London: Heinemann.

Price, D. J. de S. (1963). *Little science, big science.* New York: Columbia University Press.

Storer, N. W. (ed.) (1973). *The sociology of science: Theoretical and empirical investigations.* Chicago, IL: University of Chicago Press.

Streatfield, D. R., and Wilson, T. D. (1980). *The vital link: Information in social services departments.* Sheffield: Community Care and the Joint Unit for Social Services Research.

Weinshall, T. D. (ed) (1979). *Managerial communication: Concepts, approaches and techniques.* London: Academic Press.

Wilson, T. D., and Streatfield, D. R. (1977). *Information needs in local authority social services departments: An interim report on project INISS". Journal of Documentation, 33,* 277–293.

Wilson, T. D., and Streatfield, D. R. (1980). *You can observe a lot . . .: A study of information use in local authority social services departments.* Department of Information Studies, University of Sheffield. Occasional Publications No. 12, Sheffield.

Wilson, T. D., and Streatfield, D. R. (1981) Structured observation in the investigation of information needs. *Social Science Information Studies, 1,* 173–184.

Wilson, T. D., Streatfield, D. R., Mullings, C., Lowndes Smith, V., and Pendleton, B. (1978). *Information needs and information services in local authority social services departments (project INISS), final report to the British Library Research and Development Department on stages 1 and 2, October 1975–December 1977.* London: British Library.

5

A Multiple Sorting Procedure for Studying Conceptual Systems*

DAVID CANTER
JENNIFER BROWN
LINDA GROAT

CONSTRUCTS AND CATEGORIES

Many psychologists have emphasised that the ability to function in the world relates closely to the ability to form categories and to construct systems of classification by which nonidentical stimuli can be treated as equivalent (e.g., Miller 1956; Bruner et al., 1956; Rosch, 1977). As Smith and Medin (1981) have recently reiterated, if we had to deal with objects, issues, behaviour, or feelings on the basis of each unique example, then the effort involved would make intelligent existence virtually impossible. Thus, an understanding of the categories people use and how they assign concepts to those categories is one of the central clues to the understanding of human behaviour. As consequence, one of the important questions for many investigations is the nature and organisation of the concepts that people have, specific to the issues being explored.

In the present chapter, a procedure for exploring the categories and systems of classification that people use in any given context will be described. It is known as the *multiple sorting procedure,* and it allows a flexible exploration of conceptual systems either at the individual or the group level. The rationale for the procedure will first be discussed and then examples of its use for answering a variety of different research questions will be presented.

In this discussion of the nature and organization of people's conceptual

*We are grateful to Judith Sixsmith for her comments on this chapter.

ISBN 0-12-131580-0

systems, an important distinction must be made between the underlying categorization processes and the "ordinary" explanations that people give for their actions. It is the former that is the focus of this chapter; the latter will be discussed in another chapter by Brown and Canter.

As Brown and Canter argue, many research questions are best answered by reference to "ordinary" explanations, especially when the expertise of the individual being questioned and the unique understanding that he or she can bring to the situation are central. Alternatively, in those studies where the research questions focus on the general conceptual processes underlying the explanations people might give, it is frequently fruitful to explore the categorical organisation of those conceptual processes.

For example, if the research were questioning the compromises involved in administering a prison, then the explanations of the prison governor would be crucial to the study. On the other hand, if the differences in the experiences of inmates of different prisons were being explored, then it would be important to examine the classifications schemes which prisoners applied to their prison experience.

The study of personal systems of classification and of explanations are not inevitably distinct. They are both part of the general psychological approach that places an emphasis on understanding the individual's own framework for dealing with and making sense of the world. They do, however, place an emphasis on different aspects of people's conceptualisations, and are consequently of particular relevance for different types of research question.

Thus, although the study of the personal categorisation processes people use in thinking and acting can be recognised as being part of the general exploration of meaning, it does focus especially on subjective or personal meaning. In the book they edited, *Personal Meanings,* Shepherd and Watson (1982) show with many examples that in both a clinical and a scientific mode of operation, practitioners need to construe the personal meanings of others. This construal requires, they argue, the development of a framework for describing the professional understanding of the meanings utilised by others. For such a framework to be authentic, Shepherd and Watson insist, following Harré and Secord (1972), that it must draw upon an intensive rather than extensive approach to data collection. This involves working directly with individuals in their own terms, respecting their ability to formulate ways of thinking about the world and their experience of it. This contrasts with the use of standard questionnaires or structured interviewing procedures in which the researcher has formulated views on what the respondent will wish to comment upon, and so the researcher is, in effect, checking the extent to which the respondent will endorse the experimenter's speculations.

The intensive study of personal meanings also has strong parallels in the studies of *subjective meaning* carried out by Szalay and Deese (1978). They argue for a clear distinction between "lexical" and subjective meaning. The former being an attempt to define in the public forum (as in a dictionary) the commonly held meanings of words, the latter being an account of what is salient to an individual together with an indication of its affectivity. They see the study of these meanings as being crucial to the understanding of culture.

It is their focus on culture that leads Szalay and Deese to refer to *subjective* meaning, and the client-oriented perspective of Shepherd and Watson which leads them to deal with *personal* meaning. Yet they both have much in common. They both emphasise the need to understand the conceptual system of the individuals being studied or helped. The conceptual framework of constructs and the categories on which the respondent draws are seen by both as the starting point for understanding the respondents' actions in the world.

In Britain, at least, the concern with understanding the personal conceptual systems of individuals was spurred on by the writings of Kelly (1955) and helped along by the prolific enthusiasm of Fransella and Bannister (e.g., Fransella and Bannister, 1977). Yet, the view that each individual had a unique way of construing the world was not alien to William James many years earlier (1890) and was emphasised in some of Allport's writings (1937), when he argued for the value of an idiographic approach. Anthropologists and sociologists, especially those with a structuralist orientation, have also emphasised throughout the present century the importance of understanding individuals' systems of meaning (cf. Douglas, 1977). Furthermore, social psychologists, in studying the role of situations in human behaviour, have established the importance of the interpretations people make of those situations in which they find themselves (Argyle, et al., 1981).

RESTRICTIVE EXPLORATIONS

The brief review above reveals that there are two common themes in many disparate writings on psychology. One is the need to explore the view of the world as understood by the respondents in any enquiry. The second is the recognition that that world view is built around the categorisation schemes people employ in their daily lives. Yet, unfortunately, psychologists have been influenced by a further consideration, which has tended to dilute the impact of these two themes: the desire for quantitative, preferably computer analyzable, results. Most computing procedures have limitations that are so fundamental that they are taken for granted and rarely challenged, thus influencing the data collection procedures in ways so subtle that researchers are unaware of them. A self-structuring cycle is then set in motion. Data are collected in a form that fits known methods of analysis. Standard analytical procedures gain in popularity and are easy to use because they fit the usual data. Data are then commonly collected in the form appropriate to the standard procedures. Thus the existing capabilities of readily available computing procedures help to generate standard forms of data collection, even if those computing procedures are inappropriate for the psychological issues being studied.

Without going into a lot of technical detail, a number of restrictions imposed by conventional, widely used, statistical procedures can be summarized:

1. The most commonly used statistics tend to limit data to those having a strong, clear, linear order. Categorical data are seen as being difficult to accomodate. Thus, rating scales (e.g., 7-point) are much preferred to qualitative categories.
2. The procedures limit the structure of the set of variables, so that there are the same number for each respondent. Furthermore, the number of divisions into which each variable is coded is constrained, so that it is the same for all people. Analysis is limited to the manipulation of arithmetic means and correlations over large groups, but this requires that the actual organisation of the data for each respondent is identical.
3. Because of their computational efficiency and mathematical elegance, statistical models have tended to be restricted to those that are based on assumptions of underlying linear dimensions and that consequently generate dimensional explanatory models. Qualitative models, although increasing in popularity, are still rare.

These constraints on the analysis of data have become more apparent with the increasing availability of other computing procedures that do not have these limitations and with the strengthening of the idiographic perspective. Indeed, it is being recognised that the popularity of procedures such as the semantic differential (Osgood et al., 1957) are due to the ease of data analysis rather than any conviction that they are measuring important aspects of human experience. The semantic differential with its 7-point scales, standard set of items, and factor analysis of results, has been shown to be insensitive to differences between cultures (Osgood, 1962), and, although this may be of interest to cross-cultural psychologists, it does not suggest itself as a technique that will reveal important differences between individuals.

In effect, the semantic differential constrains the concepts people can reveal by providing them with a set of terms to which to respond and by giving precise instructions as to how that response can be structured. Procedures that allow some possibility for the respondent to frame his/her own answers are essential if the essence of any given individual's conceptual system is to be established. Thus, open-ended procedures, especially those built around the interaction potentials provided by the one-to-one interview, recommend themselves to the student of conceptual systems.

Many researchers (unaware of the range of analyses now available) are fearful of embracing open-ended procedures because they are concerned that their results will be difficult to interpret and the report or publication they seek will be difficult to structure. Thus, even when they are interested in their respondents' understanding of the world, they explore it through multiple-choice questions or very constrained rating procedures. Yet, serious researchers will still insist on what is usually termed "good pilot research." This does involve talking to people in a relaxed, open-ended way and learning from them about the concepts they use in a particular context. It is often at this stage that the real objectives, and in effect the major findings, of the research emerge. Subsequent research frequently only clarifies a little, or provides numerical support for, the insights gained at this "pilot" stage. This is a curious state of affairs when data comes from one part of the research activity and insights from another. Research would be more effective if procedures allowed the interviewees to express their own view of the issues at hand, in their own way, whilst still providing information that is structured enough for systematic analysis and reporting.

BEYOND THE REPERTORY GRID

The interview, with its potential for subtle interactions and its concern with the interviewee's understandings, is a fruitful context in which to explore people's concepts. Over the past few years a number of procedures have emerged for generating and examining people's conceptual systems within that context. One of the most popular is Kelly's repertory grid (Kelly, 1955). As many authors have noted (e.g., Fransella and Banister, 1977; Adams-Webber, 1979; Bonarius et al., 1981), the repertory grid, deriving as it does from a theory of people that puts emphasis on their conceptual systems, does have much to recommend it; yet the Role Repertory Test, which has evolved from Kelly's original proposals, is often used with less sympathy for Kelly's Personal Construct Theory than might be expected. Furthermore, the forms of statistical analysis known to Kelly limited the forms of development in grid analysis procedures, which has had direct consequences for the forms of grid which he and his followers have developed.

Fransella and Banister (1977) comment on many of these weaknesses of the grid as used. They point out:

1. The grid "has been turned into a technology which generates its own problems and then solves these problems. Such problems do not necessarily relate to any attempt to understand the meaning which the person attaches to his universe" (p. 113).
2. Grid use has been limited by the "requirement that the subject present his judgements in handy grid statistical format before we can analyse pattern" (p. 116).
3. "It is a fair guess that it is the mathematical ingenuity of the grid which has attracted psychologists rather than its possibilities as a way of changing the relationship between 'psychologist' and 'subject' " (p. 117).

Recent developments in computing procedures have weakened some of these criticisms, especially interactive on-line computing, which allows a much more flexible exploration of construct systems (cf. Shaw, 1982), but the main point made by Fransella and Banister, that the grid technology as such has masked other possibilities for exploring personal constructs, still remains.

The repertory grid technique is neither as unique in its contribution nor as definitively special to personal construct theory as its users often claim. Kelly himself traces the origins of the grid to the sorting procedures used by Vygotsky (1934) and others, and thus puts his grid technique firmly in the realm of the exploration of categories and concepts. He writes:

> Methodologically the Repertory Test is an application of the familiar concept-formation test procedure. It uses as 'objects' those persons with whom the subject has had to deal in his daily living. Instead of sorting *Vigotsky blocks* or *BRL objects* the subject sorts people. The technique bears some resemblance to the sorting employed in the Horowitz Faces Test. It is also somewhat similar to Hartley's later procedure in which he used pictures in a sorting test. Rotter and Jessor have also experimented tentatively with the formation of 'social concepts' in the sorting of paper dolls of the Make a Picture Story (M.A.P.S.) Test. (Kelly, 1955, Vol. 1, pp. 219–220)

He emphasises that his test differs from these other procedures in two ways. First, it is concerned with content, "how the items are dealt with," as well as the more usual concern for the level of abstraction involved. Second, it is "aimed at role constructs." This latter emphasis was seen as being relevant to clinical practice, not an inevitable emphasis for all studies of personal construct systems.

INSTEAD OF Q-SORTS AND PAIRED-COMPARISONS

The "Q-sort" technique was, like the repertory grid, developed as a way of examining the critical concepts people hold about role figures or events of significance to them (Stephenson, 1953). But, while this method enables people to assign elements to categories, the categories themselves are specified, usually as increments of an adjectival scale. Moreover, the Q-sort is typically used in a form whereby the interviewee is required to assign elements to the categories in a specified (almost always an approximately normal) distribution (Pitt and Zube, 1979). The use of an enforced distribution is defended, in part, on the grounds that the procedure provides data that is more conveniently processed (Block, 1961), and eliminates the problem, inherent in rating scale procedures, of different individuals calibrating the scale in different ways (Palmer, 1980). These restrictions on the interviewee's sorting behaviour thus make the Q-sort more akin to the semantic differential technique than to the intensive one-to-one interview procedure we are advocating.

Other highly restrictive sorting procedures have recently been developed as an alternative to paired-comparison judgements of similarity. For example, Ward (1977) and Ward and Russell (1981) have used sorting procedures, in which both the sorting criteria and the number of categories are specified, as a means of generating similarity matrices. Although Ward argues that the process of sorting is probably more "natural" for the interviewee than similarity judgements, the key argument for its use seems to be that it is less time consuming than paired-comparisons while at the same time provides equivalent similarity data that is suitable for multidimensional scaling procedures.

Indeed, the development of multidimensional scaling procedures grew out of the analysis of similarity judgements of pairs of stimuli. Schiffman, et al. (1981) see similarity judgements as "the *primary* means for recovering the underlying structure of relationships among a group of stimuli" (p. 19). They go on to state that they think that similarity judgements are to be preferred to verbal descriptors because such descriptors are "highly subjective and often conceptually incomplete" (p. 20). The view of the authors of the present chapter is that, whilst there may be some validity to this contention in the experimental study of perceptual stimuli, to which Schiffman and her colleagues repeatedly make reference, such a view of all human conceptualisations is unnecessarily restrictive and has not been defended with any theoretical strength.

It is our contention that perceived similarity is a more complex phenomena than can accurately be described by a single rating. Perceived similarity may, in fact, be defined by a set of multiple categorizations based on a wide variety of criteria. In many cases it is the overall patterns that emerge as a result of the concepts people themselves naturally apply to the objects or elements that is of psychological concern. Even when people are unable to put words on their categorization of elements, it is the structure they impose on the world that should be the starting point for the psychologist, rather than any general mathematical theory.

For, although interview-based sorting procedures do have a long history, it is only recently that the full possibilities of this approach have become apparent. These possibilities attempt to avoid the limitations of earlier procedures. The multiple sorting procedure does not impose a view of the likely structure and content of an individual's conceptual system on the interviewee. It minimises the "technique for its own sake" syndrome by allowing the exploration of both the nature and the organisation of concepts about any issue, maintaining the freedom and open-ended qualities considered so essential by many researchers, yet still providing for systematic analysis of individuals or groups. The use of the multiple sorting procedure and systematic analysis of data from it is possible, in part because of developments in nonmetric multidimensional scaling procedures, the use of which will also be illustrated later in this chapter.

SORTING AS A FOCUS FOR AN INTERVIEW

As has been noted, many of the explorations of which interviews are a part are aimed at coming to grips with the conceptualisations of the interviewee, whether it is a market research study, such as that looking at the corporate image of banks (Frost and Canter, 1982), or a more theoretical exploration of architects' use of stylistic terms (Groat, 1982), or even research of a more pragmatic nature, looking at why people move house (Brown and Sime, 1980). In all cases it is the particular categories and concepts people use that is at issue, as well as the way in which they use them. The interview is especially suited to these types of exploration, because the interviewer and the interviewee can explore each other's understandings of the questions being asked and because the one-to-one situation can accommodate a more intensive interaction.

Unfortunately though, the potentials of the interview are frequently its pitfall. Asking open-ended questions in the relaxed way thought to increase rapport is the formula for unanalyzable material. What is needed is a way of providing a focus for the interview to guide and structure the material produced without constraining the interviewee unduly. Bruner, et al. (1956) were some of the first to show clearly the possibilities for exploring the nature of the concepts people have by studying how they assign elements to categories. Such a procedure provides a focus for the interview, allowing other related material beyond that generated by the sorting to be noted. Yet few have followed this lead out of the laboratory by using as elements material of direct significance to the responding individuals.

Sorting procedures of various types have probably been used most frequently in the environmental psychology field, perhaps because they enable researchers to use illustrations and other visual material which are difficult to accommodate within other procedures. Specific applications of sorting technique within environmental psychology have ranged from those used simply to generate similarity matrices (Ward, 1977; Horayangkura, 1978; Ward and Russell, 1981) to those seeking to integrate the sorting process with the verbal descriptions and explanations inherent in a one-to-one interview situation (Gärling, 1976; Palmer, 1978; Groat, 1982). In the case of the latter, the researchers have intentionally used the sorting technique precisely because it is free of the limitations discussed earlier.

In the case of social psychology, one of the earliest approaches to the sorting stimuli is found in the work by Thurstone and Chave (1929), who used the judgements people made of questionnaire items as a basis for assigning weights to those items. It was the discovery that the attitude of the judges influenced the pattern of judgement that lead Sherif and Sherif (1969) to develop the "own categories" procedure and direct measure of "ego-involvement" in attitudinal issues. In the "own categories" procedure, judges assign attitudinal items to categories in terms of how extreme the attitudes expressed are thought to be. The distribution of the items in the categories is then used as a measure of the intensity of the judge's own attitudes. This differs from the clinical object sorting procedure, which Kelly discussed, in that the distribution of items to categories in a predetermined sorting concept is the main concern.

Contemporary psychologists such as Eckman (1975) have also used free sorting procedures in their work on normal verbal communication. In a related manner, Tajfel (1981) developed a theory of social categorization to explain "in" and "out" group behaviour. Tajfel (1978) states: "The role of categorization in perceptual and other cognitive activities has been for many years one of the central issues in psychological theory" (p. 305).

Tajfel's work involves organizing information in certain ways, examining differences and similarities between the content of categorizations. The chief function of this process resides in its role as a tool in systematizing the environment for action. However, Tajfel argues that assigning items to categories is influenced by the other categories in the structure of a person's experience. His experimental work was aimed at unravelling the complexities of prejudice through the process of category assignments.

Clearly then, in using the sorting procedures as an interview focus, the interviewer's task is to identify the interviewee's salient categories and the pattern of assignments used to relate categories to elements. The more freedom the interviewee can be given in performing this task the more likely that the interviewer will learn something of the interviewee's construct system rather than just clarifying his own. Such freedom should extend to the range and structure of the categories, of which the constructs are composed, as well as to constructs and elements sorted.

THE MULTIPLE SORTING PROCEDURE

The multiple sorting procedure advocated here asks little of the interviewees other than that they assign elements to categories of their own devising; it differs from the other previously discussed response formats in that no limitations are necessarily placed on how the sorting is to be done. In fact, the respondent is encouraged to sort the elements, using different criteria, a number of times. The rationale for this less restrictive version of the sorting process is the belief that the meanings and explanations associated with an individual's use of categories are as important as the actual distribution of elements into the categories.

The actual act of sorting items is a common activity. For example, in choosing a house, people will literally sort through the particulars sent to them by estate agents. In many other areas of choice, whether it be clothing, books, partners, or political parties, there is an explicit selection on the basis of a personal categorization scheme. But even when a selection is not overtly involved, such as in evaluating how successful a given setting is likely to be for a given activity, or an essay in gaining a good mark, the judgement is based on an implicit categorization scheme. The multiple sorting procedure aims to bring to light these personal schemes.

To carry out the multiple sorting, a person is presented with a set of elements and an introduction and instructions as follows:

> I am carrying out a study of what people think and feel about *children* [A] So I am asking a number of people *chosen at random* [B] to look at the following *pictures* [C] and sort them into groups in such a way that all the pictures in any group are similar to each other in some important way and different from those in the other groups. You can put the picture into as many groups as you like and put as many pictures into each group as you like. It is your views that count.
>
> When you have carried out a sorting, I would like you to tell me the *reasons* [D] for your sorting and what it is that the pictures in each group have *in common* [E].

> When you have sorted the pictures once I will ask you to *do it again* [F], using any different principles you can think of and we will carry on as many times as you feel able to produce different sorts. Please feel free to tell me whatever occurs to you as you are sorting the pictures.

The items underlined and indicated with letters in [ ] are those components of the instructions that are likely to change for different procedures in relation to different research questions. It must be emphasised, however, that these instructions are only a general statement of what is possible. The flexibility of the procedure is such that many different variations of the instructions are possible. Pilot work is always essential in order to discover what particular instructions are appropriate for each study, although typically all components [A] to [F] must be explicitly dealt with.

The elements to be sorted ([C] in the instructions), depending on the research question, may be generated by the interviewee or the interviewer; they may be labels, concepts, objects, pictures, or whatever, as will be illustrated. The person is usually asked to look through the elements to familiarise him/herself with them; also, the purposes of the research enterprise are explained (relating to instructions components [A] and [B]). In particular, it is pointed out that the interviewer is interested in the interviewee's ways of thinking about the elements presented. The interviewee is then asked to sort the elements into groups so that all the elements in any given group have something important in common, which distinguishes them from the elements in other groups. Thus, a number of groups are produced which may vary in the number of elements in them, and of course the number of groups produced may also vary from person to person and from one set of elements to another.

After this initial sort, further sorts may be carried out by the same individual, a number of times. But let us consider the initial sort before moving to multiple sorts.

An Individual Example

Consider a preliminary example, here drawn from a multiple sort carried out with a gambler we will call Ace. We were interested in Ace's views of various casinos, as part of a larger project to study what it was that gamblers enjoyed about gambling. The particular purpose of the sorting procedure was to see the basis on which a gambler selects which Casino to visit and to get some understanding of his view of the Casinos available. We wanted to know what sort of world a gambler moves around in, what type of choices he sees as being available to him.

Ace was asked to list on cards all the casinos he knew in any detail and to assign names for his own convenience. For the researcher's convenience, each card was numbered on the back. On his first sort, Ace chose to divide the cards into three groupings. These groupings were recorded as shown in Table 1, by the simple process of noting under each group the letter for the card.

At this stage, the researcher has an indication, without any verbal labeling, of one category scheme for the respondent. Such information can be very valuable, especially when working with groups of people who are not especially articulate. But there are a number of further developments of the procedure possible within the same framework. The verbal concommitants of the category scheme can be explored by asking the interviewees to indicate the basis on which they have carried out the sorting, as in the instructions [D] and [E]. This generates two levels of description. The first is a superordinate description of the principle for the sorting, from instructions [D], for example, "whether the casinos have frills or not," or "the amount of money to play the lowest stake." The second is a set of category labels for each of the groups (instructions [E]), for example, for the "frills" sort, Ace's categories were "places with no frills," "places with sedate dining," and """vaudeville"; for the "stakes" sort, Ace's categories were "less than £5," "between £5 and £25," and "greater than £25."

Table 1
RECORD OF ACE'S SORTS[a]

First Sort: "Class of Casino"
1. "Gaming Halls": G, H, D, A
2. "Middle Class": B, C
3. "High Class": E, F

Second Sort: "Type of Frills"
1. "Just Gambling": A
2. "Vaudeville": B, G, H
3. "Sedate Dining": E, D, C, F

Third Sort: "Size of the Stake"
1. "Less than £5": A
2. "Between £5 and £25": G, H, B
3. "Greater than £25": C, D, E, F

Fourth Sort: "Most likely place for me to make money at"
1. "Most likely": A, G, H
2. "Not so much": B
3. "Too expensive": C, D, E, F

Fifth Sort: "Preference"
1. "Most preferred": A, G, H, E
2. "Solid Casinos": C, D
3. "Bit Quiet": F
4. "Did not like at all"

[a]Casinos: A—Golden Nugget; B—Playboy; C—Park Lane; D—Palm Beach; E—Hereford; F—Park Tower; G and H—Las Vegas casinos.

A useful way of recording this verbal information shown by reference to Ace's sorting of casinos is also in Table 1. The categories are summarized with a description of the category scheme for the sort as well as labels for each of the groups within this sort. Other comments and points of clarification made by the respondent can easily be accommodated within this format, as well as any order that might be given to the category groupings. Given the value of the procedure as a focus for exploring a content domain, these comments may generate material of considerable value in their own right. Thus, the researcher need not reduce the responses to bipolar scales, which are often ambiguous when considered at some time after the interview.

Unlike the analyses discussed by Schiffman et al. (1981), and used, for example, by Ward and Russell (1981), the multiple sorting data need not be reduced to association matrixes, typically aggregated across groups. Both the superordinate description and the category labels can be subjected to content analysis and to multivariate statistical analyses, but it should be noted that no structure or order to these descriptions is initially assumed or implied. This is particularly important for the category labels. The bipolar dichotomies of rating scales are not assumed, nor is the order of items from ranking or scaling. If the interviewee specifies a particular order, as in the "amount of the stake" example, then note can be taken of that, but if any order might be more obscure, as in the "frills" example, then that can be utilised as well. Indeed, category schemes frequently emerge that are not simply bipolar; and this raises important questions about the extent to which such bipolarity, assumed in much research, is an actual feature of psychological processes or an artifact of the structured measuring instruments used. Furthermore, in some cases an interviewee may choose to sort some of the elements and leave others as irrelevant to the overall sort taken into account. This irrelevant group is treated as forming a further category and can be incorporated in the subsequent analysis without any loss of information or imposition of a superordinate categorization on all the elements.

Having produced one sort of the elements, it is of value in many projects for the multiple sorting to continue by asking people to examine the elements again and to try and produce another category scheme with new descriptors (instructions [F]). Table 1 gives a summary of all five sortings produced by Ace in the interview conducted with him. Analysis of this will be discussed later. It should also be noted that the number of elements sorted here (8 casinos) is limited by the number of casinos to which anyone has ready access in London, and might not give the richest picture possible.

The process can continue as many times as the interviewee feels able to sort the elements. In research carried out to date, two or three sorts are common, but up to seven or eight are frequently possible, with 15 or more occurring in some cases. The number of elements that it seems fruitful to use is in the region of 15 to 25. Depending on the individual, of course, a complete set of sorts may take anything from 10 minutes to well over an hour, which may also be extended insofar as the sorting is used as a focus for other issues explored in the interview.

Hypothesis Testing

The example used so far, from the casino sortings, is simple enough to illustrate the procedure in use with one person, as a basis for getting to understand some particular aspects of that individual's conceptual system. But the power of the multiple sorting task as a means for testing hypotheses of conceptualisations common across a number of people can also be readily illustrated. Let us consider, for example, the work of Bishop (1983).

Bishop had as a central concern the role the age of buildings played in people's views of their surroundings. However, he was aware that his own fascination with the age of buildings might have given him a particular perspective and that this way of thinking about buildings might not have been very important to most people. However, since it is clear that people can comment on a building's age, any direct questioning about age or its significance might have given a spuriously high weighting to the role of age. Bishop therefore carried out a multiple sorting with a number of respondents. He did this by preparing a set of photographs of buildings which differed in age and gave them to people to carry out a set of free sorts, as described above.

Bishop's hypothesis was strongly supported. Thirty of the 35 people he asked used age as a basis for sorting, although only 8 used it as the basis of their first sort. Bishop went a step further and classified his respondents in terms of the type of age sorting they made, showing quite convincingly that their understanding of architectural age varied very greatly, although they spontaneously used the concept. This differentiation of his groups laid the foundations for the development of his study.

To see the potential range of uses of, and variation on, the multiple sorting procedure and ways of analyzing data from it, we will now turn to other specific examples.

VARIATIONS IN ELEMENTS SORTED

The types of elements that can be used for sorting are limited only by the imagination of the investigator and the practicalities of what can be carried about and sorted on the surfaces available. Indeed, the development of microcomputers offers some intriguing possibilities for increasing the range and variety of elements that can be sorted; for example, moving objects, even for monitoring the process of sorting by recording the hesitations and false starts that might otherwise get lost in a paper and pencil record.

From the initial uses of sorting procedures, as noted earlier, a great number of different objects have been sorted. But in the more recent explorations of the content and structure of free, multiple sortings, a variety of representations of objects, or simulations, have also been used. Groat (1982), for example, used *photographs* of buildings taken from architectural magazines, books and slide collections, to explore how architects' ways of thinking about famous buildings compared with the conceptual systems of accountants. Oakley (1980) used *labels* of places to stay such as hotel, parents' home, or hospital, to examine the views residents had of Salvation Army hostels in which they were living. Grainger (1980) had architects and their clients sort the *activities* a proposed building might house, in order to establish their different understandings of what the building's functions were to be.

Focus of the Elements

In general, the more concrete and specific the elements are and the more familiar the respondent is with the elements, the more likely it is that they will be able to produce a number of rich and varied sorts. Abstract labels of possible emotions, for example, are likely to encourage relatively few sorts, whereas a set of detailed descriptions of actual places a person has direct experience of is likely to lead to the generation of a great many sorts from each respondent. The selection of elements will always need to be guided by an awareness of what the respondents are normally used to considering and whether the research is best served by a simulation, a representation of some entity, or by reference to the actual phenomenon itself.

A further consideration in selecting the range of elements to use is how big a variation to select. If general stereotypic sorts are of interest, then a very broad range across the element domain is advisable. For example, a study of conceptualisations of medical specialities among medical students would possibly be best studied using a list of all the specialities as organised in a medical text book. On the other hand, if students' individual choices of future careers were being explored, then a subset of specialities described in relation to their working context and with reference to the students' direct experience may well generate more specific sortings, revealing the idiosyncrasies of particular individuals' conceptual systems.

Generation of the Elements

In considering how the elements should be generated, two matters need to be considered: (1) whether the elements are to be generated by the investigator or not, and (2) whether the elements will have a specified structure or be a sample of some identified population.

If the researcher is setting out to test some hypotheses about people's conceptual systems, then it is likely that the elements will be identified by the researcher. For example, Groat (1982) chose photographs of buildings to test her particular hypotheses about architects' conceptions of styles. On the other hand, in the example with Ace described above, it was essential to elicit the casinos of which he had direct experience. Similarly, Groat ensured that her set of photographs included three specified styles and four building functions, whereas for the gambler, all the casinos he had actually visited were used.

The generation of the elements thus has a direct bearing on whether the sorting procedure is to be used for exploratory, heuristic, or descriptive purposes or hypotheses testing. This procedure then has potential at many different stages and in many different areas of research endeavour.

Construct Elaboration

As has already been mentioned, the sorting procedure allows constructs to be elaborated in many different ways, depending on the goals of the research activity and on the capabilities of the respondents. If the research is aimed, for example, at identifying whether residents of a hostel think of its function differently as a consequence of how long they have been there, then a knowledge of which other places of residence they think are similar to their own hostel may be of great value. For instance, Oakley (1980), in his study of hostel residents, generated data from the sorting procedure without probity for labels of the categories being used. His respondents did find verbalization difficult, but the groupings of the elements themselves provided him with some useful basic data, which enabled the Salvation Army to clarify some of the principles on which to consider the provision of new hostels.

On the other hand, if the aim of the research had been to look directly at the processes of individual rehabilitation, it would have been necessary to uncover the concepts residents use for deciding where they are going to stay. In this case, the labels associated with each category, or group of elements, would have to be elicited. It is likely that a different set of elements would have been of use in such a study, so that respondents with few verbal skills could be encouraged to express their understanding of what is available to them.

FOCI OF ANALYSIS

The reluctance of earlier researchers to use procedures as open ended as the multiple sorting task, may to some extent be due to the difficulty they perceive in analysing the data generated. However, besides the developments in content analysis, discussed by Barbara Mostyn in an earlier chapter, all of which can be directly applied to the category descriptions generated during the sorting, it is possible to use nonmetric MDS procedures. These enable the analysis to be focused on different issues depending on the research question.

What is meant here by "focusing" is that the research procedure can be tuned to any of a number of different aspects of the material potentially available. The researcher can, for example, choose to deal with differences between groups or to concentrate on particular sorting criteria within individuals. The multiple sorting procedure as such has no special limitation as to the research enterprise for which it is appropriate. It is simply a data-generating procedure which can be harnessed to the goals of a wide range of projects.

First, we shall consider studies of group differences, looking at the relationships between elements and then the relationships between categories. Second, we shall consider studies of differences within individuals.

Group Differences

ELEMENTS, CONCEPTS, AND PEOPLE

In any study of conceptual systems there exist three broad ways in which the data can be examined: by considering differences between the people, differences between the elements, or differences between the concepts and categories to which the elements are assigned. The data matrix that is always possible can be thought of as a cube, as shown in Figure 1.

The importance of the data cube is that it shows the variety of possibilities there are for data analysis. In essence, each of the planes of the cube, A, B, or C, provides a different analysis possibility by aggragating combinations of the dimensions. For example, in the prison study described below only one aspect of the concepts was dealt with—similarity to "this prison." Thus, it was plane A, elements across people, which was the focus of analysis. A study centering on the structure of the concepts a group of people have across one or many elements would be dealing with the data in plane C, because it would require the differences between people to be ignored. A study comparing people in their conceptualizations would be drawn from plane B.

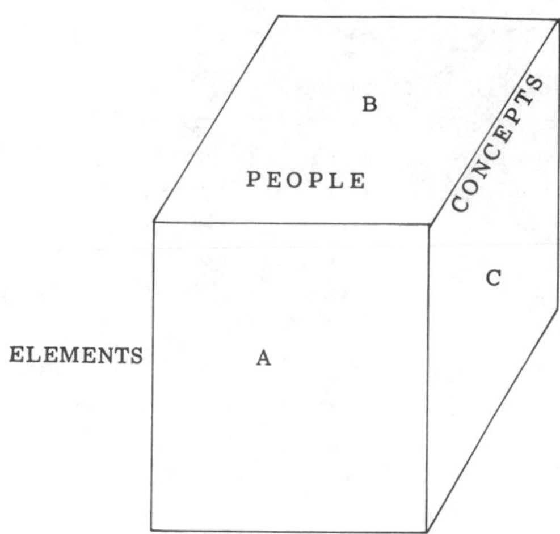

Figure 1 The data cube.

Figure 1 can be used as a guide to help clarify the research question by showing which "slice" through the cube is being used and what "collapsing" of data from another dimension is necessary. It is extremely complex to carry out analyses that combine all three aspects of the data in one operation. It is usually more appropriate to procede through the analysis in stages, working with one plane of the data cube at a time.

One of the most obvious uses for the multiple sorting procedure is to compare the conceptual systems of different groups. There is now a large literature showing how different groups of individuals addressing the same topic may have quite different conceptualizations about it, which in turn give rise to different evaluations of the issues at hand and related actions. However, as Canter (1977) pointed out, studies using standard response formats, such as the semantic differential, tend to underestimate the difference in perspectives between individuals. Indeed, such procedures tend only to indicate small differences in emphases rather than revealing the radical differences in conceptual systems commonly present when different groups interact in relation to some common object.

The repertory grid is commonly used for group comparisons and frequently with some success (Adams-Webber, 1979); but it does have severe practical limitations, both in the number of elements that can be dealt with in any given study and in the overall time taken to complete a grid (Canter, et al., 1976). For comparisons of groups it is also frequently the case that much of the detail generated by the grid is superfluous and not used in analysis. An open, free sorting procedure often has the advantages of individual sensitivity without the procedural disadvantages of the grid.

Ambrose showed the value of a sorting procedure for revealing group differences in a study reported in Canter (1980). In a study of different prisons, inmates and members of staff were asked to sort labels describing places in which people might live. One of the labels to be included in this sort was "this prison." A matrix was derived for each respondent showing which other card was put into the same sort as the cards specifying "this prison." This matrix, in effect, consists of a series of profiles for each individual indicating whether or not they saw their particular prison as similar to all the other places listed. A multidimensional scalogram analysis (MSAI; see Lingoes, 1973, and Zvulun, 1978 for details) was carried out to see whether there were any similarities or differences between the different respondents and their different institutions. Figures 2 and 3 reveal the results.

Figure 2 shows the partitioning of the space for the prisons and Figure 3 the partitioning of the space for the prison staff and the prisoners. Each point in this space represents an individual. The closer together any two individuals are the more similar are their profiles in the data matrix. The advantage of the MSA procedure is that it only deals with each response as a categorical one comparing the categories with each other. No order is assumed between the various categories, nor is any similarity of meaning

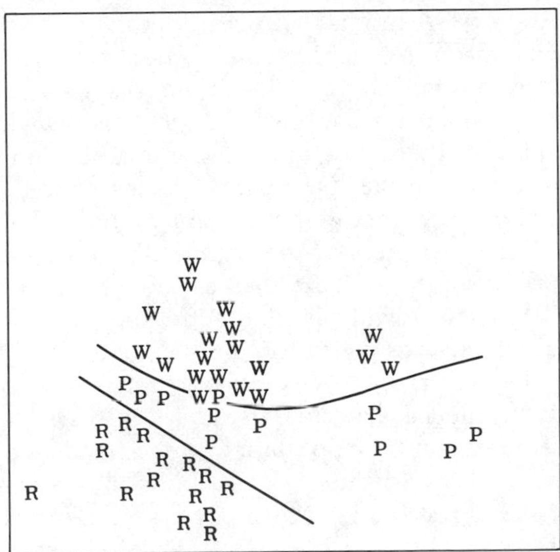

Figure 2 MSAI of card sort of residential setup by respondents in three prison establishments. W, satellite design prison in a rural location with a regional catchment area; R, block design prison in an urban location with a regional catchment area; P, radial design prison in an urban location with a local catchment.

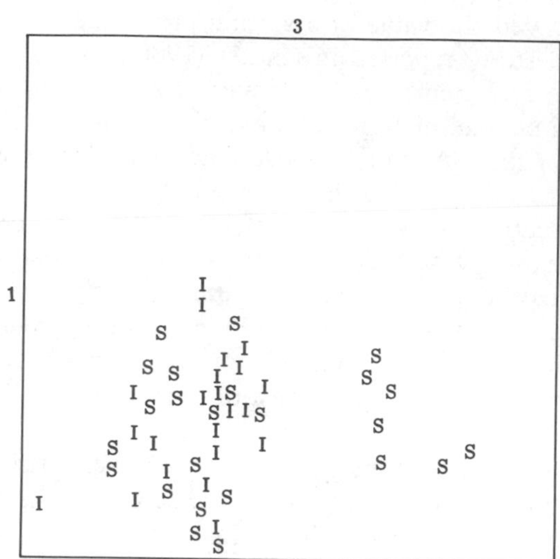

Figure 3 MSAI cardsort of residential settings showing staff and inmate respondents: S, staff; I, inmates.

assigned to the categories for each of the variables. The variables in this case were created by each of the cards used in the sort.

Looking at these MSA results, it is clear that there is no difference between staff and inmates. No clear regions of the space can be identified for these two different groups. In other words, there is not an effect of role on their perceptions of the particular prison. On the other hand, there are clear regional partitions for the different institutions. Furthermore, the order of the three regions through the space places the institutions in a sequence, from those that are most strict in their regime to those that are least strict. This shows that the strictness of the regime can be recaptured from the assignment of the institutions to the place categories. It is also interesting to see here that through individuals' free sorts, the perspective shared by prisoners and staff on the nature of the institution is revealed. In this particular case the role groups may well be assumed to be individuals who would not necessarily be expected to work together. Nonetheless, the sorting demonstrates that they do share an understanding of the nature of the institutions.

The significance of this finding is increased when it is realised that there is no easy way in which the prisoners could have guessed what the prison officers would have done in a free sort, especially across three different institutions. Yet, in a conventional questionnaire it would have been very difficult to remove social desirability bias from such a situation. Furthermore, the language requirements in terms of fluency and vocabulary that would have been necessary to question people about these subtleties would also have been demanding on many prisoners. However, in the present circumstances a simple assigning of cards to sorting categories appears to have been sufficient to reveal some intriguing differences.

Of course, a detailed understanding of the conceptual basis of these differences would not be achieved without a further analysis of the concepts used by staff and inmates. Unfortunately, because of the constrained nature of what was possible within the prison system, the details of the conceptualizations were not explored fully by Ambrose. We will therefore turn to another example to illustrate these more elaborated studies.

THE STRUCTURE OF THE ELEMENTS

In some situations it is of particular interest to try and identify the type of conceptual system groups are using. In other words, the structure and content of elements shared by groups of individuals need to be established. With the prison example this was less possible because only one sort was made by each individual, andthe particular analysis carried out (reported above) focussed on the relationship of one element to all the others. However, it is also possible to carry out analyses that look at the comparison of every element with every other element. Hawkins (1983) did just such an analysis using labels of a variety of possible places with residents of different psychiatric day centres.

Hawkins asked each individual to sort a set of cards labelling places where they might spend their day. Three different day centres were involved in this study, and Hawkins was able to compare the structure of the elements for each of these. She did this by creating an association matrix containing the frequency with which every element was assigned to the same group as every other element, across all sorts and respondents (plane A in Figure 1). A Smallest Space Analysis was carried out on each of the association matrixes created for each of the day centres (cf. Lingoes, 1973; Shye, 1978 for details).

This analysis generates a plot showing that elements more similar to each other in the pattern of sortings to which they are subjected are closer together. Figure 4 shows the SSA plot for the three different hostels; to aid interpretation regions have been indicated on these plots. It can be seen that the overall structures have a number of similarities. They all show the existence of five groups of elements: work, leisure, service, therapy, and residential. They also show that these groups are qualitatively sequenced, around a circle, rather than having a simple, quantitative linear order to them. Yet, there are some clear differences in the way the residents of the

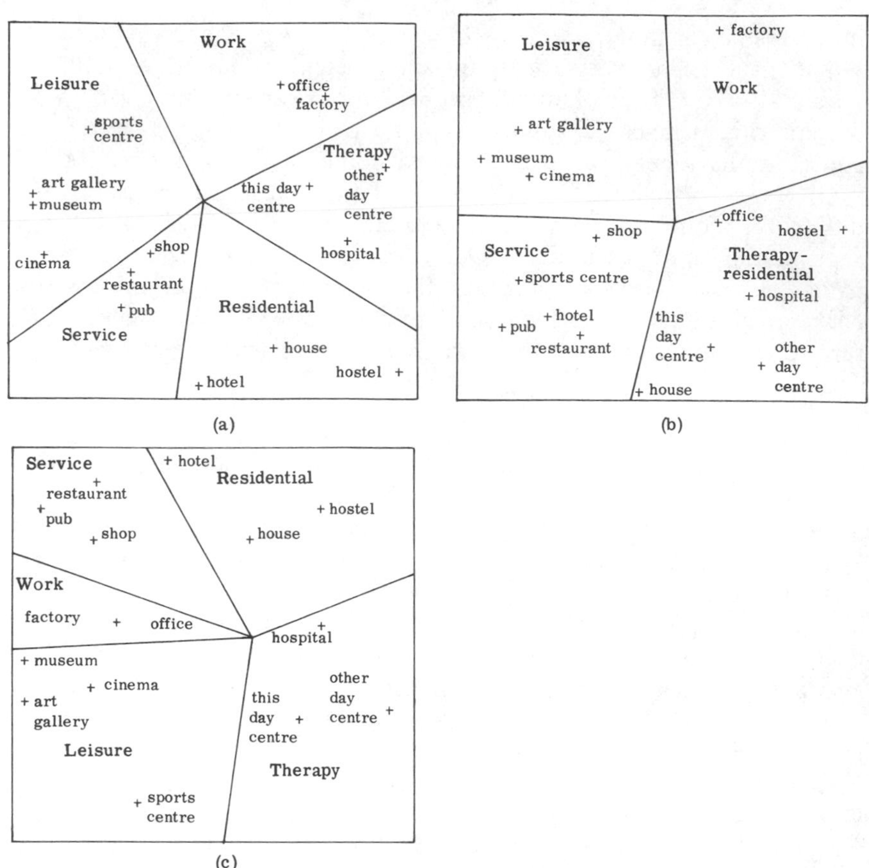

Figure 4 Position of each place on SSA-I plot looking at the frequencies from (a) centre A, (b) centre B, and (c) centre C.

three day centres see the various places. In other words, it is not solely their view of the location of their own particular hostel that is different, but the residents of each day facility actually have a different system of thinking about other possible locations. For example, to the residents of centre C, the therapeutic group, including "this day centre" is seen as being between leisure and residence, whereas for the people in centre A it is between work and residence. This reflects a differing emphasis on rehabilitation to work in the various centres. For centre B, "this centre" and the other therapy elements are confused with residential items coming close to hotel and house. This relates to the fact that the residents of these day centres have typically been using them for up to eight years and they are more chronic and indeed settled into their daily use of these places as somewhere to go.

This is particularly important for both design and development of therapeutic programs. If the whole regime of a particular psychiatric day centre relates to the way the residents conceptualize the opportunities available to them, and this consequently differs from one centre to another, then any generalized guidance suggested for use in all day centres, which aimed to help people to move into the community, would be ineffective if it did not take into account the conception of "the community" particular to any given day centre. The results indicate that the attempts to move individuals from their centre out into the community require subtle understanding of how those individuals actually conceive of the community itself.

THE STRUCTURE OF CONSTRUCTS

Another focus for analysis is the establishment of the underlying construal processes the individual brings to bear on a pattern of elements. This issue is particularly well illustrated by the work of Groat (1982) to which reference has already been made. She was concerned with whether or not architects would conceptualize works of architecture in different ways from accountants. She was able to establish quite clearly, using procedures like those described in earlier sections, that the actual sorting of the elements was different for the two groups. However, it was important to Groat's work that she should establish what types of conceptual issues were actually paramount in the judgements being made.

In order to examine the conceptual issues, she developed a matrix based on the categories within similar sorts. In other words, she first identified, through context analysis, the types of sort used by each of her groups of respondents. For example, both groups contained a number of individuals who referred to both the function and the style of the building. Two separate matrixes were produced, one for the function categories, and one for style. In each of these matrices, the categories were the columns and the 24 buildings sorted were the rows (plane C of Figure 4). The cells of this matrix were a dichotomous score indicating whether that particular building was ever assigned to that category. Smallest Space Analysis of this data showed that the structure of the "function" categories was very similar for both groups. They both divided the photographs into domestic and non-domestic buildings and within each of these groups distinguished the buildings in terms of scale. However, the style categories were quite distinct. The accountants made a big distinction between what they saw as "traditional," "modern," and "futuristic" buildings, whereas architects used a classification scheme clearly drawn from the literature of architectural criticism, distinguishing "Expressionist," "Brutalist," and "Post-Modern."

Groat's study thus shows very well how a detailed analysis of the structure of the conceptualizations of the two groups can reveal subtle differences and similarities in their category schemes. Such differences would normally be hidden by structured questionnaire and interviewing procedures and would be extremely difficult to establish with repertory grids, unless separate grids were developed for each respondent with the consequent time-consuming analysis that would involve.

Differences within Individuals

In our initial example of a multiple sorting we referred to Ace, a gambler. As part of the same study, a casino manager also went through a sorting procedure using the casino and parts of casinos of which he had direct experience. The results of these sortings are given in Table 2. The sortings from these two people, taken together, serve to illustrate the way in which very specific foci can be developed for analysis, dealing directly with the unique, idiosyncratic conceptualizations of particular key individuals.

When individuals carry out detailed sorts on elements that are special to themselves, there is always a possibility that over a variety of sorts they repeat similar categories, simply assigning different labels to each categorization. Thus, an individual who is fluent but not especially cognitively complex may generate a large number of apparently different sorts, which on closer examination are found to have little in the way of variation between the different sortings.

This is an especially important point if comparison is to be made of individuals, because it is the key aspects of their conceptual systems that we need to understand, not simply how many words they can string together. Thus, it is necessary to do an analysis for each individual and to reveal the main conceptual structure within which the individual is working. In regard to the gambler and the manager, separate analyses for each was carried out and a schematic representation prepared to facilitate a comparison of their two conceptual systems.

The analysis here again used MSAI. In this case each of the sortings acted as a separate variable and each individual had a separate matrix. The matrix consisted of the elements as rows and the sortings as columns (a slice through plane B of Figure 1). The cells of the matrix are numbers indicating the sorting categories to which the different elements were assigned. Each matrix was put into a separate MSA analysis. The analysis, in this instance, generates a configuration in which each element (in this case, casinos) was

Table 2
RECORD OF CASINO MANAGER'S SORTING[a]

First Sort: "Staff Recruitment"
1. "Career Staff": A, B, C, F
2. "Recruit from outside": E, D, G

Second Sort: "Staff Training"
1. "Little training": A, B, C, F
2. "More training": E, D, G

Third Sort: "Staff Benefits"
1. "Mainly for senior Staff": A, B, C, F
2. "Also for lower Staff": E, D, G

Fourth Sort: "Sex of Staff"
1. "Male only": A, B, C, E, D
2. "Male and Female": F, G

Fifth Sort: "Staff Contact with Customers"
1. "None": A
2. "Good with company support": G, E, D
3. "Good with no company support": F
4. "Unclear": B, C

Sixth Sort: "Staff experience"
1. "Trainee Staff": A, B, C
2. "Mixed": E, D
3. "Experienced Staff": F, G

Seventh Sort: "Whether takes cheques or cash"
1. "Cash": A, B, C
2. "Mixed": E, D
3. "Cheques": F, G

Eighth Sort: "Concern for Customer Quality"
1. "Quantity only": A, B, C, E
2. "Quality and Quantity": D
3. "Quality": F, G

[a]Casinos: A—Golden Nugget; B—Palm Beach; C—International; D—Hereford; E—Park Lane; F—Curzon House; G—Ladbroke.

a point in the space. The closer together any two casinos are in this spatial representation the more similar they are in terms of the categories that are assigned to them over the number of sorts carried out by each individual.

Table 3 shows the data matrix derived from the sorts illustrated in Table 1. Figure 5a shows the MSA for the gambler and Figure 5b shows the MSA for the manager.

The partitioning of these figures is derived from an examination of the way in which each individual sort contributes to the spatial configuration. Thus, it is clear that the manager divides casinos up on the basis of how they deal with the clientele and how the overall casino management deals

Table 3
DATA MATRIX DERIVED FROM THE SORTING PRODUCED BY ACE[a]

Elements (Casinos)	First	Second	Third	Fourth	Fifth
A	1	1	1	1	1
B	2	2	2	2	4
C	2	3	3	3	2
D	1	3	3	3	2
E	3	3	3	3	1
F	3	3	3	3	3
G	1	2	2	1	1
H	1	2	2	1	1

[a]Number in cells are categories derived from sortings as shown in Table 1.

with their staff. This gives a two-way classification of casinos: those that select their staff carefully but are not too selective of their clientele; those selective about their clientele but not so careful of their staff; and those not especially careful about how they chose their staff or their clientele. This reveals the division the manager makes between the staff and the clientele and the way in which his perspective relates to selectivity and overall standards. At first sight, the gambler's MSA reveals a very different sorting. Essentially, there is a two-way division between those casinos that are very up-market and those casinos that are more general. The gambler makes a more precise distinction within the more general casinos between those that have added frills like the famous Playboy Clubs, or those that are just large gaming halls with little extra, and a group in between. Clearly, the gambler makes much more refined judgements about the nature of the action going on within the casino than does the manager. However, they both share the superordinate categorization of how selective the casinos are.

This selectivity of casinos throws an interesting light on the whole gambling experience. It shows that an individual, in effect, is playing himself into some sort of exclusive club. These casinos, then, unlike those in the United States, may gain some of their important qualities from the way in which both the management and the gamblers draw lines between who can afford to be in which places. Certainly, further discussion of these conclusions with the respondents here as well as with other management groups would be necessary to test that hypothesis more fully.

Again, it would be difficult to see quite how such a result could be derived from a conventional questionnaire procedure. Open-ended interviews could well have revealed the same sort of material, but they might

(a)

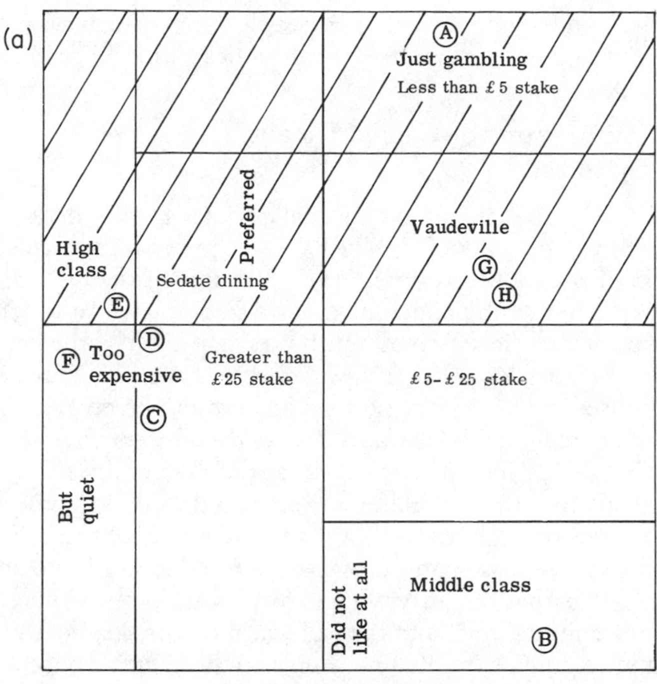

(b)

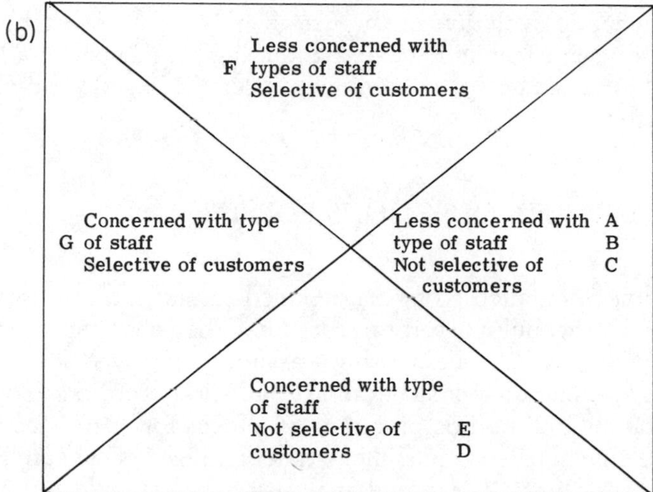

Figure 5 Summary MSAI of (a) Ace's sortings (see Tables 1 and 3 for basis), and (b) casino manager's sorting (see Table 2 for basis).

have hidden the underlying structures in people's conceptualization, while of course emphasising other aspects of casinos that may well be important.

Complex Comparisons of Categories and Construct Systems

As a final illustration of the foci of analysis that can be derived from sorting procedures, the work of Grainger will be briefly mentioned. Working from a model of place (Canter, 1977), Grainger asked a variety of individuals associated with the design of a fire station to carry out sortings of three groups of elements, each of which was generated by the individual in the course of discussion. One group of elements was the activities that were to be housed in the building; the second group, the physical properties the building required; and the third group, the concepts that would be associated with the design—the concepts of the design objects. Grainger asked individuals to do this at different stages in the design process and carried out a series of analyses to show the way in which the conceptual systems of the individuals changed over time in relation to one another. What emerged was that the activity constructs, which were initially very similar in the architects' minds to their physical constructs, became more distinct, and in so doing they became similar to the clients' conceptualization of the activities the building was to house. Grainger was thus able to reveal the dynamic evolution of the design brief by showing how the discussion between client and architect about both the intended activities and physical form can generate a common understanding of the building's future character.

SOME IMPORTANT QUESTIONS FOR THE FUTURE

The examples presented so far have served to illustrate the variety of possible uses for the multiple sorting procedure. They have shown that the multiple sorting procedure derives from a variety of psychological techniques and a melding of approaches to psychological problems. However, the use of the multiple sorting procedure as a focus for open-ended interviewing is relatively recent and still only rarely utilized. There are a number of questions about the use and analysis of the multiple sorting procedure that remain unanswered. Some of the more important ones will now be considered. All of them are amenable to empirical tests drawing on the data collection and analysis procedures that have already been described.

Questions in Analysis and Use

CATEGORY SALIENCE

One aspect of the categories employed in sorting that is especially amenable to exploration, but not as yet examined, is the salience or significance to the individual of the categories used. The role of any categorization scheme in the overall sorting structure has been explored, as discussed above, but the importance to the individual of one sort over another has not been scrutinised. Yet, the sorting procedure does lend itself to such examinations by virtue of a number of properties that *potentially* might reveal salience.

The Range of Sort Convenience. One way in which the importance of different concepts can be examined is in relation to the appropriateness of those categories for all the elements involved. Kelly (1955) discusses the importance of establishing what he calls the "range of convenience" of a construct, which he defines as covering "all those things to which the user found its application useful" (p. 137). In the sorting procedure, it is always possible for the respondent to produce a sort which only covers a subset of the elements and for the remaining elements to be assigned to a general class indicating their irrelevance to the sorting criteria. Measures and content analyses of the range of items to which different category schemes were applied would help to clarify the salience of different sorting categories.

The Significance of Sort Order. In a multiple sorting task it is clear that sorts follow each other in a distinct order. The question is therefore raised as to what the significance might be of the order in which sorts are elicited. In their study of different numbers of sorts Rosenberg and Kim (1975) came to the conclusion that sort order carried no significance. Unfortunately they only examined the first two sorts rather than looking at a larger number. Informal discussion with respondents does suggest that there may be contexts in which the order does carry significance and relates to the salience of the sorting categories being used. Some instructions may heighten this possibility, particularly instructions emphasising the use of sorts that the respondent believes reveal "important aspects of the elements being sorted."

Studies asking the respondent directly what importance they attach to different sortings are quite feasible as well as content analyses of sorts in terms of sort order. Such studies would be of value not only because little is known about the significance of sort order, but also it may reveal some interesting properties of conceptual systems not illuminated by other procedures.

The Relevance of Category Distribution. As discussed above, an early version of a sorting task was used by Sherif and Sherif (1969) in the development of Thurstone attitude scales. They had judges assign attitudinal statements to an ordered set of categories. They argued that the distribution of items in a sorting revealed something of the intensity of the sorter's judgments; the more skewed the distribution of categories the more extreme the judges' views. In other words, if people assigned a similar number of elements to each category, then they were likely to hold much less extreme views then someone who put most of the elements in one or two outlying categories.

Although the Sherif and Sherif "own categories" procedure, as they called it, is different in a number of important respects from the multiple sorting task, it does point to the possible value of studying the number of categories used and the number of items assigned to each category. Simple indexes of the distribution of items per category could easily be devised and used as a basis of this study. Such indexes could be directly related to the literature on cognitive complexity (Bieri, 1971; Streufert and Streufert, 1978) and thus provide an important link to the discussion of the role of cognitive structure in attitude change.

THEORETICAL CLARIFICATION

As discussed, the multiple sorting procedure has evolved out of a variety of origins in clinical, experimental, environmental, and multivariate psychological research. It is consequently inevitable that some of the differences of opinion between practitioners in these areas has provided a basis for some confusion in the theoretical issues underlying the use of the multiple sorting procedure. All of these issues require debate and open up interesting areas of possible research.

Categories and Constructs. Kelly (1955) makes it very clear that constructs are distinct from category schemes, although the labels given to categories may usefully identify constructs in certain circumstances. He even writes that he uses the term construct "in a manner which is somewhat parallel to the common usage of 'concept'" (p. 69). One important assumption about constructs in Kelly's terms is that they are dichotomous. They enshrine bipolarity of aspects of the similarity and differences between elements.

In this sense, categories to which elements in a sort are assigned are the constructs of the user, although only one pole of the construct may be specified. However, in Kelly's terms, the bipolarity of the constructs is an assumption of his theory, it is not open to test within his theory, nor as a consequence can it be tested using a repertory grid. This is not the case for multiple sorting. If a person assigns elements to categories that can be ordered from least to most along a single bipolar concept, then that category scheme reveals a construct (e.g., Ace's sorting according to size of minimum bet). If, however, the sorting produces a set of categories that are multipolar, then it would be inappropriate to regard this category scheme as consisting of constructs (e.g., Groat's architects' classification of building styles as Brutalist, Post-Moder, Expressionist, etc.).

Thus, the multiple sorting procedure does allow one of Kelly's fundamental assumptions to be tested. Indeed, it is the emergence of classification schemes that are not obviously constructs which is one of the starting points for considering the multiple sorting procedure rather than the repertory grid. But this leads to the question of the conditions under which people use constructs as opposed to multipolar category schemes and the possibility of converting one system of classification into the other.

Individual Differences in Sorting Competence. Anyone who uses the multiple sorting procedure will come across respondents who will find the task difficult and challenging to complete. This raises the question of how natural the task is to all people and of what differences there might be between people in their ability to carry out a multiple sorting task. Of course, the specific nature of the task itself does need to be considered. A sorting of abstract concepts is likely to be more difficult than a sorting of places to go on holiday. It is also necessary to distinguish between difficulties people may have in understanding what they are to do and difficulties in actually doing it.

These individual differences are of interest because the procedure does have roots in clinical psychological concerns with understanding the difficulties people have in coping with the world. If there are circumstances in which respondents find it difficult to form categories stable enough to describe, then the reasons for this should be searched out. The comments people make when carrying out sorts can give a valuable clue here to the difficulties they are facing and these can be related to measures such as the number of sorts and the time taken to complete a sort. The exploration of who finds what type of sorting difficult and why is likely to repay the effort involved.

Should Sortings be Reliable? The sorting task is likely to be a self-exploration for the individuals doing it, a learning process in which they come to understand more about their own conceptual system. As a consequence it is possible that an individual would not give the same sortings twice. Certainly the order in which he/she carried out his/her sortings is likely to vary from one session to the next. What is being studied is the overall conceptual system a person uses. It is likely that using two parallel sets of elements, in analogy with parallel forms of reliability testing, would not obviate the effects of the increase in self-understanding associated with a sorting task.

No published studies can be found dealing directly with these issues, but advocates of repertory grid procedure (e.g., Fransella and Bannister 1977, Chapter 6) have gone to some length to argue that reliability can easily be a measure of the insensitivity of a procedure to changing circumstances rather than a valuable psychometric property. With respect to the multiple sorting procedure, it is likely that stable individuals would generate reliable responses over two or three sorting sessions, but only if the procedure itself did not contribute to a fuller understanding of their conceptual systems or their personal growth. Only direct tests of these important questions can help answer them. Here, as with the other questions, the comments people make during the sorting procedure could provide valuable clues.

Exploring Face Validity. The validity of a sorting must depend a lot on the conditions under which it is carried out. The essence of a sorting task is to establish the individuals' own understanding of their personal conceptual system. The extent to which individuals will feel able and be able to generate that system will depend on how they understand the instructions, the personal relevance of the elements, and so on. Thus, as much as any other data collection procedure, the conditions under which the data are collected need to be carefully reported and interpreted, in terms of how the procedure was experienced by the respondent.

In this framework, face validity is given considerably more prominence than in other psychometric procedures. This is because one very important meaning to the validity of a sorting task is the extent to which the respondent and the investigator have a shared understanding of what the procedure is measuring. In this respect the details of the results, both in content and structure, can be examined to see what they reveal of the respondent's understanding of the task as presented. For example, consider the situation in which the sortings generated are all based on objective, physical aspects of the elements, such as their weight and size, yet the investigator was apparently looking for emotional significance of the elements. This suggests the procedure was not tapping what the investigator thought it was, and so careful scrutiny of the details of the procedure and its context may reveal the basis of this lack of apparent validity. For instance, perhaps the investigator introduced himself as a designer and thus set up expectations as to the type of sorting that would be appropriate.

The consequences of subtle changes in the instructions or context of a multiple sort for the results produced are directly amenable to empirical study. Here the vast literature on interviewing procedure and threats to its validity would have many points of relevance. The consequences of interviewer sex and experience are obvious examples from this literature, but there are many others mentioned throughout the present volume.

Modifications and Developments of the Sorting Procedure

The following are possible ways in which the sorting procedure can be developed and modified in order to answer some research questions more directly:

1. The creation of element sets to sort can be taken a number of steps. The selection of a carefully matched set of elements, possibly factorially designed is one step. But by adding other descriptors, experimentally varied sets of elements can be produced.
2. Sorting procedures in which one set of elements is sorted into another set offer a number of prospects for exploring the relationship between different conceptual domains. If both sets of elements are sorted independently as well as together, there is the possibility of a very close analysis of the fit between domains.
3. Asking people to sort elements into provided category schemes as well as free sorts generates links to studies using other methods of concept exploration.
4. Ranking and rating of sorts against different criteria such as importance provides the opportunity for the development of classifications of sorts themselves—higher-order sorting.
5. Group sorting procedures have been used from time to time and can add greatly to the cost effectiveness of data collection. However, these procedures are likely to be limited to groups that are quite sophisticated or to very simple aspects of sorting, such as paired comparisons.

Values and Contraindications

As mentioned throughout this chapter, the sorting procedure has the flexibility to be applied to answer a wide variety of research questions, but there are some types of questions for which it may be inappropriate. Only further use will help to clarify the boundaries of advantageous and disadvantageous uses, but a few pointers can be given now.

The multiple sorting procedure clearly has strength when the elaboration of the meaning of a concept is central to the research question. Studies of how people use the word "home," or whether "post-modern" architecture has an identifiable public recognition, or the conditions under which people will describe their actions as "panic," all lend themselves to exploration using a sorting procedure. If these concepts have a common but highly ambiguous currency, then the demands of the sorting procedure may well help to disentangle the different meanings. Also, when conceptual systems are being explored with groups whose verbal fluency may be restricted, such as children or psychiatric patients, then a sorting procedure may be especially useful.

There are two types of research questions, however, for which multiple sorting may be less appropriate; they fall into two general classes. The first are those questions in which a very personal, idiosyncratic perspective is what is being sought. The indepth psychotherapeutic interview can never be replaced by sorting tasks. The second class of research questions are those concerned with a direct understanding of processes, especially sequences of action. For example, studies of how people make decisions under stress or cope with bereavement are less likely to prove fruitful if built around a study of personal category schemes than if they focus directly on the stages through which people go and what moves them from one stage to the next.

CONCLUSIONS

This chapter has presented a detailed account of multiple sorting procedures, with respect to both their theoretical origins and their numerous applications to open-ended interview situations. As the first section of the chapter has demonstrated, the multiple sorting procedure has roots in both the early clinical object sorting techniques and the paired comparison procedures advocated recently by multidimensional scaling enthusiasts. But more important, the multiple sorting procedure derives from two parallel concerns in psychology: the significance of the respondents' own view of the world, and the recognition that that world view is built around a pattern of categorizations. In this respect, the multiple sorting procedure reveals theoretical links to Kelly's work in the development of the repertory grid and to other more recent research in social and clinical psychology.

With respect to its applications to the interview process, the second portion of this chapter has provided examples of its adaptability, and ease of administration. However, it is clear that one of its primary virtues may also be a burden to the researcher: it probably makes even greater demands than the repertory grid on the intellectual stamina of the investigator, forcing her or him to clarify exactly what it is that he/she is looking for and why. In this respect it serves as an appropriate complement to other forms of the interview procedure, such as the use of ordinary explanations. The multiple sorting task thus takes its place amongst the family of interviewing procedures, but only future developments and use will establish the role it is to play.

REFERENCES

Adams-Weber, J. R. (1979). *Personal construct theory: Concepts and applications* Chichester: Wiley.

Allport, G. W. (1937). *Personality: A psychological interpretation.* New York: Holt Saunders.

Argyle, M., Furnham, A., and Graham, J. A. (1981). *Social situations.* London: Cambridge University Press.

Bieri, J. (1971). Cognitive/structures in personality. In H. M. Schroder and P. Suedfeld (Eds.), *Personality theory and information processing.* New York: Ronald Press.

Bishop, R. (1983). *The perception and importance of time in architecture.* Ph.D thesis, University of Surrey.

Block, J. (1961). *The Q sort method in personality assessment and psychiatric research.* Springfield, Illinois: Charles C. Thomas.

Bonarius, H., Holland, R., and Rosenberg, S. (Eds.) (1981). *Personal construct theory: Recent advances in theory and practice.* London: MacMillan.

Brown, J., and Sime, J. (1980). A methodology for accounts. In M. Brenner (Ed.), *Social methods and social life,* pp. 157–188. London: Academic Press.

Bruner, J., Goodnow, J., and Austin, G. (1956). *A study of thinking.* New York: Wiley.

Canter, D. (1977). *The psychology of place.* London Architectural Press.

Canter, D. (1983). The potential of facet theory for applied social psychology. *Quality and quantity.* Amsterdam: Elsevier Scientific Publishing Co.

Canter, D., Ambrose, I., Brown, J., Comber, M., and Hirsch, A. (1980). *Prison design and use.* Final report to the Home office. University of Surrey.

Canter, D., Brown, J., and Richardson, H. (1976). *Constructs without tears: Is there life beyond the grid?* Paper presented to the British Psychological Society Annual Conference, Exeter.

Douglas, M. (Ed.) (1977). *Rules and meanings.* Harmondsworth: Penguin.

Eckman, P. (1975). *Unmasking the face.* New Jersey: Prentice Hall.

Fransella, F., and Bannister, D. (1977). *A manual for repertory grid technique.* London: Academic Press.

Frost, A., and Canter, D. (1982). Consumer psychology. In S. Canter and D. Canter (Eds.), *Psychology in practice: Perspectives on professional psychology.* Chichester: Wiley.

Gärling, T. (1976). The structural analysis of environmental perception and cognition. *Environment and Behavior 8*(3), pp. 385–415.

Grainger, B. (1980). *A study of concepts in the building design process.* MSc. Dissertation, University of Surrey.

Groat, L., and Canter, D. V. (1979). Does post-modernism communicate? *Progressive Architecture,* December, 84–87.

Groat, L. (1982). Meaning in post-modern architecture: An examination using the multiple sorting task. *Journal of Environmental Psychology, 2*(3), 3–22.

Harré, R., and Secord, P. (1972). *The explanation of social behaviour.* Oxford: Blackwell.

Hawkins, C. (1983). *Differing conceptualisations of users of three psychiatric day centres.* MSc dissertation, University of Surrey.

Horayangkura, V. (1978). Semantic differential structures. *Environment and Behavior, 10*(4), 555–584.

James, W. (1890). *Principles of psychology.* New York: Holt Saunders.

Kelly, G. (1955). *The psychology of personal constructs.* New York: Norton.

Krampen, M. (1979). *Meaning in the urban environment.* London: Pion.

Lingoes, J. (1973). *The Guttman–Lingoes nonmetric program series.* Ann Arbor, Michigan: Mathesis Press.

Miller, G. A. (1956). The magical number seven, plus or minus two. *Psychological Review, 43,* 81–97.

Nasar, J. (1980). On determining dimensions of environmental perception. In *Edra, 11.* pp. 245–256. Washington: Environmental Design Research Association.
Oakley, R. (1980). *Profiles and perspectives of hostel residents.* MSc. dissertation, University of Surrey.
Oostendorp, A., and Berlyne, D. E. (1978). Dimensions in the perception of architecture. *Scandinavian Journal of Psychology, 19,* 145–150.
Osgood, C. E. (1962). Studies in the generality of affective meaning systems. *American Psychologist, 17,* 10–28.
Osgood, C. E., Suci, G. J., and Tanenbaum, P. M. (1957). *The measurement of meaning.* Urbana: University of Illinois Press.
Palmer, J. (1978). Citizen Assessment of the Coastal Visual Resource. In *Coastal zone 78.* New York American Society of Civil Engineers.
Pitt, D. G., and Zube, E. H. (1979). The Q-sort method: Use in landscape assessment research and landscape planning. In G. H. Elsner (Ed.), *Our National Landscape.* Berkeley: Pacific Southwest Forest and Range Experiment Station.
Rosch, E. (1977). Human categorization. In N. Warren (Ed.), *Advances in cross-cultural psychology* (Vol 1). London: Academic Press.
Rosenberg, S., and Kim, M. P. (1975). The method of sorting a data gathering procedure in multivariate research. *Multivariate Behavioral Research,* October, 489–502.
Schiffman, S. S., Reynolds, L. M., and Young, F. W. (1981). *Introduction to multidimensional scaling.* New York: Academic Press.
Shaw, M. L. G. (1982). The extraction of personal meaning from a repertory grid. In E. Shepherd and J. F. Watson (Eds.), *Personal meanings.* Chichester: Wiley.
Shepherd, E., and Watson, J. P. (1982). (eds.) *Personal meanings.* Chichester: Wiley.
Sherif, M., and Sherif, C. (1969). *Social psychology.* New York/Tokyo: Harper and Row/John Weatherhill.
Shye, S. (Ed.). (1978). *Theory construction and data analysis in the behavioral sciences.* San Francisco: Jossey–Bass.
Smith, E. E., and Medin, D. L. (1981). *Categories and concepts.* London: Harvard Press.
Stephenson, W. (1953). *The study of behavior: Q-technique and its methodology.* Chicago: University of Chicago Press.
Streufert, S., and Streufert, S. (1978). *Behavior in the complex environment.* New York: Holt Saunders.
Szalay, L. B., and Deese, J. (1978) *Subjective meaning in culture: An assesment through word association.* Hillside, NJ: Erlbaum.
Tajfel, H. C. (1978). The structure of our views about society. In H. Tajfel and C. Fraser (Eds.), In *Introduction to Social Psychology,* pp. 302–321. Harmondsworth: Penguin.
Tajfel, H. (1981). *Human groups and social categories.* Cambridge: Cambridge University Press.
Thurstone, L. L., and Chave, E. J. (1929). *The measurement of attitudes.* Chicago: University of Chicago Press.
Vygotsky, L. (1934). *Thought and language.* Boston, MA: MIT Press.
Ward, L. M. (1977). Multidimensional scaling of the molar physical environment. *The Journal of Multivariate Behavioral Research, 12,* 23–42.
Ward, L. M., and Russell, J. A. (1981). Cognitive set and the perception of place. *Environment and Behavior, 13*(5), 610–632.
Zvulun, E. (1978). Multidimensional scalogram analysis: The method and its application. In S. Shye (Ed.), *Theory construction and data analysis in the behavioral sciences,* pp. 237–264. San Francisco: Jossey-Bass.

6

The Content Analysis of Qualitative Research Data: A Dynamic Approach

BARBARA MOSTYN

INTRODUCTION

Content analysis is essentially just another term for a very ordinary, everyday activity we all engage in when we communicate with one another. Content analysis occurs whenever the recipient of a message says to her/himself: "What they are actually saying is ——"; "What this means is ——"; "The speaker intended ——"; and so forth. Furthermore, since the majority of the communications we receive daily (whether in social encounters or the hotchpotch of ideas and news items from the mass media) are fragmented and unstructured, we are quite experienced in having to restructure communications before we can make sense out of them. When we stop to think about it, we realise that to eliminate this wealth of unstructured material from our daily lives would mean "losing much of the richness of social experience" (Goode and Hatt, 1952).

Since we are all experienced in the handling of unstructured communications, the analysis of unstructured, open-ended research material should not impose any unnatural restraints on the researcher. (Open-ended research material is that resulting from responses to nondirective questions, which by their very nature impose as few constraints on respondents' answers as possible, unlike, for example, multiple-choice questions. A typical nondirective question would be: "When you think of a holiday, what are all the things that come to your mind?").

As Berelson (1971) has said, "Content analysis does not differ from close reading plus judgement, a traditional and time-honoured method."

Furthermore, when we draw conclusions from unstructured communications based on our own personal judgements about the content, we are making inferences. And we do it all the time. For example, when we read that negotiations between country X and Y have broken down we infer

ISBN 0-12-131580-0

that there may be future hostilities; when we hear that the electricity workers have won a big pay award we infer that the cost of electricity will go up; when we are told that they are closing many of the schools in our borough we infer that there will be quite a few teachers out of work; when someone we have recently met invites us to their home for dinner we infer that they would like to make friends with us, etc.

Because language is both complex and inexact, we know that it is not enough to merely take in words before drawing inferences, whether they are words from an advertisement, a request from a friend, or a newspaper article reporting current events. To gain any real insights into the meaning we must analyze the communication presented to us. Gordon (1978) has described this process as a four-step procedure: (1) listen and read critically; (2) ask probing questions of the data—What is the meaning? (3) look for meaningful relationships; and (4) synthesize, arrive at some sort of solution about the data.

However, when the material to be digested is the result of qualitative research investigations—that is, when it is in the form of answers to open-ended questions—then Content Analysis requires another function beyond inference: *interpretation,* which as Freud (1950) has described, "gives meaning to the content." Thus, we become concerned with content as a reflection of deeper phenomena. Words are treated as symbols and the data has attributes of its own; we are analyzing both manifest and latent data—"the complex gestalt" (Jones, 1981). And increasingly there is an awareness that it is equally important to include nonverbal communication and tone of voice in the interpretation whenever possible, since these factors give clues to deeper feelings. As Henry (1956) has said, "Statements are organised by the intellect but take their clues from the emotions." For instance, when someone reads a communication that they find unpleasant or even frightening, such as a description of the health effects from smoking, and resultingly they push it away (try to distance themselves from it) and frown as if in pain, this reaction says more than the comment "I don't like this very much." Thus, qualitative content analysis is really trying to discover what psychologists like Rorschach (1956) stressed for years: "*how* rather than what the person experiences."

QUANTITATIVE DATA VERSUS QUALITATIVE DATA; OR "WHAT" VERSUS "WHY" DATA

The complexities of analyzing qualitative research data can be particularly appreciated when compared to quantitative data. The latter are typically collected when the purpose of the research is to determine what, where, when, and how many, rather then *why.*

Briefly, the major differences between the two approaches are:

QUANTITATIVE RESEARCH	QUALITATIVE RESEARCH
Samples: large, hundreds or thousands.	Small, typically less than 100.
Interview Length: short, less than an hour, to avoid respondent "wear-out," since usually short answer and multiple-choice are the only techniques used. Also respondents are unpaid.	Long, more than an hour, to allow the interviewer to get beyond the superficial with a variety of research approaches. Respondents are usually given an incentive for their cooperation.
Questioning: follows a set format and is the same for each respondent.	Follows respondents' reactions to various stimuli within a general framework.
Objectives: a checking exercise, how many, where and when; e.g., a *refinement* of existing data.	A learning exercise; what are all the feelings associated with X? e.g., an *expansion* of existing data.
Analysis: statistical.	Content analysis.
Report: based on statistical summaries and correlations written for the purpose of furthering understanding about the research subject; e.g., *what* is going on?	Based on theories of motivation written for the purpose of understanding the attitudes and behavior of repondents vis-à-vis the research subject; e.g., *why* is this going on?
Reliability and Validity: can always be determined, providing time and resources are available.	Can rarely be determined, due to the subjective nature of the research material and the one-off nature of most projects.

WHAT IS QUALITATIVE CONTENT ANALYSIS?

As Krippendorff (1980) has observed, "The history of science shows a consistent trend to make more and more phenomenon subject to measurement and analysis." It is as if scientists believe that reality is accessible only "through the medium of a measuring instrument."

Content analysis is the "diagnostic tool" of qualitative researchers, which they use when faced with a mass of open-ended material to make sense of. The overall purpose of the content analysis approach is to identify specific characteristics of communications systematically and objectively in order to convert the raw material into scientific data.

The raw material of the qualitative researcher is most typically words because as Laffal (1969) has noted words are the "determinants of consciousness." As researchers, we are essentially dealing with what respondents can tell us, not necessarily with what is going on inside their minds. Words are our environmental determinant, says Rapaport (1969): "All organisms live in environments which determine their lives and humans live in an ocean of words; we create an invisible semantic environment of words which is part of our existence in quite as important ways as the physical environment." It is the task of the researcher to find meaning within this sea. The words to be analyzed typically occur in the form of interviewer's notes of what was said, a transcript of the proceedings, or a tape recording.

The analyst takes this raw material and subjects it to scrutiny to see if any regularities occur in terms of single words, themes, or concepts. He/she then attempts to set up conceptual categories; this process then leads to hypothesis testing or reformulation due to the discovery of new relationships among the data. For example, in a study concerning seat belts, it was found that nonusers feared that putting on a seat belt symbolised that the car was in charge. Regular wearers, on the other hand, felt that putting on a seat belt meant the driver had the upper hand because she/he was at one with the car. Thus, a new dimension concerning seat belts emerged from the research—who is the boss?

This sort of dichotomy, dependent on the discovery of a new relationship in the data, is most useful in the interpretive stage, as can be readily appreciated. Ultimately, of course, the purpose of content analysis of open-ended material is to understand the *meaning* of the communication; that is, both its manifest and latent meaning within the context of the respondent's own frame of reference; for example, phenomenologically how does he/she experience it? Thus, in addition to attempting to apply the usual scientific principles of looking for meaningful relationships in the data, the analyst must also understand the roles, values, and life styles of respondents in order to interpret the data. This requires that researchers understand their subjects as people, in terms of their motivations and life style, as well as familiarise themselves with typical behaviour by frequently observing people in average situations—social encounters, as customers, drivers, pedestrians, and so forth.

THE QUANTITATIVE HERITAGE

Content analysis as a scientific discipline has an old and honourable heritage originating in the attempts by linguists to analyze the content of communications from a quantitative view point.

In fact as far back as 1740, content analysis was used to analyze communications. From that time until the present (with the advent of qualitative researchers who are now asking the question "why?" of the data), content analysis has consisted almost entirely of "word counts" and "scores" for the occurrence of specific themes. This was because the primary purpose of the analysis was to answer the question "what" from the research material. When first applied, the most typical use was to determine authorship by discovering word and theme regularities; one of the most famous uses concerned the authorship of the American Federalist Papers—was it Madison or Hamilton? In Britain, content analysis has been used to attempt to shed light on the old argument: How many people actually wrote Shakespeare's work? The typical quantitative approach consists of determining units—words, sentences, or descriptive phrases to be used in the analysis and then setting up categories for scoring purposes. The categories typically consist of adjectives or symbols, which are listed and then given to a team of coders who go through the data. The researchers who create the categories are the judges, while the coders are clerks, rather than decision makers. Not surprisingly, the advent of the computer has been most welcomed by quantitative researchers who have been quick to apply it to content analysis.

Examples of the variety of topics researched by quantitative content analysis include:

1. *Cultural products*—Social Anthropologists analyzed Greek vases for themes of achievement motive, and love songs for recurrent themes of longing, distress, etc. Musical themes from various cultures have been analyzed, as well as the types of photos that appear in archives.
2. *Dreams* have been analyzed by type, central character, and major theme.
3. *Nonverbal communications*—Psychologists have analyzed voice in terms of pitch and timing, as well as facial expressions.
4. *Childrens' books* have been analyzed for themes regarding the work ethic and the types of social behaviour that are rewarded and punished.
5. *Films, plays, and magazines* have been analyzed for cross-cultural comparisons; for instance, the German for themes concerning respect for authority and the American for themes concerning the portrayal of ethnic minorities.

However, the greatest impetus to content analysis came during the Second World War when the psychologists Lasswell and Lazarsfeld used content analysis to study propaganda. They were not only concerned with word counts and the occurrence of themes, but took into consideration the various types of audiences to whom the messages were addressed, In addition, they took careful note of changes over time. For these studies of propaganda, teams of judges were used to decide on the categories.

Furthermore, once it was determined that propaganda types and their effects could be studied, researchers in other fields were encouraged to engage in content analysis: patient–therapist interactions were studied; political debates, astronaut–ground control interactions, and the Watergate tapes analysed.

From the above, it can be seen that content analysis has had a rich and varied history before the qualitative researchers came along and insisted that the question "why" as well as "what" should be answerable. At this point, the concept of *intent* was introduced into the content analysis of communications. This is not surprising, since qualitative researchers have typically had some grounding in clinical psychology, which is always concerned with the question of why does X do/think/feel Y? Furthermore, qualitative researchers trained in the use of projective techniques are familiar with the idea of interpreting responses according to predetermined concepts developed by the originators of such techniques as Draw-a-Man (Goodenough); Sentence Completion (Payne and Tendler); Ink Blots (Rorschach); Thematic Apperception Tests (TAT, by A. H. Murray); Cartoons (Rosenzweig)—these were designed to shed some light on what is going on in respondents' minds—*why* does she/he feel that way? (For more details on these techniques see Mostyn, 1978.)

QUANTITATIVE VERSUS QUALITATIVE CONTENT ANALYSIS

In the field of applied psychology, as indeed with most of the social sciences, there is the inevitable dilemma: Should research produce *numbers,* with their rigour, precision, and reliability? Or the more descriptive, phenomenological qualitative data, with its richness of detail and nuance? Since frequently the researcher has a choice of whether to design a research project that lends itself to quantitative or qualitative analysis, it is important to know the arguments for and against both approaches. The argument is often, as described by Berelson (1971), "between frequencies and real meaning."

The Qualitative Argument

Those who feel that data has more meaning, and therefore more usefulness, when it is submitted to qualitative content analysis point out that applying mathematics to social science data does not ensure rigour, that quantitative procedures such as counting do not guarantee objectivity, and that besides it is a fallacious argument, since the determination of all categories involves qualitative judgments in the first instance. For example, what is "achievement motive" as portrayed in Greek vases or "respect for authority" as portrayed in American Films? Holsti (1969) reports of an experiment in which inspirational themes were explored in litereraturе by two methods: either coding and scoring according to predetermined categories, or asking judges to read an entire book and give it a summary score. It was concluded that little of substance was lost using the latter approach.

Moreover, since the qualitative researcher is also concerned with intentions in the interpretation of communications, quantitative analysis is not sensitive enough. As George (1959) has advised, "The qualitative analysis of a limited number of crucial communications at one moment in time may often yield better clues to the particular intentions than more standardised quantitative methods." This is particularly likely to happen because the quantitative analyst typically gives each unit or category of analysis equal weighting, which is totally unrealistic. Qualitative content analysis no doubt captures the richness, complexity, and gestalt of the material, while quantitative methods, particularly those employing the computer, are intolerant of ambiguity—a salient feature of most social and market research. Freud (1950) had the same attitude towards the interpretation of dreams; he rejected the dream code books of his time, since they gave no real insights into what was going on for the dreamer.

Furthermore, it is essential that the qualitative researcher understand respondents as people; therefore, the more phenomenological approach, one in which the researcher tries to see the world from the respondents' point of view, is more likely to give a better understanding of the everyday experiences of the motorist, buyer, tenant, and so forth. As Calder (1977) has described, qualitative research is typically characterised by a period of intense interaction between the researcher and the subjects in their own milieu, "thus encouraging people to reveal in their own words their feelings about the subject." These type of data do not lend themselves to descriptive quantitative analysis, since they are not only dependent on content but on the intuitions of the researcher about what was happening and why.

The Quantitative Argument

Those who feel that quantitative content analysis is the more meaningful point out that the research findings will be more rigorous, because the researcher will be forced to select his/her categories carefully, thus the analysis will be systematised and not just impressionistic. As Goode and Hatt (1952) have stated, "Intuition is not enough to demonstrate the truth of ideas." May (1978) has also warned that the qualitative approach has often "substituted the word for the numbers game." This is particularly likely to happen when impressionistic methods are employed, which are heavily dependent on the analyst going through the data to get "a feel," and perhaps being overly struck by a particular "neat turn of phrase," which assumes unreasonable importance. Or, the analyst may focus on a few dramatic but untypical cases; with systematic quantitative analysis this is avoided.

It is on the *reliability* issue that the quantitative researcher is most critical of qualitative content analysis; what little research there is indicates that on the whole there is a low level of comparability for qualitative research. For instance, May (1978) reports of an experiment in which the interpretations by five different qualitative research psychologists concerning the same problem differed markedly. In another experiment three different research methods were used—group discussions, minigroups, and depth interviews. Although each researcher was given the same research problem, the results, subjected to content analysis, differed a great deal. On the other hand, in a recent training workshop for qualitative researchers, Bill Schlackman, a noted London research psychologist, asked each participant individually to analyze and interpret qualitative data in the form of a tape-recorded group discussion. They were also asked to make recommendations from their findings. He found no significant differences concerning the interpretation of the data, but researchers made vastly different recommendations, which surprised him. This was an important finding, since the researchers were working for different organisations and were not obtaining high correlations because of interaction effects. This is a problem Krippendorf (1980) has emphasized: inter-rater agreement for content analysis data is usually highest where people work together.

According to Lazarsfeld (1940), the lack of precision in the analysis of content analysis data accounts for the low reliability. George (1959) explained the dynamics of the problem in terms of "circularity," for example, (the researcher) making an early hypothesis and then "seeing what he thinks he should see." However, the problem is more complex, according to Krippendorf (1980). First, content analysis is basically about the symbolic meaning of messages; "yet messages do not have a single meaning that needs to be unwrapped." Qualitative data can be looked at from numerous perspectives, and these may not even be shared by experts. Krippendorf points out that experts in anthropological artifacts or nonverbal communication frequently disagree on the symbolic meanings in a content analysis. Second, reliability is dependent on the data being obtained independently of the measuring instrument or person, and, since typically the qualitative research analyst has also conducted some, if not all, of the interviews, contamination effects are inevitable. Third, to properly test reliability some duplication of effort is essential, and this is not realistic for most social and market research projects, where costs and often timing are of prime importance.

The reliability of quantitative content analysis, on the other hand, is enhanced because coders use agreed-upon categories. When these categories have been developed for a particular "dictionary," which is then fed into a computer, reliability among coders can be as high as 99%.

There have been several attempts to improve the reliability of qualitative content analysis. Montgomery and Crittenden (1977) have devised a scheme for improving the reliability of analysing open-ended questions. They take the weighted average from two analysts who have independently coded responses according to quantitative principles. They have obtained reliability coefficients of nearly .60.

One of the oldest open-ended research tools—the Rorschach—in which agreed categories are used to score open-ended responses, obtains .98 reliability. However, on the whole, the basic problem about obtaining high reliability with qualitative content analysis is that the findings are not always independent of the measuring instruments, for example, the analyst. But, as Kassarjian (1978) comments, "the reliability coefficient cannot be the sole criterion for the quality of the study."

Problems of *validating* the results of qualitative content analysis, where intuition and interpretation play a major role in the analysis, are obvious. The only type of validity relevant to qualitative data according to Krippendorf (1980) is "semantical validity," or the degree to which a method is sensitive to the symbolic meanings in a context (a subjective judgement in which the researcher must ask, "Is it measuring peoples' feelings?") Attempts to correlate feelings and attitudes with other variables to estimate validity are unrealistic, since in most cases the qualitative research project is a one-off study, and variables cannot be realistically selected.

As to the argument between qualitative and quantitative content analysis, there is of course a need for both, and in the last analysis they have more in common than they have differences. For example, saying that X increased sharply is for all intents and purposes the same as comparing 23% with 41%: "both are quantitative, one is just more precise than the other" (Berelson, 1971). In fact, Berelson's advice is to use only the time-consuming quantitative content analysis approach when (1) a high degree of precision is required; (2) where there is a chance that impressionistic analysis could be subject to bias; or (3) when it is intended that content data will be statistically related to numerical data (such as motorists' attitudes about their own driving patterns). Otherwise, Berelson advises that content analysis should be done as roughly and impressionistically as the circumstances of the study will allow. Krippendorf (1980) would agree, as he has stated that the ultimate reliability test of a good content analysis is "Does the data obtained in the research provide a trustworthy basis for drawing inferences, making recommendations and supporting decisions?"

TYPES OF OPEN-ENDED MATERIAL SUBJECTED TO CONTENT ANALYSIS

Holsti (1969) has pointed out that there are many ways to study peoples' behaviour: (1) experiments in a laboratory; (2) giving people a questionnaire to fill in; (3) observing behaviour; (4) simulating models of peoples' behaviour; (5) studying artifacts—literature, tools, wall paintings, and so forth, and making deductions about behaviour and beliefs; (6) interviewing people; and (7) exposing respondents to projective techniques.

In the social and marketing research fields, it is the latter two approaches that are most prevalent. And, most typically, when the project is qualitative as opposed to quantitative, there are open-ended questions, such as, "What do you remember about your first car?" "What comes to your mind when you think of money?" "How would you describe a typical Council tenant?" Qualitative research also makes extensive use of the great variety of projective techniques, and each type elicits its own varieties of response.

Association Techniques

The most widely used is "word association"; the respondent is asked to say whatever comes into his/her mind concerning a list of preselected words. Since there is no further prompting from the interviewer, the respondent may of course go off on any number of tangents. In a study concerning speed limits, respondents were asked to respond to such words as "laws," "safety," "going fast," "police," and so forth. Responses varied a great deal between men and women, young and old, convicted speeders and nonspeeders, and along personality variables such as authoritarianism.

Another association technique makes use of "analogies"; respondents may be asked to describe an object in terms of textures, colour associations, animals, or personality types. In a study on shopping, respondents were asked to select colours and textures to describe their feelings in a shop. In a study on seat belts, respondents were asked to describe the personality of a seat belt, for example, the type of person it would be if it came to life; other respondents were asked to describe animals most descriptive of seat belts.

Story-telling Techniques

Respondents may be asked to respond to an actual photograph, drawing, or cartoon; these techniques yield a great deal of open-ended material. In a motoring study, respondents were shown a sketch of a man behind the wheel of his car as seen from behind the motorist; the speedometer showed that he was going 70 mph; the road was visible through the windscreen. The respondents were asked to describe what was going on, what the man was thinking and feeling.

Sentence Completion

While with this technique, respondents answers may be relatively short, they typically vary a great deal. For instance, when asked to describe the worst things about driving a car, some respondents mentioned the physical strain, others the mental strain, time, money, being everyone's chauffeur, and so on. In a study conducted among the elderly, they were asked to complete a sentence about their personal fears. Some mentioned outside forces—vandals, muggers, higher prices, and so on; others mentioned more personal things—health, becoming depressed, loneliness; yet others mentioned world events—nuclear war, lack of morals, unemployment, and so on.

Psychodrama and Role Plays

These techniques yield the greatest volume of open-ended data. As with association techniques, the interviewer/researcher can only set the stage (literally and figuratively). Once respondents get into the action or drama, it may go in many directions and for long periods of time. For example, in a project conducted among shop floor supervisors, they were asked to play the role of top managers sitting on a committee discussing ways to increase profits. There were six groups of supervisors in all, and each one went off in a different direction. One group concentrated on incentives for the work force, another on better use of the working day, another on cutting out dead wood, and yet another on creating new markets for the product.

Drawing Techniques

These techniques have become increasingly popular as a way of eliciting responses within an open-ended format. Respondents are asked to draw a picture and then to explain their drawings. For instance, men were asked to draw how they felt when they went shopping for clothes; some used arrows, others circles or heavy and thin lines to describe feelings. However, without a verbal expression it was impossible for the researcher to know that in one instance Mr. X was describing an assertive approach to the situation and in another a state of confusion, while in yet another a leisurely browsing behaviour was being conveyed. The research project previously described, conducted among supervisors, included a drawing exercise as well. They were asked to draw their job as they saw it, indicating the way in which communication with others occurred. However, in order to understand the extent to which the communications were "perceived" as positive, negative, fruitful, or frustrating, it was necessary to ask the men to describe their pictures. Again there was an extensive range of responses; some described their jobs mechanically, others emotionally or intellectually, and yet others described an "ideal" versus their actual job.

The above projective techniques are the most prevalent qualitative research approaches; they yield open-ended data that must be codified, analyzed, synthesized, and summarized via content analysis in order to give meaning to the material.

OTHER FACTORS AFFECTING THE CONTENT ANALYSIS OF QUALITATIVE DATA

Not only must the researcher be aware of the various types of responses each projective technique can produce, but also they must consider the research situation before undertaking content analysis. For instance, respondents may be interviewed on a one-to-one "depth" basis or in groups. The latter complicates the analysis, because in groups respondents interrupt each other, change the subject in midstream, and generally do not respond in an orderly way. Furthermore, group dynamics get in the way of the content; that is, respondents react to each other and not just to the subject being investigated.

There are also research formats in which respondents are asked to write down their own answers as they introspect about a particular subject; in effect they interview themselves. For example, in a study on shopping, housewives were asked to record both what they bought and how they felt about the particular shopping experience, how it compared to others, what had surprised or disappointed them, etc. They had to reflect upon and analyze their own recent experiences; therefore, the content to be analyzed had been subjected to research influences that were very different from those generated by group discussions or face-to-face interviews.

In a different vein, brainstorming or creativity sessions actually encourage respondents to be irrational, to say the first thing that comes into their minds without censorship. Fantasy material of this type presents the analyst with an entirely different content analysis format from that of the focused interviews, either group or depth.

Another type of qualitative research that creates a broad base of content to be analyzed is action research, in which groups of respondents are reconvened four or five times to focus on the same general problem. As times goes on, respondents become less and less inhibited, as well as more creative, which expands the content. For example, in a study of attitudes towards work, the immediate focus could be job satisfaction and ways of enrichment. Over time the subject expands to family, social, and community life as well. In one such study, a group felt that their isolation from a new community detracted from job satisfaction. Community representatives were brought in to describe their activities. The group not only responded to the representatives but began to think in terms of establishing their own special-interest and social groups. Analyzing the results of action research is a very demanding job, because the subject matter increases over time.

The Delphi Technique also creates unique analysis problems. In this research approach, respondents are sent a questionnaire containing a large percentage of open-ended questions about a subject in which they have a vested interest. For example, journalists were sent a Delphi questionnaire concerning the future of persuasion and retailers were sent a questionnaire concerning the future of packaging. With the Delphi format the questionnaire responses are first analyzed and summarized; respondents are then sent the questionaire again with a summary of the answers from the total sample. They are asked to consider the issues again in the light of the first round of responses. The research subject, as the name Delphi implies, usually deals with the future. As the study progresses and respondents think more about it (they receive three questionnaires in all, which contain a considerable number of open-ended questions), the range of ideas obviously expands and the content analysis task increases accordingly.

There is yet another factor the qualitative research analyst must consider: respondent types. In traditional content analysis of propaganda, both the character of the orator and type of audience were taken into consideration; the qualitative content analyst must do the same. The types and range of responses will vary a great deal according to the types of people who respond: Are they average motorists or only those who have been prosecuted for speeding? Are they special groups such as vandals or unemployed school leavers? Are they in special situations such as prisons or hospitals, or are they elderly or handicapped? Where are they in the life cycle, just entering marriage or at the "empty-nest" stage? Are they in special positions, such as sales clerks, second line management, travelling representatives, retailing decision makers? Whatever stage of life or situation respondents are in, their frame of reference will be a major factor influencing the types of responses they give to open-ended questions.

THE APPROACH TO CONTENT ANALYSIS OF QUALITATIVE RESEARCH MATERIAL

As with any other type of scientific data analysis, the results of content analysis must meet certain basic requirements; these are, according to Holsti (1969):

1. *Objectivity* (e.g., freedom from analyst bias).
2. *Systematic* (the analysis must be designed to secure data relevant to the scientific problem, the hypotheses).
3. *Generality* (the results must have sufficient general application; therefore, the sample must be representative of some relevant universe).

However, even before the analysis can begin, there must be questions posed of the data, or, in more scientific terms, hypotheses formulated for testing. These provide what Holsti calls the "binding" through which the analytic categories are related to the basic problem.

Hypotheses will be formulated as a result of many influences:

1. The specific research problem as presented to the researcher. For example, in a study of speeding behaviour one research question was, do motorists respect the law? An hypothesis put forward was that convicted speeders do not respect speed limits and feel that they know the appropriate speed for each type of road condition. (This in fact proved to be a correct hypothesis.)

2. Reading through or listening to responses from the pilot interviews will focus the researcher's mind on major themes out of which hypotheses will be formulated. For instance, when youngsters were interviewed about their experiences with nature conservation work, they focused on how differently everyone—teachers and classmates—behaved while working in the open, compared to classroom behaviour. The hypothesis formulated was that one of the benefits of doing nature conservation work was a social one, e.g., getting to know more about people.

3. An understanding of the basic theories of human behaviour, which provide models and key concepts, not as rigid moulds, but rather as foundations upon which hypotheses can be developed. For example, in a study of interior decorating it was proposed that when the housewife sets out to decorate her home, she selects rooms to express the different aspects of

herself, such as her ideal, future, past, or present self, in accordance with the self Theories of Goffman.

Qualitative researchers can never devote too much time to immersing themselves in the study of human behaviour, and in particular, theories of perception, motivation, and personality. There is an enormous and stimulating body of knowledge to be read and absorbed. For example, the theories of Eric Berne (*Games People Play,* 1964) are based on the observation that from an early age we learn how to play the games of life and thus become dependent on them for survival, which in Berne's terms means the avoidance of stress, the maintenance of our sense of equilibrium, and the pursuit of pleasure. Then there are the theories of the cognitivists such as Lewin, who state that behaviour is due to the interaction of man and his environment; that the psychological field of every person is made up of person-centered forces and environment-centered forces, described as vectors, exerting particular pressures from various directions. On the other hand, the theories of the existentialist Maslow are currently influencing qualitative researchers; he stresses the inner richness and uniqueness of every individual as well as a basic need to "self-actualize"; e.g., to know, experience, and seek out the novel, rather than to seek a state of equilibrium as proposed by Berne and others.

Kelly's concepts of "personal constructs," defined as creations by individuals in order to react to the past and reach out to the future, are purposeful, according to Kelly, because "man is in business to make sense of his world." (For more details of these theories see Mostyn 1977.)

The qualitative researcher would find it useful to learn how to score and interpret projective tests such as the TAT, Draw-A-Person, and Sentence Completion. The Rorschach Ink Blot Test is one of the oldest and most extensively documented techniques due to its world wide use, and numerous categories have been developed to help in the interpretation; in addition, age, sex, and nationality norms have been established.

Furthermore, it is essential that eventually the qualitative researcher ask her/him self, What are *my* theories of human behaviour? What are the basic motivations in *my* opinion? I have often felt that this question basically boils down to asking oneself, Do I believe that most behaviour is learned, or is it innate? That is, are we born a blank slate upon which society writes out the instructions, as the Behaviourists assume, or do we come preprogrammed to think and act in certain ways, as the instinct theorists propose? Since it is quite likely that both operate, what is the balance between the two? It is important to recognise one's own biases and prejudices in terms of the perceived sources of human behaviour—the environmental or the unique genetics of the individual.

Another basic question the researcher should ask her/him self: Is the pursuit of a state of balance or equilibrium a basic motivation, or does the human being, as Maslow states, seek disequilibrium in the pursuit of satisfying a basic need for adventure?

In summary, the above questions indicate that a thorough knowledge of motivational theories is essential in order that the researcher may formulate meaningful hypotheses concerning the subject under investigation. This does not mean that all of the hypotheses formulated must be based on psychological theories; frequently it is even more meaningful to pose basic, simplistic questions. For example, in a study concerning the personal benefits derived from nature conservation work, it seemed reasonable to expect a priori that there would be a range of very basic benefits, such as: intellectual (learning about flora and fauna); emotional (getting rid of pent-up energy or anxiety); and physical (fresh air, exercise) benefits. This proved to be a fruitful hypothesis. However, reading through the group discussion transcripts revealed another benefit—social (mixing with a variety of people).

In a study into the cause of vandalism, the rather basic hypothesis formulated stated that there were probably both internal and external causes; this gave a meaningful structure to the study. And in yet another study of environmental nuisances, a priori hypotheses were proposed that peoples' hopes and fears regarding the future of the environment would indicate their concerns about the present; this proved to be a fruitful line of questioning.

Content analysis, as Berelson (1971) has advised, "has no magical qualities; you rarely get out of it more than you put in and sometimes you get less. In the last analysis there is no substitute for a *good idea*," that is, a testable hypothesis. In addition to a thorough grounding in the theories of human behaviour, the qualitative researcher must be an expert in group dynamics and sensitive to the interaction factors that occur in a group setting—"shifts to risk" or adoption of the status quo. This is because group discussions as a research technique, have become increasingly popular in social and market research circles. Bonoma and Rosenberg (1978) have recommended that in order to deal effectively with groups, researchers should also consider social influence theory, and focus on communication *modes* and not just the message; that is, in the analysis, it is important to evaluate the quality of the communication: was it friendly, dramatic, hostile, and so forth. In this approach each group member is given a number; as the analysis proceeds, vectors are drawn between these numbers and labeled according to psychological function—reinforcing, hostile, and so forth. This approach, while useful in *describing* behaviour, does not help in interpreting it.

Providing that the qualitative researcher is well grounded in her/his field, e.g., in the theories of motivation as well as group dynamics, and has formulated some testable hypotheses before undertaking the research investigation, she/he must then ask, Have I the *personal* requirements to be an effective analyst of open-ended material? These requirements, according to Holsti (1969), are that they must see themselves as scientific observers capable of both intuitive and analytical thinking (classification of data) based on knowledge, understanding, and experience. However, it is the intuitive requirement that sets the qualitative researcher apart from the quantitative; this is because qualitative data must be *interpreted,* and not just reported. As Henry (1956) has commented, "Guidelines (categories for analysis) can only be scaffolding; artistic judgement and intuition will always remain part of the process of interpretation." Interestingly, while Rorschach emphasized the need to develop agreed-upon and specific categories for his projective test analysis, he always maintained that there was a high dependence on intuition and heuristic thinking when analyzing the data.

On the other hand, there have been and will be in the future many attempts to develop methods that are less dependent on the analyst and her/his intuition. Jones (1981), in developing the cognitive map approach to analysis, pointed out that open-ended material was too complex to be left to the individual analyst. She recommended instead that each respondent would be represented by a cognitive map—a structure of the person's beliefs and attitudes, which featured plus and minus vectors for each communication made by an individual. These maps can then be combined by a computer to obtain "group concepts," thus constructing the results rather than relying on the researcher's capacity for "empathy, sensitivity, imagination and creativity," e.g., intuition. This is, however, an expansive and time-consuming exercise, as Jones admits, and more importantly, too mechanistic for qualitative data. It may report what was said and what happened, but there is no reliable way to interpret what respondents meant or felt from cognitive maps.

There have also been attempts to develop dictionaries for the content analysis of open-ended material, similar to those used in quantitative content analysis. Once the general inquirer dictionary was developed at the Harvard Social Relations Laboratory in the 1940s for the purpose of analyzing political documents in terms of their most common word characteristics, there have been numerous dictionaries developed: the anthropology dictionary to analyze cross-cultural folk tales; a dictionary for use in analyzing behaviour and personality as revealed in clinical group discussions; a dictionary to analyze neurotic themes among patients for psychotherapists. (More details in Stone et al., 1962.) However, since these dictionaries are dependent on "tagging" key words in the text, they do not allow for inference, a vital element in interpretation. Qualitative researchers interpret data on the assumption that inferences between intent and content can validly be made. Dictionaries deal only with content; thus, such an analysis is very lopsided.

There is one other major requirement for the qualitative researcher, and that is experience: experience in formulating and testing hypotheses as well as experience in conducting qualitative research. As Krippendorf (1980) described, experience is essential in order to distinguish the relevant from the irrelevant. While most intelligent, conscientious people can be trained to code quantitative data without previous experience, this is definitely not the case with qualitative research; here, experience is the best teacher.

THE CONCEPT BOOK APPROACH TO CONTENT ANALYSIS

The method of conducting content analysis of open-ended material that I propose is one that I call the "concept book approach"; it was initially developed by the Father of Motivational Research, Dr. Ernest Dichter.

Since the basic problem facing the researcher who sets out to analyze open-ended material is that she/he has to classify data on which very little order has been previously imposed, the first prerequisite is that the analyst must let the data "do" the work for him/her. That is, the proof for or against a certain hypothesis, or the evaluation of an hypothesis, must arise out of the data, and it must *guide* the analyst to revise ideas or discover new hypotheses. The data must also be used to support any conclusions drawn in the form of quotations. As Goode and Hatt (1952) have advised, "fit classes to the data."

Therefore, one absolute requirement for the qualitative analyst is that he/she must continually be analyzing the data. As one experienced qualitative researcher, Maureen Ressler, in London, explained in a personal communication, "You keep testing the data like an oil refinery keeps testing all the time." Thus, the qualitative researcher cannot just put the project into the field and forget about it, she/he must constantly keep in touch with interviewers and follow developments, so that hypotheses can be continually reevaluated and new hypotheses developed. For instance, in the course of a series of group discussions with men concerning the "meaning" of socks, it was found that instead of being seen as a protective coating, socks were actually viewed as a second skin, that is, more a part of the wearer than the environment. This hypothesis could then be proposed to the other interviewers on the project and therefore to the remaining respondents. Further research supported the hypothesis, which thus accounted for the then male resistance to synthetic socks, and most particularly throw-away socks.

A "RECIPE" FOR THE CONTENT ANALYSIS OF OPEN-ENDED DATA: THE CONCEPT BOOK APPROACH

Here is a 13-step recipe for the content analysis of open-ended material—the Concept Book Approach.

I. Briefing

Review the research problem thoroughly; make sure you understand it. Ask questions of the client or sponsor until you are sure you understand the antecedents—what led up to this research project? What is the *real* purpose of it?

Put the problem into perspective; for example, the frame of reference of the respondents (the phenomenological approach).

Thus, a research investigation among holiday makers concerning U.K, holidays will take place in an entirely different social, economic, and attitudinal climate in 1985, compared to the same study conducted in 1977. Freud (1950), for example, when analyzing dreams, emphasized the importance of placing the dream in the relevant context for the individual and understanding the antecedents to the dream.

II. Sampling

Once you feel you have grasped the essentials of the research problem, check the proposed sample. Is it representative enough to generalise to the whole population or only a certain segment of it? Should it be expanded? For instance, are delinquents from one-parent families sufficient to answer your research question or should your sample contain delinquents from all family types?

III. Associating

As an experienced researcher, ask yourself if you have met a similar problem before, and if so, what were some of the ideas from that research which might form the basis of fruitful hypotheses this time? For example, the research investigation to determine the personal benefits of nature conservation work revealed a variety of personal benefits—social, emotional, physical, and intellectual. When the Volunteer Centre proposed a research investigation into the motivations underlying volunteer work, it was hypothesized the some of the same types of personal benefits might be appropriate and that nondirective questions concerning them should be included. The focus provided by these questions proved to be useful in this particular study.

IV. Hypotheses Development

Write down (on separate sheets of paper) testable hypotheses, whether based on previous experience with a similar problem or on an understanding of the dynamics of human behaviour, particularly motivations. For instance, a study concerning the purchase of furniture was to be conducted for a major British manufacturer. Among the sample would be newlyweds, an obvious group for new furniture purchase. The hypothesis put forward was that the couple's selection of furniture was their way of advertising what sort of couple they were—trendy, traditionalists, moderates, status conscious. The hypothesis was worth testing, but the results turned out differently: newlyweds tended to buy innocuous, middle-of-the-road furniture as a way of avoiding making a statement about who they were as a couple or a unit. This made sense when analyzed further; after all, this newly formed pair were not a unit yet; it would take time. In fact, as all social scientists know, one never sets out to prove that one's hypothesis is right, rather one applies the null hypothesis, and tests it to determine if the status quo obtains, and therefore that the hypothesis should be rejected. Only when the evidence indicates that the hypothesis cannot be rejected does one accept it. The hypotheses developed at this stage and noted down form the basis of the Concept Book. The most useful way of assembling the Concept Book is to place each sheet of paper (containing one hypothesis) into a loose-leaf notebook so that they can easily be shuffled around to indicate relevance; that is, as the study progresses, those hypotheses that seem most fruitful should be kept towards the front, the controversial in the middle, and those that are weaker at the end.

The importance of approaching the data collection or interviewing stage with testable hypotheses cannot be overstressed; having these hypotheses sensitizes the qualitative researcher and her/his assistants to the behaviour and approach of respondents, e.g., to what they might be trying to say. As Macoby (1959) has pointed out, even the most thoroughly conducted content analysis "cannot be a substitute for theory development and hypothesis testing, deductive reasoning and experimentation."

V. Hypotheses Testing

Before the interviewing commences, the researcher must make certain that the open-ended questions to be put to respondents are presented via the "funnel" approach; that is, starting with the most general and moving to the specific. An example would be questions concerning feelings about driving at the beginning of the interview leading on to more specific questions towards the wearing of seat belts. This allows the respondent to bring up seat belts early in the interview, if they are particularly significant for her/him. It also provides a general focus for respondents as they adjust to the interviewing situation, rather than their being asked to consider seat belts when they first sit down for the interview with many other things on their mind.

Once the fieldwork begins, the researcher must keep in constant contact with other interviewers on the project in order to note themes and trends, in particular to get a feel for whether or not the proposed hypotheses have any merit or if any new hypotheses seem to be emerging. Above all, the researcher must remain flexible, willing to give up original hypotheses and embrace new possibilities. For example, during the course of a series of group discussions among children on the subject of aircraft noise in relation to other noises in their environment, it became increasingly clear that the noises of aggression, for example, people fighting or arguing, were far more disturbing that the noises of large aircraft overhead or other environmental noises, such as traffic. This had not been anticipated. However, the researcher was able to contact the other interviewers and ask them to test this hypothesis in further interviews. It was decided that the children would be asked to take a piece of paper and draw an X in the middle to symbolize themselves; around this X they were to draw all of the noises that bothered them either in symbol form or with words. They were to place nearest to the X those noises that disturbed them the most. The hypothesis was supported by the research: the vast majority of children drew pictures of people fighting or arguing nearest to the X symbol of themselves.

As Berelson (1971) has described, the task at this stage of the research is to discover, define, and redefine one's ideas. This is the stage at which the analyst becomes deeply senstive to the data and begins to make inferences, such as the possibility that wool may have an "unreliable" (mind of its own) image, while synthetics are seen as "solid" and more dependable.

The researcher should never be put off by contradictions or puzzles of any sort at this stage, since, as Freud stated, "The ability to be puzzled is the beginning of wisdom."

VI. Immersion

The qualitative researcher must next immerse her/himself in the research data, read it in note or transcript form, or listen to it if it is on tape. This total immersion is essential. The researcher must embrace all of the material in order to pick up even the subtlest clues and get a feel for what is really going on. In fact, the researcher would be wise to adopt at this stage a rather cynical attitude, described by Krippendorf (1980), in which content analysis is seen as a game in which the analyst tries to guess what his opponent (the respondent) is hiding, "to perform better than chance he must rely on *any* information his opponent happens to reveal."

At the same time, the researcher must be sensitive to new ideas and relationships, as well as patterns between inferences previously defined, and be willing to test any hypotheses regarding these possible relationships. For instance, to test the hypothesis that people with positive feelings towards wool, despite its unreliable image, are more likely to wear it next to their skin—socks, jumpers, gloves—than those with negative feelings towards wool.

Unlike quantitative research, where the interpretation follows from the analysis, the qualitative researcher uses the content as a reflection of deeper phenomena, for example, to interpret data. Accordingly, most qualitative researchers agree that there is definite value in listening to the tape recordings in addition to reading the transcripts, since the nuances of feeling, tone of voice, pauses, and so forth become evident.

It is in this phase that experience is most valuable—it helps to sharpen the researcher's sixth sense, that is, to gain insights from the material without getting caught up by the novel (perhaps interesting), but irrelevant, responses. It is at this stage that the Concept Book is expanded and further refined; the researcher will want to note on the pages containing the hypotheses these refinements and additions. In one study it was noted that single, divorced, or very defensive respondents were the most likely to feel that seat belts inhibited their driving; these additions enhanced the Concept Book. Furthermore, new hypotheses will have emerged which must be entered in the Concept Book; for example, in a study among volunteer workers it was found that many of the most active volunteers had themselves been helped at a critical point in their own lives.

Where several hundred depth interviews have been conducted and total immersion in the data is not reasonable (the researcher would suffer from data indigestion), there are several possibilities. Some researchers request interviewers to write a brief summary of the main points of the interview or to select out interviews that might be worth reading because they are so typical or unusual. Other researchers select every fifth or tenth interview and read it thoroughly, making sure that all subgroups are included—males and females, middle class, working class, and so on.

VII. Categorizing

The next stage involves working *with* the Concept Book. It is at this stage that the real work of content analysis begins; that is, the selection of "categories" with which to organize the analysis. Categories are the key to content analysis, whether quantitative or qualitative. According to Berelson (1971), "Content Analysis stands or falls by its categories."

The immersion in the research data will have produced a wealth of impressions and ideas which will have been noted in the Concept Book. Now it is necessary to give each idea, concept, or hypothesis a "label"; for example, make a category out of it and assign it a number, a letter, or a combination of both to use as a code. Once each item in the Concept Book has a label and a code, the raw data—open-ended responses—must be coded. Presumably the researcher has transcripts, interviewer's notes, or his or her own notes taken while listening to the tapes. Ideally these sheets of paper should have a wide margin on the left-hand side where codes, corresponding to categories, can be easily inserted. Coloured pens aid visibility and can also be useful in identifying subgroups; for example, all notes taken from children's interviews are coded in green, adults in blue, and so forth.

According to Holsti (1969), there are several things to remember when selecting categories. First, they must reflect the purpose of the research; second, they must be exhaustive; third, and most important, they must be mutually exclusive, which will not only make report writing easier, but will enhance reliability, and therefore make the entire research exercise more scientific. In addition, the researcher must link each unit or category with an hypothesis indicating whether it does or does not support it. The experienced researcher while going through the data will also be evaluating the quality of the answers before coding them—are they clichés? Are they unclear? For example, in a study concerning housing, the answer, "We moved to a better area," was deemed a poor answer. It should have been probed further—What is a better area?

Certain other refinements may be useful to code, as suggested by Kassarjian (1978), such as the use or nonuse of the personal pronoun concerning a personal issue, as well as the degree of confidence surrounding an attitude.

By this time, the Concept Book should be quite full of ideas, not all of equal value; in addition, many initial hypotheses will have been discarded. Under each hypothesis, theme, or idea in the Concept Book, subthemes or ideas should have begun to emerge as well.

VIII. Incubation

The researcher should read through the Concept Book to refresh his/her memory. Then, following the example of Maureen Ressler, (personal communication) the project should be set aside for several days to let the various ideas incubate and jell in his/her mind.

IX. Synthesis

The researcher must then sit down with the Concept Book and ask him/herself several important questions:

1. What is my rationale for coding the data in this way, what makes this concept work, what is the proof?
2. As I read through the data, what patterns now emerge? What relationships seem important? For example, in the speeding study, drivers from the North and older drivers expressed a great deal of anxiety about speed limits; why? the researcher must ask. What other reasons might correlate? In this case, the depth interviews revealed that they were less likely to drive on motorways, did not drive as many miles per year as other drivers, and tended to view driving as stressful.
3. Is there any one theme that seems to dominate the findings, one theme that could be called the "key concept" to which all others relate? This was the approach favoured by Dr. Dichter.

For instance, in a study concerning motivations regarding seat-belt wearing, it was clear after going through all of the transcripts that wearers and nonwearers had two entirely different viewpoints about the meaning of seat belts. The wearers felt that seat belts gave them a greater feel for their cars, made them better drivers. Nonwearers on the other hand, felt that seat belts were a part of the car reaching out to "take them over," and therefore not to be trusted. These two key concepts gave order to the rest of the data. All of the other findings seemed to relate to these two key concepts, including attitudes towards driving, safety, seat belt design, and even "other drivers."

X. "Culling"

Since it is not possible for the final report to play back all of the recorded observations, the researcher must think in terms of condensing, excising, and even reinterpreting the data, so that it can be written up as a meaningful communication. Original hypotheses that cannot be supported will have been abandoned; fresh ideas that seemed to emerge out of the data during a first read-through may not have been sustained. In addition, confusing and contradictory ideas that defy clarification have to be abandoned. In the end, the researcher must bear in mind that the final report must be clear to readers who have not had the benefit of being present at the interviews or reading through the raw material. The objective is to produce a clear communication of what heppened without too many qualifications.

It is equally important to bear in mind that despite the fact that qualitative research may often engage a respondent in a rather lengthy interview, perhaps up to 3 hours, one has only obtained a very small slice of life from that individual. Since people's lives are very complex, the only way of understanding the whole person is to conduct a longitudinal study; one interview will simply not fill in all the gaps, tie up all the loose ends, and generally make sense of the totality of a person's attitudes, feelings, and opinions about a particular subject. Thus, the researcher must accept that some responses will never make sense and that some themes produced by a number of respondents will remain a puzzle.

Moreover, a good content analysis is never finished according to Krippendorf (1980), "it will answer some questions but raise others," leading to the formulation of new hypotheses, which the current data may not be able to support or reject; thus, more research will be needed.

XI. Interpretation

"The richness of qualitative analysis resides not in the content categories with which they deal but rather with the *interpretation* which they make of the content material" Berelson (1971). Berelson adds the caveat that "interpretations are not limited by either the mode of analysis or the content." But how does one go about interpreting data? How can one make that creative leap in the dark from the observation that nonwearers of seat belts feel "uncomfortable," "tied down," "tense," and "anxious" in a seat belt to the interpretation that nonwearers fear being taken over by the car, losing their sense of being in charge of the machine when entwined in the car's seat belts?

Is it just intuition? Is it an understanding of basic motivations, like the dynamics of fear and its correlate loss of control over one's environment? It is all of these and more. It is the ability to see new relationships by allowing one's creative powers enough free rein to envision, for instance, that mens' socks could indeed be more of a second epidermis than an article of clothing.

It is the ability to turn ideas around, perhaps even upside down, in order to explore new relationships. For instance, rather than focusing on what people say about their bath soap—how it makes them feel, reactions to the fragrance and colour—watch what they do with it. They hold and caress it in their hand; thus, the shape is important, too—it should cradle in the hand and fill the palm comfortably.

It is the ability to stand back from a problem in order to gain perspective. To ask, for instance, why a woman wears makeup—as a mask to hide behind or as a means of enhancing her best features? (Both in fact seem to be true, the latter for younger women, the former for the middle-aged woman.)

It is the ability to work with contradictory data; for example, why do regular tea drinkers claim that it "calms me down," "wakes me up," "is a tranquilizer," "is a stimulant"? Perhaps it's because people use tea to make them feel the way they want to feel.

It is the ability to see behind rationalizations: when people state that they already have too much bed linen and too many blankets and therefore could never justify buying a Continental Quilt, might there be more to it? Some basic resistance? Could it be a fear of the unknown? How do Continental Quilts work? How do you get them to stay on the bed? How do you care for them? How can you feel confident with them?

And, on another subject, what does "I enjoy helping those less fortunate than I am" mean from a voluntary worker? Is it perhaps another way of saying "I am aware of how lucky *I* am when I compare myself with the less fortunate; this gives me confidence and encouragement"? Is it really the voluntary worker who is benefitting?

It is also the ability to ask, "What is the *meaning* of this? What is the meaning of gardening, planting, growing? Isn't it a generating or parenting activity? What is the meaning of pet ownership? Isn't it having power and authority over another living thing? What is the meaning of life insurance? A way of buying off the fates, paying one's dues to the Gods of Good Luck? What is the meaning of giving to charity? Isn't it a way of keeping the problem from one's own door so that there is no need to do anything about it?

There is no easy formula to aid the researcher in the interpretation of qualitative research data as opposed to merely reporting the findings. To be able to interpret does, however, require several qualities and abilities from the researcher, among the most essential, to stand back from the problem to gain a new perspective; work with contradictions; explore new relationships, turn the problem around, perhaps even upside down; understand basic motivations and apply them; see behind rationalizations; ask and try to answer the question, what is the meaning of this? Give one's

ing respondents' feelings. And in the Volunteer Workers Study, the "fact" that no respondent under 60 mentioned that it was "one's duty to help the unfortunate" was very significant.

4. If possible, the researcher must attempt to look for indications of *salience*: How willing have respondents been to bring their behaviour in line with stated attitudes? What, if anything, have they done? In the study among volunteer workers, the question was asked, To what extent were they willing to work for organisations or people they rated as most "worthy"? The correlation was in fact very high. In the study on speed limits, the question was asked, How frequently had those drivers who feel they "know best" been willing to try it out—for example, drive over the speed limit and perhaps be warned, summoned, or prosecuted? The correlations were also very high in this instance.

Often, intended behaviour will be the only guide to salience. For instance, respondents may be shown a product idea to which they positively respond—they like the smell, shape, packaging, etc. But it is important to know how willing they would be to switch brands for it, for example, give up the habit of the old product. Usually the correlations are rather low, habits do not die easily.

5. Finally, as Henry (1956) has also pointed out, when we are dealing with some aspect of respondents' fantasies, hopes and fears, or nostalgic reminiscences of their childhood, we must remember that the respondent is required to communicate this fantasy in some recognisable form; that is, to verbalise it in a way that will "make sense"; for example, to make rational irrationale thoughts, to apply logic where it does not apply. In this instance, the qualitative researcher must say to him/herself, What does the respondent *mean*, What is she/he trying to say?

For instance, in a study of *vandalism*, adult respondents referred to frustrations, pent-up energy, and feelings of *impotence* among the young, which turned out to be equally an expression of their own feelings and fears as Council tenants.

XIII. Rethink

The researcher must go back to Step I and review the research objectives, and then either rewrite (often impossible, due to time constraints) or at least edit the report to make certain that he/she has not got carried away with a handy theory or colourful quotation and exaggerated it out of all proportion compared to what actually happened.

Even more importantly, since the qualitative researcher does not merely report what happened, but rather interprets what it means, he/she must be certain that the interpretations made have not been taken further than the evidence would justify. Last, the researcher should bear in mind Henry's (1956) advice: "It is not necessary to interpret everything, many things may seem to have no part in the analysis, to treat all data collected as relevant evidence is just not scientific" —or in fact, realistic.

In summary, to conduct a meaningful content analysis of open-ended material using the Concept Book approach, the qualitative researcher must follow this thirteen step recipe:

1. Understand the research brief thoroughly.
2. Evaluate the relevance of your sample for the research project.
3. Associate your own experiences with the problem; look for clues from the past.
4. Develop testable hypotheses as the basis for the Concept Book.
5. Test the hypotheses throughout the interviewing and analysis process.
6. Stay immersed in the data throughout the study.
7. Categorise the data in the Concept Book; create labels and codes.
8. Incubate the date before writing it up.
9. Synthesize the data in the Concept Book; look for the key concept.
10. Cull the data; it is impossible to report everything that happened.
11. Interpret the data: What does it mean? What are its implications?
12. Write up the report.
13. Rethink and rewrite: have the research objectives been met?

In the last analysis, the best approach to the content analysis of open-ended material is a professional one; that is, qualitative researchers should in the first instance be well versed in the theories of human behaviour and motivation. Second, they must not take an overly academic approach to social and marketing research and try to make the data fit a convenient theory; rather, they should maintain a mental flexibility which allows a convenient hypothesis to be rejected and new hypotheses to emerge. Third, they must allow their own well-founded insights and intuitions to come forward when immersing themselves in the data. Fourth, they must be daring enough to take that creative leap in the dark that interpretation demands. Fifth, they must be willing to take on board the responsibilities of the social scientist—to approach the data objectively, systematically, and rigorously. Sixth, they must be willing to develop an approach similar to the "recipe" suggested in this paper and stick to it. Last, qualitative research is a field where experience is the best teacher; the researcher must assume that she/he is always learning and growing. As Cervantes said hundreds of years ago: "Experience, the universal Mother of Science."

REFERENCES

Berelson, B. (1971). *Content analysis in communication research.* New York: Free Press.

Berne, E. (1964). *Games people play.* New York: Grove Press.

Bonoma, T. V., and Rosenberg, H. (1978). Theory based content analysis: A social influence perspective for evaluating group process. *Social Science Research* 7(3), 213.

Calder, B. J. (1977). Focus groups and the nature of qualitative market research. *Journal of Marketing Research 16,* 353.

Ekman, P. (1965). In I de Sola Pool (Ed.), *Trends in Content Analysis.* Urbana, Illinois: University of Illinois Press.

Freud, S. (1950). *The interpretation of dreams.* New York: Random House.

George, A. L. (1959). *Quantitative and qualitative approaches to content analysis.* New York: Rand Corp.

Goode, W. J., and Hatt, P. K. *Methods in social research.* New York: McGraw-Hill.

Gordon, W. I. (1978). *Communication: Personal and public.* New York: Alfred.

Gottschlalk, L. A. (1969). *Manual of instructions for using the Gottschlalk–Gleser content analysis scales.* Berkeley, CA: University of California Press.

Henry, W. E. (1956). *The analysis of fantasy.* New York: Wiley.

Holsti, O. R. (1969). *Content analysis for the social sciences and humanities.* Reading, MA: Addison.

Jones, S. (1981). Listening to complexity. *Journal of the Market Research Society, 23*(3), 62.

Kassarjian, H. H. (1978). Content analysis in consumer research. *Journal of Consumer Research, 4*(1), 8.

Krippendorff, K. (1980). *Content analysis: An introduction to its methodology.* Beverly Hills, CA: Sage Publications.

Laffal, L. (1969). In G. Gerbner and P. Stone (Eds.), *The analysis of communication content.* New York: Wiley.

Lazarsfeld, P. (1940). The quantification of case studies. *Journal of Applied Psychology,* p. 817.

Macoby, N. (1959). In de Sola Pool (Ed.), *Trends in Content Analysis.* Urbana, IL: University of Illinois Press.

May, J. P. (1978). Qualitative advertising research: A review of the role of the researcher. *Journal of the Market Research Society, 20*(4), 203.

Montgomery, A. C., and Crittenden, K. S. (1977). Improving coding reliability for open-ended questions. *Public Opinion Quarterly, 41*(2), 3.

Mostyn, B. (1977). *Motivational research: Passing fad or permanent feature?* Bradford, Yorkshire England: MCB Books.

Mostyn, B. (1978). *Handbook of motivational and attitude research techniques.* Bradford, Yorkshire, England: MCB Books.

Rapaport, D. (1969). In G. Gerbner and P. Stone (Eds.), *The analysis for the social sciences and humanities.* New York: Wiley.

Rorschach, H. (1956). Gauging primary and secondary processes in rorschach responses. *Journal of Projective Techniques, 20,* 12.

Stone, P., et al. (1962). Coding content data. *Behavioural Science, 7,*(4), 484.

7

Intensive Interviewing

MICHAEL BRENNER

INTRODUCTION

In recent years, there has been considerable criticism and rejection by social scientists of the established measurement theory, "to establish causal laws that enable us to predict and explain specific phenomena" (Labovitz and Hagedorn, 1971, p. 1). It has been pointed out that an uncritical quantitative approach to data collection is, in the majority of instances, incompatible with the actual psychological conditions, in interviews, under which data are collected (see Phillips, 1971, 1973). This realization enabled, in a variety of ways, the psychologically more sensitive employment of interviewing methods, which, it must be emphasized, are still used quite traditionally, and with legitimacy, to approach measurement (see Chapter 2).

There has been another, much fiercer line of criticism and rejection of the established measurement theory. Deutscher (1966, p. 241) has given some of the reasons for this, namely,

> that the adoption of the scientific model in the social sciences has resulted in an uncommon concern for methodological problems centering on issues of reliability and to a concomitant neglect of the problem of validity. . . . We concentrate on consistency without much concern with what it is we are being consistent about or whether we are consistently right or wrong. As a consequence we may have been learning a great deal about how to pursue an incorrect course with a maximum of precision.

Deutscher's remarks are clear enough: while engaged in apparently rigorous scientific activity, social scientists have successfully failed to accomplish the ultimate goal of research—valid knowledge (see also Phillips, 1971, 1973; Argyris, 1980; Kriz, 1981). More importantly, and in addition to the issue of invalidity, social scientists "have tended to bend, re-shape, and

ISBN 0-12-131580-0

distort the empirical social world to fit the model they use to investigate it. Wherever possible, *social reality is ignored*" (Filstead, 1970, p. 3; my italics).

Consequently, it has been suggested that we must use methods that may be regarded as enabling more intimate familiarity with social life, more valid knowledge "through detailed, dense acquaintanceship" (Lofland, 1976, p. 8) with social life. Such methods (participant observation, intensive interviewing, field work, total participation in the social life under study) are frequently characterized, in contrast to the measurement position, in terms of "qualitative methodology":

> Qualitative methodology allows the researcher to "get close to the data," thereby developing the analytical, conceptual, and categorical components of explanation from the data itself—rather than from the preconceived, rigidly structured, and highly quantified techniques that pigeonhole the empirical social world into the operational definitions that the researcher has constructed. (Filstead, 1970, p. 6)

As to the case of the interview, Filstead's methodological advice is readily accepted. Indeed, interviewing means quite literally to develop a *view* of something between (*inter*) people. If viewing means perceiving, then "the term 'interview' refers to the act of perceiving as conducted . . . between two separate people" (Lofland, 1971, p. 75).

In survey interviewing, as I have noted, this act of perceiving is "structured." By that I meant, among other things, that the questions are listed in a questionnaire, most of them "closed" questions, which are asked in one and the same order from each respondent. The employability of such an approach in interviewing assumes, first and foremost, that the multitude of acts of perceiving is unproblematic: the relationships between interviewers and respondents are as unproblematic as the understandings of questions and answers. Insofar as we can ensure that these acts of perceiving *are,* minimally by and large, unproblematic, survey interviewing is a legitimate methodological tool.

For certain data collection purposes (the pretesting of questions, the discovery of respondent problems, for example), we must reject survey interviewing as a suitable methodological strategy and replace it by another methodology. If we are really interested in a form of social life, this requires the use of methods that enable, as I have indicated, intimate familiarity with that life. This, in turn, necessitates

> free-flowing and prolonged immersion. This immersion, first and ideally, may take the form of direct, bodily presence in the physical scenes of the social life under scrutiny, either in an indigenous role or in the role of someone known to be studying that world. (Lofland, 1976, p. 8)

The radical quest for intimate familiarity presupposes the practical availability of a particular research situation: the study would need to be longitudinal and multi-method. For various practical reasons (see, for example, Canter, 1980; Brown and Sime, 1981; Brenner, 1981), intimate familiarity will not be attainable through "prolonged immersion," or, more technically, participant observation. It is more typical for a multitude of research projects that the investigators will have only *post festum* access to the remembered experiences of the forms of social life they are interested in. If this access is comprehensive and prolonged, for example, by using intensive interviewing, it can approximate intimate familiarity.

Having chosen to use intensive interviewing, a qualitative method, the investigator has not, unfortunately, solved problems of invalidity and bias in data collection, and, indeed, may even have created new problems. The issue will be illustrated, and later dealt with in more technical detail, by considering the case of "account analysis," which seems to me to be the most prominent version of intensive interviewing in Britain. Account analysis refers to the in-depth gathering of informants' explanatory speech material and its subsequent content analysis.

> In account analysis we try to discover both the social force and explanatory content of the explanatory speech produced by social actors. This then serves as a guide to the structure of the cognitive resources required for the genesis of intelligible and warrantable social action by those actors. (Harré, 1979, p. 127)

Obviously, the gathering of accounts involves an interview situation. However, as far as I know, no research has been conducted into the possibly biasing effects of the psychological processes operating in the accounting interview, while a multitude of studies are available to demonstrate equivalent effects for conventional research interviews, that is, semi-structured interviews or survey interviews, which are, of course, fully structured (see, for example, Cannell and Kahn, 1968). In particular, we do not know which interviewing techniques should be used to accomplish accounts with the least bias. Brown and Sime (1981) have provided us with a description of their interviewing techniques and the interviewer training received; this description is, however, sketchy and needs future elaboration. There is some attempt to do so in the present volume (see chapter by Brown and Canter), but there is, still a lack of detailed procedures. Moreover, abstracting now the issue from its interviewing aspect, the accomplishment of accounts is clearly the result of cognitive, interpretational work; informants have to select from their past experience those aspects that seem significant and, hence, worth reporting, within the frame of reference provided by the investigator. This means that informants should stick to the frame of reference provided in their making sense of some piece of experience. Marsh (1979) has noted in this context that this does not necessarily happen; accounts do not necessarily refer to events within the proposed investigator's frame of reference of the remembering process. He observed a considerable overreporting of incidents of physical violence by football fans as the result of the fact that the youngsters had a goal, in their reporting, different from that expected by the investigator. What they really wanted, in the accounting situation, was to display the phenomenon of violence rhetorically, for the purpose of symbolic exhibition, in its own right, rather than to reflect in their speech their actual experience of violent incidents. Marsh argues, in contrast to some early proponents of an accounts methodology (see Harré and Secord, 1972), that it would be mistaken to take accounts literally. What one needs, instead, is knowledge of the accounting practices employed by informants before one can comprehend with reasonable confidence what it is that is meant in accounts.

Moreover, accounts may be given from different particular perspectives of experience. They can, thus, contain descriptions and causal attributions referring to "why things happened" from a multiplicity of perspectives. If compared, it can happen that the summation of the accounts gathered provides a multimeaning and multicausal representation of what went on. The integration of the accounts may, therefore, be difficult, particularly if one should wish to derive causal explanations of events from them. Using an accounts strategy, it is, however, refreshing to realize that we cannot deceive ourselves methodologically: we will have to face, when they occur, the real ambiguities and multimeanings in accounts.

Accounts, being essentially "stories" about events and experiences, as a methodology are much more demanding and time- and cost-consuming than any other interviewing approach (perhaps with the exception of Lisanne Bainbridge's approach to data collection and analysis; see her chapter 9). Once gathered, accounts have, however, not only the advantage of providing massive qualitative knowing about a form of social life than would be unobtainable by other, structured interview methods, but also the advantage that the material, once transcribed from tapes, can be analyzed qualitatively as well as quantitatively. Canter's (1980) *Fires and Human Behaviour* provides excellent examples of the uses of accounts for both these ends. Thus, the employment of an accounts methodology can help elegantly to circumvent the ongoing qualitative versus quantitative methods debate. Both forms of representing social life can be accommodated adequately in the methodology, given also, that it constitutes—and this is perhaps most important—an effective substitute for more direct methodological means to attain intimate familiarity.

INTERVIEWING TECHNIQUE

Intensive interviewing is essentially a discovery procedure, substituting for the more direct scrutiny of a form of social life. "Its object is *to find out* what kinds of things are happening, rather than to determine the frequency of predetermined kinds of things that the researcher already believes can happen" (Lofland, 1971, p. 76; my italics), as is usually the case in survey research.

Whatever kind of interview is used in a research programme, the ultimate purpose of the data collection must be to obtain valid information from those questioned. That is, ideally, informants should answer questions truthfully, while also meeting with precision the particular requirements for information posed by the various questions used ("open" general, "open" specific probes, for example). The reporting of information is, however, necessarily and inevitably embedded in a social situation, the interview, with its own peculiar social psychological organization. Thus, we can never assume that the accounts given are simply answers to questions; they are the joint product of the questions as perceived by informants and the social situational circumstances within which the questions were put to them.

The most crucial component of the social situational circumstances affecting the accounting process is the interviewer, or, more precisely, interviewing technique. Interviewing technique must meet, ideally, two requirements: it must not bias the accounting process, and it must ensure a social effective interaction that helps the informant to report adequately, that is, within the frame of reference within which the intensive interviewing is conducted. Both these requirements I will now consider.

To avoid bias, the interviewing must be done nondirectively. That is, the interviewer, whatever questioning technique he/she may be using, must leave it entirely to the informant to provide answers to questions. For example, questions must never be asked in a leading or directive manner as this exerts pressure on informants to answer in particularly ways. For example, "you don't . . . you haven't experienced any problems in getting information from psychiatric social workers?" implies as the "right" answer "no," as against the nondirective "have you experienced any problems in getting information from psychiatric social workers whom you met here, in this hospital?" The latter question leaves it entirely to the informant to answer, and, in addition, provides a circumscribed frame of reference for the account. In more general terms, the interviewer must maintain a neutral stance; whatever the topic of the conversation, he/she must not express his/her personal views about the issues under consideration, as this amounts to an explicit interviewer effect on the informant which might endanger, as in the case of leading or directive questioning, the validity of the information reported. Brown and Sime (1981, p. 160) have aptly summarized the interviewer's place or role in intensive interviewing:

> An account is the personal record of an event by the individual experiencing it, told from his point of view. The account interview is the context in which the story is

> related. Essentially, it provides a social situation for the recounting of the experience with the interviewer's role being that of *facilitator.* (My italics)

That is, an account should be very near to unconstrained, free reporting, "but in practice some degree of guidance is usually required" (p. 164). Which means of guidance should be used? One such means is the use of an interview guide; another is the employment of questioning techniques in an ad hoc manner with the aim, for example, to elicit further, specific information or to keep the accounting within the frames of reference posed by the general questions or to clarify possible inconsistencies in the material provided by informants.

Most kinds of intensive interviewing will require the use of an interview guide, as accounts on more than just one topic need to be obtained. An interview guide differs from a structured questionnaire, as only one of the rules related to the use of structured questionnaires (see my chapter on Survey Interviewing in Part 1) is preserved, namely, the interviewer must try to obtain accounts on all the topics listed in the guide. How he/she does this is unimportant, as long as he/she acts nondirectively and takes care that the accounts are adequate (free of internal inconsistencies, for example) and as complete as possible. Interview guides are typically developed by means of pilot research (see, for example, Lofland, 1971; Brown and Sime, 1981;). Lofland (1971, p. 76) has described the beginning of such pilot research; it

> begins with the prospective investigator taking some place, class of persons, or abstract topic as problematic to him. One of these kinds of things, or some things about them, puzzle him. He would like to know more. If he takes such puzzlement seriously—as a topic of investigation—he may first sit down in a quiet place and use what is called his "common sense."

Once the research problem is cognitively located, the investigater may study the scientific or other writings on the problem, this leading to a more thorough sorting and ordering of the research questions. At this juncture, a first draft of the interview guide may be put together and must then be pretested. This will reveal whether the interview guide is sufficiently comprehensive to cover the research problem as seen by the investigator and his informants. Such pilot research provides, in addition, first-hand insight into what might be called, the "cultural endowment" of the informants. Such insight is essential for the preparation of effective questioning techniques; it becomes absolutely essential in cross-cultural research, when the process of questioning and answering is problematic for the investigator as well as his informants (see, for example, Circourel, 1974).

Once the pilot research is completed, the interview guide can be finalized; also, the investigater will know, minimally by and large, his/her role as "facilitator"; namely, which questioning techniques to employ. Sime in

Brown and Sime (1981, pp. 181–182) gives this description of the final stage of intensive interviewing of people who had experienced a fire:

> Individuals were instructed to recount exactly what happened from the moment they realized anything was wrong until the fire was over. Care was taken during the interview not to give the participant the idea that researchers had any clear prior knowledge of the event from other sources. The early parts of the accounts were characteristically monologues. Areas for elaboration and to be covered were determined beforehand. It was found in many cases that the account agenda themes reproduced below were actually covered in the course of the account without prompting from the interviewer.
>
> Account Agenda Themes
>
> Recognition of fire
> Sequence of actions
> Location of occupant at each stage
> Perception of situation
> Related past experience
> Role of person

While Sime encountered relatively few problems in obtaining from his informants adequate material related to the account agenda themes, or what I have called "interview guide," in other research projects using intensive interviewing, for example, because of cognitive problems experienced by informants, such as memory or "social taboo" problems, the design of questioning techniques must be more detailed. Lyn Lofland (Lofland, 1971, p. 82), for example, found it necessary, because of problems of recall likely to be experienced by her informants, to employ in her Urban Careers Interview Guide a sophisticated approach to interviewing which contained questions and probes, such as these:

> Can you tell me exactly how you went about finding a place to live, how you got your first place, and so forth?
>
> Probe for:
>
> Conception of city areas (or Bay Areas).
> Areas would *not* consider.
> Contacts with real estate people, landlords, etc.
> Financial constraints.
> Any necessity for finding a place quickly.
> Internal or external conflicts and compromises.
> Network involvement (e.g., friend found place, relatives did, etc.).

Thus, clearly, the interviewer's role in intensive interviewing can require a highly skilled performance which, in cases (see Lofland, 1971, 1976), extends well beyond the use of particular interviewing techniques to the social management of total interviewing situations. Not only for this, not necessarily typical, reason is it imperative that the interview is tape-recorded (after having obtained the informant's consent, of course); but also, there is no strict order of questioning. The interviewer is continuously busy monitoring whether his/her actions are adequate, in the context of the interview guide and the interview situation, and whether the informant's information is adequate, that is, provides acceptable and complete answers to the questions. The interviewer must also immediately absorb the accounts and search for inconsistencies; moreover, he/she must think forward, what questions to ask next; in more general terms, what to *do* next. Tape recording the coversation is necessary for another reason:

> Note taking was both distracting to researcher and informant. It may well have inadvertantly cued respondents into discussing at length issues that the researcher happened to note down and skirt those for which no note was taken. Taping provides a permanent verbatim recording of the account that enabled the researcher to give his total attention to the verbal and nonverbal behaviour of the informant. (Brown and Sime, 1981, p. 175)

The danger of tape-recording is, of course, that the interviewer may cease to listen carefully to the informant's talk. This may, minimally, result in brief accounts only, as the acceptability and completeness of the answers is not monitored. Thus, some note taking, besides the taping, I think, is essential, if only "to keep account of what has already been talked about and what remains to be talked about. Having the advantage of the tape recording, this becomes note taking in its best sense" (Lofland, 1971, p. 89).

CONSIDERATIONS BEFORE ACCOUNT ANALYSIS

I have already noted that the material collected by means of intensive interviewing is the joint product of the questions as perceived by informants and the social situational circumstances within which the questions were put to them. Thus, it is unwarranted to proceed uncritically from the collection of accounts to their analysis, as they cannot be taken literally; they are not simply linguistic "pictures" of past experience. Rather, to remain in the analogy, they are pictures that are "blurred" by the "gatekeeping" and distorting influences of informants' cognitions of their experience, which are further modified by the effects of interviewer–respondent interaction within the totality of the interview situation. The investigator, before proceeding to the account analysis stage, must attempt to detect any such influences, to become able to answer questions related to the reliability and validity of the material gathered, that is, its scientific utility for the purposes of description and explanation.

One of the strategies that can be applied to the detection of "gate-keeping" and distorting influences on accounts is to use investigative procedures that have been helpful in other contexts of interviewing, in particular, survey interviewing (see Cannell and Kahn, 1968; Phillips, 1971, 1973). Essentially, there are three options: (1) to compare accounts against "verification data"; (2) to scrutinize accounts for overt, observable undesirable influences in the interview situation; and (3) to employ a cognitive approach for the assessment of informants' motivational states during the interviews—their perceptions of the questions, for example.

All these options have their peculiar limits; this amounts to the admission that the detection of undesirable influences in toto is impossible. For this reason, it is questionable whether the concepts of reliability and validity as used conventionally in the methodology of the social sciences (see Selltiz et al., 1976, Chapter 6) can be usefully applied in the context of intensive interviewing or, for that matter, of interviewing in general (see Andersen et al., 1979). Brown and Sime (1981, p. 161); therefore,

> suggest to adopt the alternative concepts of authenticity and attestability. Authenticity relates to the corroborative support given an account either by artefacts, or by its internal consistency or cross-reference to other sources of information. . . . Attestability is taken as the degree to which the researcher has made explicit his methods and distinguishes his interpretation of events from those of his informants such that that the academic community can scrutinize and evaluate the legitimacy of the findings.

However, despite Brown and Sime's valuable suggestions, I use the more traditional concepts of reliability and validity, if only for the reason that the three options given above are procedures which enable, primarily, the search for sources of bias and invalidity in interview material.

Turning now to the first option, useful for checking the external validity of accounts: this entails their comparison with "verification data," that is, a set of items of information which should also be expressed in the accounts. Cannell, et al. (1961), for example, using verification data, found in their study of health reports that memory decay, leading to the inaccessibility of information to respondents, was an important biasing cognitive factor. The underreports of hospitalizations ranged from about 7% underreporting for the first 20 weeks to about 30% for the hospitalizations that occurred 41–53 weeks prior to the interview.

Given the availability of verification data, and given that it is found that items of factual information are underreported, or, as in the case of Marsh (1979), overreported, one can hypothesize that other cognitive factors, besides memory decay, were involved in the reporting. These can relate to particular motivational states, the goal to present oneself in a certain way, for example. Consequently, informants may not have revealed what they regarded, subjectively, to be unpleasant or threatening events, or may have exaggerated the frequency of their occurrence if they were seen as particularly salient or relevant to the conceptions of the informants. The use of verification data may point to another cognitive factor that leads, as does memory decay, to the inaccessibility of information, namely, that there may have been actual limitations in the informants' knowledge of the information sought.

Verification data, useful as they are in attempting to determine the accuracy of the factual information reported, are, however, not usually available. Indeed, their unavailability, sometimes their principal unavailability, as in studies concerned with behaviour in fires (see Canter, 1980), is often the reason why intensive interviewing is selected as a substitute for the more direct scrutiny of forms of social life. Sometimes, it is possible to generate verification data, by means of observation, for example (see Marsh, 1979). It is, however, unlikely, whatever kind of verification data is used, that the data will be free of error (see Mathews et al., 1974). Thus, the investigator must assume, in his/her comparison, that the verification data are more accurate than the items of factual information obtained from informants, without being in a position to demonstrate, in the majority of instances, the propriety of this assumption. (Such a demonstration would involve a validation of the verification data, which is usually practically impossible, as no other sources of information, besides the verification data and the accounts, can be accessed.)

The ultimate limit for the use of verification data in attempting to determine the external validity of accounts is, of course, that such data can only relate to "facts," nonarbitrary events, happenings or circumstances. Much of the account material will, however, contain expressions of attitudes, judgments, sentiments, value statements, and cognitive experiences, among other things. For these kinds of information verification data cannot possibly exist; the only way of assessing the authenticity of such expressions is to scrutinize the interviewer–informant interaction, as recorded on the tapes, for possible biasing effects. Where the extent of interviewer–informant interaction was low and the reporting was related to the description and explanation of the same event, as in Sime's fire research (Brown and Sime, 1981), one possibility for assessing the validity of the accounts is to compare them and see whether a high degree of concordance between different accounts can be found. That is, the descriptions and explanations of events and experiences may be regarded as highly valid, when they are, by and large, the same across accounts.

Turning now to the second option, useful, to some extent, for checking the validity more generally: this involves the scrutiny of the material for overt, observable undesirable influences in the interview situation. For example, in the extreme, an account may have to be discarded because of strong bystander interference, or because of "negativistic" informant motivation, that is, the goal of the informant to destroy the encounter as an adequate interviewing relationships.

It is more typical that accounts are undesirably affected by factors that can operate in interviewer–informant interaction. I have pointed out that the interviewer, in intensive interviewing, should act as facilitator only; he/she should always act nondirectively. This extends to anything the interviewer does in the management of the encounter; "it is most productive of information for the interviewer to assume a non-argumentative, supportive, and sympathetically understanding attitude." (Lofland, 1971, p. 89) There is considerable agreement on this subject between interview methodologists, because it was found that other styles of interviewer action can bias the answering process (see, for example, Gorden, 1975).

Interviewers can deviate from the facilitator role in many ways, of which only some are observable in their biasing effects when using tape-recordings. Unobservable are, for example, any biasing effects of background characteristics of interviewers, such as their age, education, socioeconomic status, race, religion, or sex (see Hyman et al., 1954, pp. 153–170). Similarly unobservable are any biasing effects of nonverbal social perceptional processes, when, for example, the interviewer tacitly communicates the expectation of a "right" answer to the informant.

As accounts are the joint product of the questions as perceived by an informant and, minimally, his interaction with the interviewer, the questions and the informant must also be considered as sources of bias. Again, the majority of biasing effects originating from questions and informants will be unobservable.

Questions can involve cognitive problems for respondents, particularly in terms of question wording and frame of reference of questions. It is known that the use of leading words, of technical or uncommon terms, or of ambiguous or vague expressions may lead to bias (see Moser and Kalton, 1971, p. 391). Thus, in the pilot research phase, the investigator has to try to develop questioning approaches that enable the easy comprehension of given kinds of content by all informants and ensure the maximally accurate communication about issues.

Despite the investigator's effort to prepare adequate questioning approaches, it can happen that the content of questions adversely affects the informant's motivation to answer truthfully, that is, to provide an accurate and complete account of an issue. This applies in particular to questions involving "prestige, social gain, personal circumstances" (Moser and Kalton, 1971, p. 390), and inviting informants "to maintain self-esteem, to be perceived by the interviewer as a person who does not violate important social norms in thought or act, and to present an image of consistency and worthiness" (Cannell and Kahn, 1968, p. 545). The motivational effects of question content have been studied extensively under the heading of "social desirability" (see Phillips, 1971, 1973), which refers to the tendency of informants to deny socially undesirable traits involved with questions and to admit socially desirable ones.

There are, of course, kinds of informant motivation that can have biasing effects but are independent of question content. For example, there is "acquiescence," which refers to the tendency to agree, or disagree, with questions independent of their content. The acquiescent answering style is also referred to as "yeasaying," or, in the case of disagreement, "naysaying" (see Couch and Keniston, 1960). The acquiescent informant might be disinterested in an adequate participation; he might even be "negativistically" motivated. There is also "need for social approval," which has been defined as "the need of subjects to respond in culturally sanctioned ways" (Crowne and Marlowe, 1964, p. 354). That is, informants with a high need for social approval are said to be more likely than others to respond affirmatively to perceived social influences.

These are just two kinds of informant information independent of question content. In principle, the informant is free to develop any motivational state during the interview. The effects of undesirable kinds of informant motivation on the quality of the results of intensive interviewing can be considerable, as the interviewer cannot control, but only attempt to influence, the informant's motivational state during the interview, by being nonargumentative, supportive, sympathetically understanding, or facilitating. However, it must be borne in mind that informants can, at least in principle, use *any* means of action to damage, or to destroy, the interview as a viable data collection situation. As Sudman and Bradburn (1974, p. 16) have pointed out for the case of the survey interview:

> The primary demand of the respondent's role is that he answers the interviewer's questions. Answering certain questions will require considerable effort on his part. If the respondent is not sufficiently motivated to perform his role, the *whole* enterprise falls apart. (My italics)

It is one of the characteristics of intensive interviewing that the interviewer should follow rules in his/her relationship with the informant. For example, he/she must try to obtain accounts on all the topics listed in the interview guide; his/her questionning must always be nondirective; that is, must never suggest a "right" answer or direction of answering; he/she must take care that the accounts obtained are adequate (as complete as possible, linguistically comprehensible, free of internal inconsistencies, for example); he/she must enact a facilitator role by being nonjudgmental and supportive, among other things. Also, although this is a "weak" rule, once the informant has consented to the interview, he/she should be motivated to participate fully in the encounter.

Given that intensive interviewing can be defined by means of such rules, one can ask whether the interviews actually occurred within the rules. One of the ways of tackling this issue is to scrutinize the material for any instances of "rule-breaching" (leading, directive questioning by the interviewer, deviations by the informant from his ideal role, for example). In more practical terms this would require a content analysis of the interviewing interaction in search of such actions which, in combination with other actions, may make us suspicious of the validity of the account material gathered under the circumstances of high interviewer interference or "low" informant motivation, for example.

As far as I know, examples of such direct scrutiny of interviewer–informant interaction do not exist. More typical seems to be the practice of transcribing the accounts from the tapes without any checks on possibly biasing influences of the interview situation (see, for example, Lofland, 1971, p. 91). Or the coding of the transcripts commences after comparison with available verification data in conjunction with more general checks on the validity of the material (see, for example, Brown and Sime, 1981, pp. 166–168). There exist, however, analysis techniques, initially developed in the context of survey interviewing (see Marquis and Cannell, 1969; Cannell et al., 1975; chapters by Brenner and by Dijkstra et al. in this volume), which can initially serve as models of "how to do it," although they will clearly require extensive modification before they can be usefully employed in the scrutiny of accounts material.

In addition, such a direct analysis of interviewer–informant interaction can, at least to some extent, be used to assess possibly biasing effects of question content, as it is likely that indicators for such effects will be found in the action stream. Questions that were frequently followed by some evasive informant action or the refusal to answer, which results in vague and ambiguous material, despite extensive probing, or which involve frequent requests for clarification of "what is meant by the question" provide such indicators. Unfortunately, cumbersome as the direct scrutiny of accounts will be in any case, the method captures only those biasing effects that are overtly expressed, in the action stream. Thus, surely, as Brown and Sime (1981, pp. 166–168) argue, a multimethod approach to validation must be employed, given the general situation that all validation methods are defective. Nevertheless, I would welcome a direct scrutiny of interviewer–informant interaction, as it is clearly right here where the accounts are accomplished.

Finally, I consider methods useful for the assessment of participants' cognitive states as possible sources of bias and invalidity (motivation, interpersonal perception, perception of the questions) in intensive interviewing. While an analysis of interviewer–informant interaction is undertaken, one can get people, using various rating scales, to judge various dimensions of cognitive states. The emerging data, though possibly highly reliable, may nevertheless be poor when it comes to validity. There are two other methods which partly circumvent the dilemma.

One is to question the informant, intermittantly or upon ending the interview, about certain cognitions: how the informant experiences or has experienced, the interviewing relationship, how the interviewer and the questions, indeed the whole research problem, were perceived. In this way the informant is, as it were, asked to "meta-communicate," to provide material explanatory of other things said. Part of this procedure was used by West (1979, p. 728), with some surprising and revealing results, in his investigation into "the social construction and consequences of the label epilepsy." He ended his semistructured street interviews with the question, "Would it surprise you to know that I suffer from epilepsy myself?"

While the validity of such meta-communication is questionable because it occurs in one and the same interview situation where informants' cognitive states may have already solidified, it nevertheless can provide the investigator with indicators of them, as in the case of West. Limited as the method is, there is no other way in field research to tap informants' cognitions directly. When accounts are obtained in a "laboratory" context, then, of course, we can replay the tape to informants, and using, for example, a self-confrontation interviewing technique (see von Cranach et al., 1980, pp. 218–224), try to elicit particular cognitive states in the context of particular accounting material. Providing the informant is willing to participate in this somewhat cumbersome procedure, this can greatly increase our understanding of the question–answer process, as the informant views it.

As regards the interviewer, he/she can reconstruct his/her cognitive states during his/her transcription of the account. "Listening to the tape piece by piece forces one to consider, piece by piece, whether he has accomplished anything or not" (Lofland, 1971, p. 91). It is this cognitive self-analysis of one's own actions and the actions of informants in the interview which contributes, in conjunction with the cognitions of informants, to a deeper understanding of what it is that was attempted and meant in the account material.

> One other point: in the course of writing up the interview, new questions and puzzlements are likely to occur. These also should be recorded and later considered for incorporation into future interviews as questions or probes. If there are a great many new questions that require interviews, one can then give thought to reinterviewing the same persons." (Lofland, 1971, p. 91)

If the situation Lofland describes should arise, this could be extended to a full test–retest approach. That is, the interview, as regards many questions, is conducted twice, and by comparing the material, the internal consistency (or stability) of the accounts can be checked.

CONCLUSION

Clearly, many of the ideas for the minimal improvement of the adequate understanding by the investigator and the validity of intensive interviewing material that I have proposed are difficult, if not impossible, to realize in the practice of research. It is, therefore, always necessary to consider the feasibility of supplementing an accounts methodology by other methodological means—observation, inspection of the material by experts, for example, before the analysis of the accounts commences.

Moreover, the methods for attempting to make explicit how the accounts have been gathered are all defective in themselves and cumbersome to operate, given that intensive interviewing and the transcription of the material is usually in itself very laborious. Nevertheless, already the theoretical, programmatic consideration of such methods supports the hypothesis that intensive interviewing, as *any* method (in particular the survey interview and the laboratory experiment), in all likelihood will fall short of the ideal of accurate data collection; and it will usually be impossible to know just how far.

REFERENCES

Andersen, R., Kasper, J., Frankel, M. R. (1979). Total survey error. San Francisco: Jossey-Bass.

Argyris, C. (1980). Inner Contradictions of Rigorous Research. London: Academic Press.

Brenner, M. (1981). *The need for qualitative knowing in evaluation research.* Paper presented at the Perspectives on the Evaluation of Action Research in Community Education seminar, Manchester Polytechnic, November 26–27.

Brown, J., and Sime, J. (1981). A methodology for accounts. In M. Brenner (Ed.), *Social method and social life,* pp. 159–188. London: Academic Press.

Cannell, Ch.F., Fisher, G., and Bakker, T. (1961). *Reporting of hospitalization in the health interview survey.* Washington, DC: U.S. Department of Health, Education, and Welfare.

Cannell, Ch.F., and Kahn, R. F. (1968). Interviewing. In G. Lindzey and E. Aronson, (Eds.), *The Handbook of Social Psychology* (Vol. 2), pp. 526–595. Reading, MA: Addison-Wesley.

Cannell, Ch.F., Lawson, S. A., and Hausser, D. L. (1975). *A technique for evaluating interviewer performance.* Ann Arbor, MI: Institute for Social Research.

Canter, D. (Ed.) (1980). *Fires and human behaviour.* Chichester: Wiley.

Cicourel, A. V. (1974). *Theory and method in a study of Argentine fertility.* New York: Wiley.

Couch, A., and Keniston, K. (1960). Yeasayers and naysayers: Agreeing response set as a personality variable. *Journal of Abnormal Social Psychology 60,* 151–174.

Crowne, D., and Marlowe, D. (1964). *The approval motive.* New York: Wiley.

Deutscher, I. (1966). Words and deeds: Social science and social policy. *Social Problems 13,* 233–254.
Filstead, W. J. (Ed.) (1970). *Qualitative methodology.* Chicago, IL: Markham.
Gorden, R. L. (1975). *Interviewing: Strategy, techniques, and tactics.* Homewood, IL: Dorsey Press.
Harré, R. (1979). *Social being.* Oxford: Blackwell.
Harré, R., and Secord, P. F. (1972). *The explanation of social behaviour.* Oxford: Blackwell.
Hyman, H. H., et al. (1954). *Interviewing in social research.* Chicago, IL: University of Chicago Press.
Kriz, J. (1981). *Methodenkritik empirischer Sozialforschung.* Stuttgart: Teubner Verlag.
Labovitz, S., and Hagedorn, R. (1971). *Introduction to social research.* New York: McGraw-Hill.
Lofland, J. (1971). *Analyzing social settings.* Belmont, CA: Wadsworth.
Lofland, J. (1976). *Doing social life.* New York: Wiley.
Marquis, K. H., and Cannell, Ch.F. (1969). *A study of interviewer–respondent interaction in the urban employment survey.* Institute for Social Research, Ann Arbor, MI.
Marsh, P. (1979). *Problems encountered in what people say and what they do.* Paper presented at the Analysis of Open-Ended Data symposium, University of Surrey, December 12.
Mathews, V. L., Feather, J., and Crawford, J. (1974). *A response/record discrepancy study.* University of Saskatchewan, Department of Social and Preventive Medicine.
Moser, C. A., and Kalton, G. (1971). *Survey methods in social investigation.* London: Heinemann.
Phillips, D. L. (1971). *Knowledge from what?* Chicago, IL: Rand McNally.
Phillips, D. L. (1973). *Abandoning method.* London: Jossey-Bass.
Selltiz, C., Wrightsman, L. S., and Cook, S. W. (1976). *Research methods in social relations.* New York: Holt, Rinehart and Winston.
Sudman, S., and Bradburn, N. M. (1974). *Response effects in surveys.* Chicago, IL: Aldine.
von Cranach, M. (1980). "Zielgerichtetes Handeln." Bern: Huber.
West, P. (1979). An investigation into the social construction and consequences of the label epilepsy. *Sociology Review 27,* 719–741.

8

Life Story Interviews and Their Interpretation

STEPHEN K. TAGG

INTRODUCTION

The goal of this chapter is both to describe a qualitative interview method, wherein informants are encouraged to recall aspects of their life story (Gottschalk et al., 1945; Bertaux, 1981), and also to review procedures for the interpretation of a variety of forms of such long-term retrospective accounts. The concept of life story is used to designate the retrospective information itself without the corroborative evidence often implied by the term *life history*. Life story interviews have several qualities that might lead to more frequent use: first, the involvement of the personal conceptions of the past and all its stages, and second, the readily interpretable nature of the open interview product. The method, however, can present problems, for example, when a reliable memory for unimportant events is required or when a series of stories are to be combined or contrasted.

Life story interviews are likely tools for the generalized developmental social science perspective of the life span (Featherman, 1982). The use of life story interviews shows that researchers feel respondents can make sense of their past and indicates that administrative records are not always meaningful. On the less positive side, use of life story interviews suggest increased impatience for semicausal interpretations of contemporary problems, rather than the delays associated with longitudinal studies. Increased use of life story interviews, with attempts to systematize interpretation, can be found in medicine (particularly in psychiatry) and in history (particularly in social and family history). Finally, there are many applications in sociology, psychology, and life course studies, for example, in personality, occupational, and educational phenomena.

Many of the more recent studies suggest that effective use of life stories

ISBN 0-12-131580-0

is more likely when a researcher can combine control over the interpretability of life story research with respect for the difficulty of the interviewer and respondents' tasks. Controls can be of two kinds: conceptual constraints and research procedures. This chapter reviews research procedures in coding, interpretation, and comparison of life stories. Respondent selection and account elicitation are also discussed in as far as they influence the interpretation. Also, the influence of conceptual constraints, such as theoretical and pragmatic orientation, are considered.

In the sense that life stories are accounts, one could do worse than to apply procedures for accounts, such as those described in Brown and Sime (1981). However, life stories have some attributes that suggest specific research procedures may be required: for example, although accounts typically cover sequences of events, the complexity of life stories is greater because they contain intertwined sets of sequences of events. The unconstrained life story also covers many themes and perspectives. If the interviewer's interests are unrestricted and the informant's time and enthusiasm are unlimited, it is possible to produce massive protocols from single respondents. Life stories are also more complex in that they are rarely recalled in simple order of occurrence. All these attributes add complexity to the interpretation of life stories; without some conceptual control to restrict the range of structures for life story collection and collation, the researcher will be faced with reams of indecipherable protocols. Agar (1980) further suggests that the partial overlap of distinct interpretative approaches to life story narrative produces "the worst sort of quagmire." Although this chapter suggests a variety of interpretative strategies, the researcher is advised to select an unequivocal approach to interpreting the interview product.

Even within conceptual and procedural limits such as those of studies on occupational mobility (Goldthorpe, 1980), researchers are still left with difficult problems in using life story material. Should it be coded and treated as further survey type variables, should it be used purely for illustration, or should it be given a more central role? This chapter brings together advice and tools to suggest a way in which a wider range of researchers might make profitable use of life story interviews. It contains three sections: the first on the range of methods for the life story interview and the second on tools for interpreting such interviews. The conclusions suggest lines for development of techniques that are feasible to both administer and analyser but that retain some direct interpretability.

THE LIFE STORY INTERVIEW

This section concentrates on the most critical part of life story research: the interview. The forms of life story interview are described through a

{One / A sample} informant in an interview situation with a {researcher / interviewer} is shaped

by {reinforcement / questioning / probing / scheduling}, which represents the {hunches / research strategy} of the research, and

is motivated to retrospect on {all / particular aspects} of the interviewee's past life, through

his or her present-day construct system, building up from {events / actors / places}, each of which has a

place as a {start / direction / turning point / end} in a story. Stories are elaborated through similarity

of {story structure / actors / places / events / points in time} This is {repeated / done only once} until research criteria are met. To aid

interpretation, {transcripts / tape-recordings / age charts / checklists} are recorded and used as {a source of ideas / the majority of text / illustrative text / a source of variables}

for the final publication.

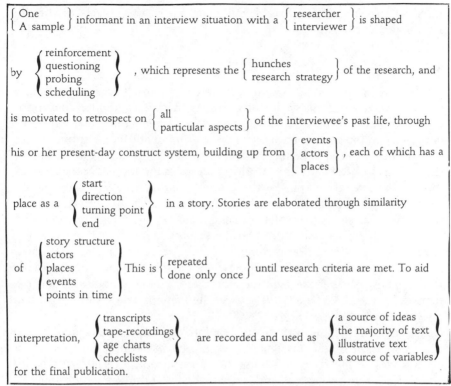

Figure 1 Facet analysis of the life story interview.

facet analysis in Figure 1. The features of this analysis are noted here and illustrated in the following sections.

Interviews can take various strategies, such as probing for deeper or wider explorations. The interviewer can sometimes be the researcher, implying differences in the understanding and involvement with research goals. The informant reconstructs memories through his or her present construct system. Where aspects of this construction can be elicited in interviewing or analysis, it can improve the reliability of the method, but this retrospective bias cannot be removed completely. The life story discourse can be seen to involve three key remembered entities at the lowest level: events, actions, and places. The respondent may reconstruct different types of involvement with such entities, for example, involving action and affect. Such entities are usually recalled as structurally related entities or stories; sometimes the same entity is in more than one story. Thus both story and entities can form the basis for further elaboration of the discourse. This elaboration can be aided by similarities of story, actors, places, involvement, or by adjacency in time. The final facets are those of how such a process is recorded and what use is made of it. It is this facet, the status of the product, with which illustrations of the aspects of the life story interview begins.

Status of Product

Life story information can be incorporated in many ways into the stages of research. For example, political scientists (Becker, 1970) interview principal actors in retrospections of their own and other actor's roles in important events. However, such interviews are frequently not attributed, but instead they are used to help elaborate the researcher's ideas. Publication of the interviews rests on thir exploration through more accessible corroborative material. In spite of the unpublished nature of the interviews, they demand thorough preparation by the researcher. An informant does not want to have to explain all the background details. An interviewer who knows the topic can ask more pertinent questions, although anthropologists (Agar, 1980) note that it may be difficult to communicate that background knowledge in research reports. A similar use of life story methods is also made by clinicians who do not take systematic notes of their patients' life stories. Generally, life story interviewing takes a minor part in case studies (Bromley, 1977).

The status of the life story in such exploratory studies is as a first step to the elaboration of the researcher's well-prepared conceptions. In most other styles of life story research, the retrospections are less closely involved with sensitive events and more involved with the everyday events. The product of such interviews is more disclosable. Such interviews can lead to whole books, to quoted small excerpts, or to interpretation through coding systems. Bertaux (1980) asks, "How much?" Should the aim be a book-length autobiography or something shorter? He also mentions the completeness of accounts and a distinction similar to Farraday and Plummer's (1979) contrast between sociological and literary product.

The first type of product is a publication like Thomas and Zaniecki's (1958) account of the Polish peasant, where recollections take a major part. Other examples are the studies of Chalasinki (1981) and Bertaux and Bertaux-Wiame (1981), where the merely reformatted text is used as the major empirical component of research; these are very similar to biography. To Bertaux, the literary text emphasizes the informant's own construct system, whereas the sociological product represents the researchers' views.

The other two types of products are associated with the use of life story information in a more traditional, quantitative way. First, there are studies such as those by Goldthorpe (1980) and Synge (1981) who use illustrations from life story texts to ellaborate more traditional survey studies. Second, there is the retrospective information that involves similar processes for the respondent during interviews. Within such an orientation there are strategies varying from open-ended records (such as life story grids, as in Balan et al. [1973]), through checklists (such as that used in some epidemiological studies, as in Casey et al., [1967]), to closed retrospective survey questions. The first of these strategies is considered in this chapter. Quantitative strategies introduce as many problems as are solved by avoiding the difficulties of textual interpretations (Brenner, 1979). The different strategies vary in the degree of interference in the product; the retrospective question and variable-producing strategies are likely to involve more constraints. However, although a retrospective question may appear simpler, it requires the informant to use a reconstructive process similar to that involved in less constrained account-gathering interviews.

The facet of product status (i.e., source of ideas to source of variables) is similar to the differentiation made by Farraday and Plummer (1979) between the subject's pure account and the sociologist's pure account. However, they betray their own ideological position when they say "sociologists using life history methods become more like a journalist, a novelist or a biographer" (p. 774). Bertaux (1981) argues that the latter three roles are more effective agents for change than sociologists have ever been!

The product facets were taken first to provide a functional introduction; further parts of this section will follow more nearly the order of Figure 1. What is not questioned at this point is the reliability of retrospection as a denotation of things past. Those writings that suggest caution are considered in the third section, which deals with interpretation. Meanwhile, recollections are viewed as if memory was perfect and not subject to selective omissions and exaggerations. The problems of reliability will be revealed as the structure of the life story interview is examined.

Selection of Respondent

The first facet in Figure 1 is that of the selection of respondent, which distinguishes between interviewing single informants and a sample. Bertaux (1981) argues that, because of the nature of the method, one should consider concepts of saturation as more relevant than those of sampling. Taking Ferrarotti's (1981) view that the life story is best used to illustrate the story of groups rather than that of individuals, Bertaux argues that interviews with succeeding respondents quickly get to the point where they only add information about the individual and do not provide fresh information on groups. The potentially overwhelming extent of textual life story material suggests that interviewing a survey sample will produce insurmountable problems in interpretation. Therefore, most life story studies restrict their volume either by limiting the number of informants, or by limiting the extent of their life stories by research procedures, or by using both restrictions. What is noticeable in many reports is the statement that interviews, though completed, have yet to be analysed!

Pelto (1970) sees representativeness as the key problem in the anthropological use of life stories and suggests their use should be mainly as explanatory and illustrative materials in connection with other kinds of data. He proposes a respondent selection strategy similar to Bertaux's (1980) concept of diversity; this suggests interviewing a range of differing respondents. This strategy has some features in common with stratified sampling; however, until life story interpretation produces statistics whose generalization to a population can be studied, it is only in such a strategy that any of the concepts of sampling can be applied. It is possible that Bertaux's tactic of interviewing to saturation may be made more systematic through taking items from a population until the required precision of estimate is obtained. However, this would require the researcher to select a parameter to indicate the crucial information in life story.

Interviewer Task

The next four facets of Figure 1 describe several ways in which life stories can differ because of the behaviour of the interviewer. The interview for textual life story elicitation is typically semistructured. A truly open-ended life story interview, without agenda, risks both immense length and difficult interpretation. The respondent will need motivating. It is important that the interviewer knows what is to be encouraged and uses those means (Cannell et al., 1981) that can control what is produced. If an informative discourse is to be produced, it is also important that the respondent gets to share in the interview goals.

The interviewer's elaboration strategy poses some important questions: To what extent should the interviewer explore the details of particular remembered events? Should the interviewer differentiate the typical from the exceptional, and how should the interviewer encourage elaboration? To answer these problems requires knowledge of the goal of the study, and requires either a well-trained interviewer or a researcher with interviewing skills. The session is subject both to the use of relatively neutral probes and also the influence of reinforcement. Cannell et al., (1981) show how interviewers can encourage more recall. Brenner's (1981) sequence analysis of closed-ended question-asking conveys the complexity of alternative paths in interviewing. These studies suggest that effective interviewer training and control is imperative.

A further difficulty of an extensive interview that requires many sessions is scheduling. Does the interviewer summarize the last session's close and hope for a relatively unprompted continuation? The way in which summarizing and scheduling is done will shape what is produced. The interviewer must choose how to stop and restart discourse in the sessions. The respondent will think the interviewer has an agenda even if it is not made explicit.

The type of questions used in a open-ended life story interview is determined by the research style with which the interview is organized. A researcher–interviewer is likely to be in a hunch-following mode, whereas a briefed interviewer is more likely to have been told of a research strategy. The anthropologist may use a hunch-following strategy to a life story because he or she is unlikely to have sufficient background information to formulate a wide range of specific questions. However, the anthropologist may investigate particular general issues, such as roles or rituals, which are then more extensively elaborated. A researcher or an interviewer in a known culture is able to concentrate on more specific issues or use devices to aid recall.

Life story research interviews differ in the importance placed on letting the informant control the product. Nicole (1980) aruges that the informant's discourse should be respected as it is richer than the sociologists! Bertaux (1981) argues for the respondent's control on ideological grounds. As a text-oriented research product of this type is a kind of biography, it is a more powerful instrument for social change and insight (which Bertaux contends is the purpose of social science) when there is less of the social scientist and more of the informant. The desire for researcher control over the interview product signifies the researcher's belief that his or her way of looking at things is more important than that of the respondent. However, even if the researcher does give the informant control over the product, Bertaux advises researchers to assert some control in the process of interpretation. Such control will be essential if the comparison of life stories is an important component of research.

Conceptual constraints are an important influence on the questions the interviewer asks and the themes that are elaborated. Although Bertaux and Bertaux-Wiame (1981) approached the bakery profession with open minds, they soon realized that they did not need to do any more life stories than those that told them what they wanted to know. As they were only interested in the careers of the general group "bakers," they were not interested in all the details of individual cases, which they dismiss as providing information only at a psychological level. There are similar restrictions in interviewing themes in the majority of story studies. For example, an interviewer only diverts from finding out about occupational careers to use other events to act as prompts to recall.

This off-theme line of questioning is advocated by Hindley (1979) who suggests that "advantage can be taken of subjects' tendency to structure information, by trying to get them to think of other things going on around the time of the events of interest" (p. 103). This is necessary if the research goal is to achieve maximum information on particular events. Hindley stresses that respondents should not be asked questions in a way that might lead them to see themselves as having to defend their actions; this point is also emphasized by Brown and Sime (1981). If the respondent has interpreted a line of questioning as checking inconsistency, the relationship with the interviewer is most likely to be strained.

Bertaux (1980) mentions the degree of directiveness in interviewer contributions. He advocates three acceptable types of direction: looking for patterns of similar episodes at different points of time, to encourage the respondent to make comparisons; looking for value judgements and emotional involvement; and encouraging the respondent to elaborate on particular instances.

Bogdan and Taylor (1975) advise that interviewers should not interrupt when taking life stories; they should pay attention and be both nonevaluative and reflective. They corroborate Agar's (1980) caveat on background information, saying researchers should not "take for granted commonsense understandings and assumptions" (p. 114). To monitor the possible effects of interviewers on protocols, it is suggested that interviewers should note their own current impressions and observations. Bogdan and Taylor also address a consistent theme in advice to life story interviewers—what to do about apparent contradictions. These authors suggest that if the researchers see contradictions they should be pointed out, either through negotiation with the subject, or by a comment to the readers; in any case they should not be removed.

Gittins (1979) describes both the problems of prompting and also the social situation of the oral history interview. In an example from her own research, she suggests that the most important difference between two groups of women's retrospections were that one group told much less about their family in spite of a large amount of prompting and encouragement. Gittins further suggests that the skilled resolution of apparent incompatibilities can disentangle some of the influence of the respondent's construct system. Gittins gives an example of the contradiction between ideal family size and achieved family size. Asking respondents to explain the difference can give valuable information on their feelings, although they may also get defensive. Gittins concludes that life story interviewing has at least as many problems as other methods, but that through it oral historians are able to find information that official statistics do not record.

One of the most helpful questioning strategies in life story interviewing is provided by the use of life story grids. The report given in Goldthorpe (1980) provides a typical example of the use of an life story grid; in this study it was called "a 'Life-History Chart' on which the interviewer was to record full details of a respondent's occupational history from his first full-time employment to date and, in conjunction with this, further details of changes in the composition of his family and household over the same time span" (p. 292). They also noted that in their pilot work "older respondents often found difficulty in providing reliably the kind of rather detailed retrospective information" (p. 292). This underlines the complexity of the cognitive task for the respondent. Although this method has considerable advantages in focussing discourse around particular entries, it does make considerable demands apparent to the respondent. Its primary benefits are the production of research records that can be easily compared and summarized without sacrificing all the features of an open-ended interview.

Perlman (1974) used the Balan et al. (1969) type of life story grid, which has a row for each year (see Figure 2). On this the respondent's age is filled in left-hand column and the other columns indicate topics under the major headings of migrational, occupational, educational, and family history. An appropriate cell is filled in with the details of any change. Filling in the form is a joint task between the interviewer and respondent, who is often easily motivated (by the clear demand characteristics of the task) to cooperate. Perlman claims that "reliability was excellent because memory could be aided by moving back and forth among the several areas of the respondent's life. Omissions and inconsistencies showed up easily and could be corrected immediately before proceeding to the next items" (p. 5).

The interviewer–respondent relationship is crucial for the life story interview. Gilbert (1980), interviewing scientists about their careers, observes that his respondents were unfamiliar about the interview situation and had little idea of the demands of their role. Gilbert suggests that his informants may have produced a very particular view of their careers, resulting from "their initial conceptions of the roles which they assumed they and I should play during the interview" (p. 233). Such problems may be addressed by the preparation of the interviewer to be able to interact at the level of the respondent's peers.

Brown and Sime (1981) make clear how the interview situation may distort accounts: The implied roles of both interviewer and respondent, the significance of the tape-recorder, and the process of negotiation to eliminate internal inconsistencies are stressed. They further show examples of "account agenda themes" that work to constrain retrospections in a particular account-gathering task.

In open-ended life story interviews the task for the interviewer is a

		Migrational history						Occupational history				Educ hist	Family hist
YEAR	AGE	NAME OF PLACE	MUNICIPALITY	STATE	SIZE CLASSIFICATION	TYPE RESIDENCE	REASON FOR MOVE	TYPE OF WORK	JOB CLASSIFICATION	JOB LOCATION	REASON FOR JOB CHANGE	SCHOOLING	MARRIAGE BIRTHS ETC
1969													
1967													
1966													
.													
.													
.													
1904													

Figure 2 Perlman life story grid.

difficult and complex one. It is important that a clear strategy is used, whether it involves agenda, life story grids, or playing the role of a peer; undue inconsistency in interviewer behaviour is a source of confusion both for the informant and for interpretation.

Respondent's Construct System

The term *respondent's construct system* is used to imply, not only cognitive structures in the Kelly (1956) sense, but also the individual's value systems, scripts, and life themes (Schank and Abelson, 1977). This aspect of the life story interview model is central; it represents the way that the past can only be recalled through the blinkers that are characterized as the "Retrospectroscope" in Wall and Williams (1970).

Breaux (1977) points out how different respondents may produce accounts with features at different levels of a dimension varying from the smallest detail of what was happening, to descriptions of the overall process of the whole episode. Breaux found evidence that higher-ranking staff produced accounts that dealt more with overall processes. This characterizes the role of differences in construct system in retrospection of the same events. The particular effect is probably due to differences in the respondent's views of what was expected in such a retrospection and their responsibility in the original setting. In such ways an individual's construct system is not completely fixed and immutable.

Past events are recalled in a way that makes sense for the person recalling, as he or she reconstructs a story of past events. It is possible that through asking specific questions about the past, or exploring details about particular, exceptional events, one might reduce this bias. However, all life stories and life event judgements will be contaminated with the respondent's present construct system. All users of life story methods of any type should be aware of this limitation.

Kohli (1981) distinguishes two functions of life stories: a referential function (the description of events in temporal order) and an evaluative function (the relevence of those events to the present). The evaluative function conveys both the influence of the present construct system and also the interpretation of the informant's relationship with the recalled entity. Kohli suggests one useful line of interview questioning is to attempt to disengage the evaluative component. This might be taken to suggest to an informant he or she should retell an episode with a change of theme. The respondent might, for example, be persuaded to reconstrue himself or herself in a more active role rather than as a helpless victim of fate.

Story Structure of the Life Story

One way to describe the structure of life story texts is by using concepts proposed by psychologists studying memory for stories (Thorndyke, 1977; Mandler and Johnson, 1977; Schank and Abelson, 1977; Rumelhart, 1975). As an indication of a wider application of story structure, Newcombe and Rutler (1982) argue that it may provide a promising paradigm for the wider issues of the understanding of human social behaviour.

Such a story structure will contain a hierarchy of detail. At the lowest level are key remembered entities: events, like visiting someone in hospital; actors, who was visited; and places, as hospitals. Thus, the same memory can be investigated by asking questions relating to the three entities. For example, "Can you remember visiting someone in hospital?" "Can you remember any times you saw your grandmother?" and "Can you remember anything about the hospital?" Each event can be seen to be composed from actors and places. The memory psychologists describe an extensive set of remembered entities in hierarchical relationships with one another. By "story rewrite rules," events are put together into episodes and episodes into stories. Other concepts at higher levels include topics, themes, and goals that interconnect various themes. Even the extended set of story rewrite rules used by the memory psychologists are probably still too simple for the majority of accounts and stories.

A story is defined in Mandler and Johnson's (1977) scheme as a setting and a series of episodes. Episodes have beginnings, causes, developments, and endings. It could be argued that life stories consist of a series of intertwined stories. Because most people use everyday story form for narratives and accounts, these ideas may contribute to the analysis and interpretation of life stories. Agar (1980) points out that "the notion of 'well-formed story' is as relevant to Jack [his informant] as it is to the psychologists who are examining stories in their simpler forms . . . the structure, then becomes a guide to the analyst" (p. 228).

The type of remembered entities involved may change during the account of a story. The mixture may be subject to the current construct system, the behaviour shaping of the interviewer, and other aspects of the interview situation. This problematic mixture is found when looking for the entities to be coded in accounts (Brown and Sime, 1981). Story structure analysis of the discourse may provide entities of a defined type, facilitating comparison. Further, interviewers could encourage respondents to give structurally unambiguous accounts, asking for details of entities demanded by story structure rules but only implied in narration. By such elaboration further interpretation should be made easier.

Story Elaboration

The story-structure model of life story material suggests several methods for elaboration. Given a particular event, the interviewer can ask for the beginning, causes, development, and context of each episode. Further particular episodes can be related to more extensive themes like social values; however, this is liable to recall biases, as the reconstruction of stories of the past is suffused with present-day values. Other strategies for elaboration were mentioned with the interviewer's task in the section beginning on p. 168. This section deals with elaboration strategies most relevant to interpretation.

Poivier and Clapier-Valladon (1980) suggest the life story interviewer should encourage a critical stance by the respondent; encouragement should be given to obtain clear definitions of recalled settings, and the interviewer should help the respondent explore the nature of the narration. Respondents should be asked about the limits, rules, and sequences of settings. The authors suggest the elaboration of retrospections, both through interviews on the same events from varying perspectives and through cross-comparisons with corroborative material.

There are other possibilities for elaboration. One could ask for similar stories or other episodes involving the same actor, places, or types of events. A frequent retrospection strategy is to use closeness in time to produce a structure for reliable recall. Asking a mother "When did your child have flu?" is liable to produce error; some of this may be overcome if, as suggested by Hindley (1979), other neutral marker events, such as birthdays and holidays, are used to build up a more accurate picture.

Mode of Recording

The final aspect of the interview is what is actually recorded by the researcher. This can vary from the tape recording or its transcript, to nothing in the case of the sensitive political informant. Although strategies like life story grids impose structure on what is recorded, there is still some open-ended textual coding to be done.

Bertaux (1980) advocates the process of "hot transcription" of textual material. This involves producing the typed version as soon as possible after the interview, usually without using a tape recorder. Bertaux argues that this reduces the influence of the researchers' perspectives. He advocates longer transcripts as they give more opportunity for alternative interpretations.

Because of the difficulties both of diversity and extent associated with the recording of textual material, there are several techniques in life story interviewing that limit what is recorded. Typically events of only a few classes are recorded and only chronological adjacency is sought as the recorded relationship between them. A life story grid is a system of this type. Although this makes coding a more achievable task, data management and interpretation still present considerable difficulties.

The interpretation of the different type of materials, textual and life story grid will be surveyed separately in the following section. This section will not only show ways of finding the deeper meaning of the interview product but will also detail tools for estimating the effects of interview strategies.

INTERPRETATIONS OF LIFE STORY INTERVIEW MATERIAL

In the preface to a book entitled *Interpreting Multivariate Data,* Barnett (1981) poses the following questions, which are pertinent to the interpretation of life story data:

> What do the data really show us in the midst of their apparent chaos? How can we cogently summarize and represent these data? How can we reduce dimensionality and scale to a level where the message of the data is, at least informally, clear, and sensible models can be developed? (p. v)

Note that Barnett is describing the problems of numerically coded data, with comparable variables for a homogenous set of entities. To be able to reach the state with life story material where the techniques described in his book can apply, considerable (possibly degrading) processing is necessary. However, any interpretation aims for organized display, summarization, and informal model-fitting. Display implies changes in ordering or format; summarization implies a process of condensation where some variability in the information is removed. Informal model-fitting represents a procedure of fitting ideas to displays and summarizations.

What is the nature of the prior processing that is required? Where the retrospections of sensitive informants interviews have already reached their audience (the interviewer), no further processing is required. In contrast, for life story grids a routine textual coding operation is required. The data are best coded as changes on variables at particular times; some of the data management consequences of this perspective are addressed later. For textual material that requires summarization and comparison between subjects, considerable processing will be necessary.

Textual material is relatively unrestricted by constraints at the time of interviewing. It is possible that, if textual material is sufficiently complete, information at the level of the life story grid can be derived by coding. Life story grids cannot, however, be elaborated into interview protocols and are in this sense restricted.

The process of interpretation addressed in this section can be seen as the assimilation of the respondent's position into the researcher's model for the appropriate class of respondents, as well as the generation of that researcher's model. Through the application of coding processes and exploratory statistical tools, the researcher creates a summarization of the life story material. To the extent that this summarization allows the researcher to address the questions of his or her research strategy, it can be seen as informal model-fitting.

One problem of interpretation, especially with unrestricted material, is the multiplicity of alternative interpretations. Runyan (1981) addresses this alternative interpretation problem in psychobiography by examining a series of alternative explanations from the literature for Van Gogh's earcutting. Runyan concludes that there should be more ways of comparing the effectiveness of such interpretations but does not suggest criteria. The perspective in his paper is that it is unwise to assert that there will be just one interpretation. What can be hoped is that some interpretations may be refuted, on the basis of explicit research strategies.

It could be said that life story method is less suitable for exploratory studies because an explicit interpretative structure may make both the data gathering and the interpretation tractable. Without some structure, the confusing multitude of possible interpretations may lead the research into a morass. As the data cannot help decide between interpretations, it is best to have the basis for interpretation decided, either before or by some other research procedure.

Life Story Text Analysis

There are a variety of summarizing processes that can be applied to life story interview transcripts. Time sequencing, parsing, coding, and the construction of transition matrices and cross-sectional views reduce the text to make it more comparable and interpretable for the researcher. Content analysis and computer-aided text indexing provide tools that do not break up the sequence of the elicited interview but just index particular categories in the text. Brown and Sime (1981) distinguish three methods for transforming accounts: (1) purely qualitative quoting of protocols; (2) descriptive use, as illustrations to theories under development; (3) theoretically oriented content analysis or indexing. The first two methods correspond to the less transformed research product.

The three methods of text analysis and text indexing can be seen to provide systematic and interpretative analyses of life story texts. Such texts cover many issues, topics, and time periods. To describe them as overlapping, multiple accounts does not convey all their complexity; for example, they are likely to contain unexplained and unfinished episodes. The chances of a limited series of rules representing all life story material are as remote as machine-aided translation (Boden, 1977); however, there is value in outlining analytic strategies.

As the order of events in time is often of primary importance to the researcher interpreting life stories, time sequencing is very frequently applied to such accounts. This may not be easy, as is illustrated by Catini (1981), whose informant remembered childhood events through her mother's songs in a disjointed series of episodes. A time sequence process draws together accounts so that episodes follow in time order, although there have to be limits to the disruptions of particular stories. This can be a simple reformatting for publication, or preparation for further analyses. Typically text can either be cut and pasted into time order, or it can be duplicated into place. Such a duplication needs to maintain appropriate references to the text's primary position; the text might be duplicated to provide an explanation of a later episode.

The effect of time sequencing will be to produce relatively self-contained accounts in an established time order. Certainly there are other relationships likely to exist between such parts of life story text through continuities of entities such as actors, places, and themes. Such time sequencing requires some concept of what are separate movable parts of accounts, and in this way time sequencing requires some degree of parsing. Time sequencing will be easier if interview questioning is oriented to produce easily separable story components.

The second process that can be applied to life story text after time sequencing is a parsing similar to that of Schank and Abelson (1977). As suggested by Agar (1980), certain extensions for life story interpretations could be made to Rumelhart's (1975) rules. Agar suggests that the normal structure of stories is likely to be universal in a culture; we might therefore expect it to be feasible to apply some form of story analysis to life story text.

It might be possible to make this automatic, as in some developmnet of Schank and Abelson's computerized restaurant story analysis. However, that system depends crucially on the use of two additional factors. First, Schank and Abelson use a construct called a script, which provides a flexible system of rules of what is to be expected in a setting such as a restaurant. Second, they use a coding of actions into a limited set of primitive acts. The script has many similarities with the concept of standing patterns of behaviour settings (Barker, 1968). As the primitive acts would need to be coded before parsing could start, it is possible that coding, parsing, and time sequencing should be done in reverse order. This is likely to produce more problems; story structures are easier to find if the text had been separated into discrete texts; coding is easier to do if the context is clarified by applying story structure. Ideally, parallel application of the three processes could be used, with a system of "co-routining" that applied each of the three techniques until one of the others was required to resolve an ambiguity. Thus, time marker words might be used to identify many time sequencing problems, but it is possible that some parts of text could be distinguished in time only because of their story structure features.

To apply a derivative of Schank and Abelson's system would require scripts for a wide range of settings. Unfortunately, such scripts are often what a life story study is trying to uncover; especially in historical or anthropological studies. A further failing of computerized language analysis systems is that most systems cannot accommodate to the sloppy grammar and unfinished sentences that populate life story transcripts (Boden, 1977). However, such considerations do not prevent the application of the three processes by hand!

In hand sequencing and parsing, it is possible to adapt rules and create exceptions so that a complete structuring of the text is possible, although it is subject to researcher bias. Such a parsing with story structure, whether automatic or not, is likely to uncover background assumptions. This is made clear in the analysis of simple stories by Rumelhart (1975) and Mandler and Johnson (1977), and it would be a benefit of story structure analysis. For example, Mandler and Johnson show some of the missing structures in the "War of the Ghosts" story. If this analysis could be done at a point where questions to the respondent could be generated to fill in such gaps, a better text and interpretation would be forthcoming.

Such a parsing takes sentences as its basic units, although occasionally clauses are all that can be found to represent some components of the story structure. Earlier content analysis systems such as the General Enquirer (Stone et al., 1966) worked with single words; such a perspective cannot represent the structural features of life story accounts.

After time sequencing and parsing, a further summarization process for life story text would be categorizations of the various discovered entities. This can be done both through a content coding system and also by counts of structural varieties. If comparisons are made between individuals, comparative numbers of entities of similar content or structure provide interpretative yield. An example of a structural interpretation is Gittins' (1979) observation that certain respondents were unlikely to recall details of stories about events with a family theme.

It may be possible to derive quantitative measures of aspects like complexity and continuity of organization. If one takes a higher-level entity like a story or an episode as a unit analysis, one could calculate indices of similarity of units, in terms of having similar components, or indices of the similarity between components over units. Both procedures would produce matrices within individuals, whose interpretation could be aided through one of the techniques described in Barnett (1981), for example, Multidimensional Scaling (MDS). Richardson (1977) describes an analysis of accounts using this tool. Transition matrices, indicating the frequency with which categories of components follow one another, can also be constructed. These take the form of assymmetric square matrices where a cell entry represents the relative frequency with which the column entry follows the row entry. An example of this is Figure 3.

However, such interpretative strategies depend on the unambiguous

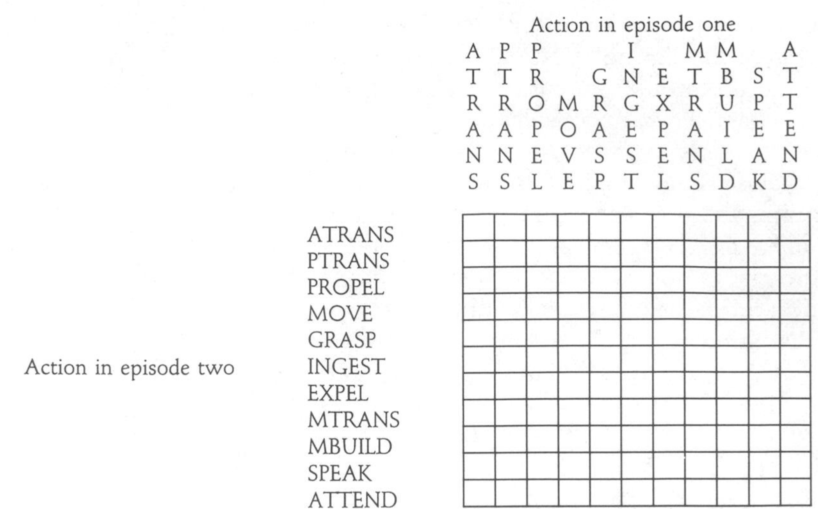

Figure 3 Illustrative transition matrix. For all pairs of episodes coded by Conceptual Dependency Theory (Shank and Abelson, 1977), cell entries represent the number of times, or some transformation thereof, that one primitive act in a row follows a primitive act in a column.

separation of entities. It is necessary to make assumptions before one can differentiate types of entities recalled by different individuals in a comparable way. These assumptions would include a model, stable between individuals, of different types of entities.

The results of a parsing of a series of life stories would be an indexed file from which it should be possible to derive counts of presence and joint presence for a variety of units of analysis and attributes. One could derive co-occurence counts between entities for each of a group of individuals' key stages of life; such a summary could be interpreted through the application of the INDSCAL model (Carroll and Chang, 1970), which gives a basis for individual differences scaling interpretations.

This story structure approach, using all these tools is as yet conjecture and is untried on life stories, as far as I know. However, some account analyses (Breaux, 1977) have used similar methods. Life story texts have been analysed, but with more informal episodic structures (Catini, 1981).

Life Story Indexing

One less adventurous and perhaps more practical approach is exemplified by what Agar (1980) calls themal analysis. This consists of intuitively extracting small chuncks of text on particular themes to see if, when presented together, they may lead to interpretative insights. This is a process that could be done automatically by a concordance package (Hockey and Marriott, (1980) as long as all synonyms could be passed to the package. For a theme of time, one could try words like *years, dates, winter, days, o'clock,* and so on. By examining contexts, an interpretation of the view of time and any changes thereof might be forthcoming.

Read (1980) and MacIntyre (1979) describe studies using computerization of standard indexing procedures suggested in both Thompson (1978) and Bogdan and Taylor (1975). The idea is simply to cut the text into segments and to index the segments by theme or content. The hand version involves duplication, cutting, and pasting onto index cards, which are then sorted in index boxes. The computerized approach, assuming the transcript is machine readable, simply associates a certain index category with sets of chuncks of text. A computer text management system for this procedure provides additional flexibility over the hand system; it might provide opportunities for overlapping indexing, so that categorizations based on actors, places, and other themes of relevence to the researcher can all be intermeshed. However, more complex indexing demands parsing and similar problems to story structure analysis.

Zarpati (1981), Elder (1978), and Runyan (1980) stress the concept of life cycle that provides a strategy for the categorization of parts of life stories. Runyan points to other cycles in occupation and leisure (Hedges, 1981) that can all provide themes for the dynamic interpretation of life stories. Such conceptions would lead to particular indexing strategies.

A development of the indexing approach would be to use the indexed life story file as a database to answer questions like What job was this person doing in 1965? Questions of this type can be used to construct a life story grid. To do this requires completeness in the interview transcript, which must be indexed for order and time of occurrence, parsed into separate episodes, and indexed for themes. The indexed file differs from the text analysed by story structure only in that the text is still untouched.

An example of an application of a qualitative indexing is the study by Denzin (1981) who used informant retrospections as an interpretative component of a wider investigation of the liquor industry. Denzin looked for three major themes in both questioning and indexing. First, he explored informants' conceptions of and attitudes to the product; second, he studied informants' perspective of the controlling forces, both internal and external, on patterns of activity in the industry; third, he elicited views of the organisation. These interpretatons were combined with corroborative material.

Brown and Sime's (1981) description of indexing in account analysis is also informative. Under the variety of themes in accounts, series of categories are developed; parts of transcripts are indexed for presence or absence of these categories. Cross-checking is necessary in such a coding process to establish its reliability. However, Brown and Sime observe that "the use of independent coders to avoid researcher bias has been more problematic than was first envisaged" (p. 184). This was most noticeable when coders were given contextless episodes to code; it is likely that the coders' assumptions about the context affects their performance.

The interpretation of life story interviews will be aided by the degree to which they are systematically organized. However, the size of the organization that is involved is daunting, especially as it is open to bias. Prospective researchers should therefore be warned against the use of this technique when what they seek is either specific information to answer theoretically grounded questions or to generate hypotheses. Unstructured life story interviewing is a useful technique for gaining understanding of an informants' past, but it is a technique best suited to filling out details rather than either the creation or testing of theories.

Tools to Interpret Life Story Grids

Balan and his colleagues have analysed, in a study of mobility in a developing country, the life stories of 1,640 men in Monterey, Mexico (Balan et al., 1973, 1969; Balan and Jelin, 1980). The interpretation of their life story grid data was a problem. The grid had sixty rows, one for each year of the man's life, and twelve columns for areas of change. First, the changes were coded, with considerable effort. Then a system had to be designed to deal with the 720 separate cells of information on the grid. If each cell had been keyed, data capture and storage would have been costly, so the data was coded and keyed only when there was a change in a column. A keyed record consisted of three variables: the row number, indicating age; the column number, indicating which topic; and the code for that topic. Thus, one could indicate that at the age of 35 a man had a male child, by the row number for 35, the column for births, and the code for a male child.

This way of storing grids where there are few informative cells is called address coding (Visvalingam and Rhind, 1976). In these days of cheap computer storage media, it is the savings on data capture cost that still makes this an appropriate strategy to follow.

A special FORTRAN program (Balan et al., 1969) was written to access data in this form. It lets the researchers act as if the grid had been punched with 720 variables. Further, this program can calculate other variables which help interpretation of life story material. The program can cumulate, for instance, the number of places the man has lived in to date for every year of his life; the program can also create "moving" variables, for example, the number of dependent children under 13. This variable changes from year to year with births, deaths, and maturation.

Using fixed-length records (as required by most statistical packages) extracted from this data, more interpretative analyses were run of the relations between occupational movement as predicted by age and year of arrival in Monterey. Cohorts of comparable groups were extracted to enable this analysis to control for some historical effects. A multivariate model of advancement was built. This involved a path model that related age at marriage, family background, and size of community to achieved occupational state. Balan and his colleagues stress, in their interpretation, three types of cycles: the life cycle, with implications for the sociology of the family, and individual occupational and migrational cycles.

This style of research, claim Balan et al. (1969), is best contemplated only by "amply funded projects organized so as to provide well trained interviewers under close supervision, expert coders able to work with the data over long periods of time, and access to large-capacity computers and competent programmers" (p. 114). The only constraint that is now less important for any similar-size study is the large-capacity computer, although it is still necessary to use someone skilled with data management to deal with such data.

Perlman (1974) used the Balan type of life story grids in her study of urban poverty in Rio de Janiero. She used the same basic address coding system, ADMINS (Pool et al., 1969), to help check the coding and to pass derivatives of the data to a statistical package for the preparation of tables. Hedges (1981) has also used the grid technique but reports his analysis as "in progress." This is a typical state for life story data analysis as it is heavy on resources, and places strong demand on statistical packages (Tagg, 1981).

Karweit (1973) describes the problems of storage and retrieval of life history information collected in an educational and occupational mobility study. She describes Balan's approach as a direct method. Balan uses a large time interval (a year), and thus the size of the grid is fairly easy to key by address coding. However, with such a large time interval, there is always a possibility of missing some detail.

The method Karweit advocates is an indexed procedure; the life story grid method is adapted so that the questionnaire only elicits changes in state, but records a more accurate timing, to the nearest month. This loses some of the cooperative advantages of the age grid and asks, perhaps, for too accurate dates. She created a hierarchical database with information at the level of the individual connected with all associated change records, which are stored in sequence. As the time period is a month, there is less point in conceiving specifically of the life story grid. However, the coding of the data as changes is identical.

Goldthorpe (1980) and Carr-Hill and MacDonald (1973) give an indication of the range of interpretation-aiding tools that can be applied to such data once it is accessible. Storing only changing information, they suggest three basic types of retrieval: first, the retrieval of a "life" as a set of events; second, the set of observations for each year to form a cross-section; and third, the unscrambling of particular events and items for separate analysis.

Careers, a concept synonymous with cycles, are viewed as sequences of events. Carr-Hill and MacDonald make the contrast between focussing on events and the view of life as "a continuous stream observable at any point" (p. 62). They also distinguish the effects of age and calendar. On the one hand, an analysis of precursors of occupation at age 40 will be confounded by whether World War Two was a possible precursor; whereas creating cohorts from the same cross-section and doing seperate analysis can have the effect of losing common age effects. Carr-Hill and MacDonald suggest an analysis modelling both age and cohort effects.

Carr-Hill and MacDonald demonstrate some useful graphical devices where instantaneous state can be displayed on a graded scale, such as is possible for occupational prestige. An example for one respondent is given in Figure 4.

Displaying one individual's life pattern is similar to a time series plot; displaying a group of individuals plotted with slight increments shows, where paths are denser, whether particular movements are more popular.

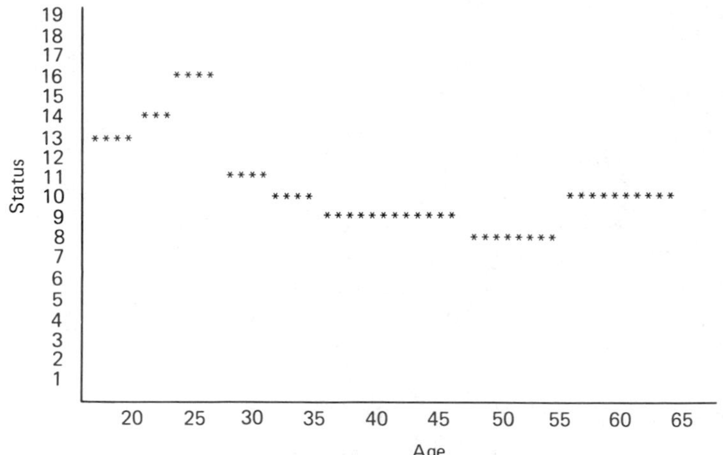

Figure 4 Occupational trajectory taken loosely from Carr-Hill and MacDonald (1973).

Carr-Hill and MacDonald consider the problems of comparing the patterns of such trajectories; however, they were not able to satisfy themselves with any formal definition or measurement of pattern difference. They suggest instead a process whereby the representation allows for an obvious pattern to be input as a template; this template is then used to remove fitting trajectories, and then further patterns are extracted on the remaining trajectories. This can be thought of as an informal model-fitting procedure.

In respect to modelling changing statuses, Carr-Hill and MacDonald explore both path analysis and logistic regression. The latter is more appropriate because events are typically only dichotomous or nominal-level attributes. They also examine transition matrices, for which they consider varieties of Markov models, including mover–stayer models. These interpretative techniques are focussed for applications in situations where no forgetting or recall bias is assumed. Although they have interpretative potential, it is unlikely to be applicable to the majority of life story interviews.

Another application of logistic regressions is made by Runyan (1980) who compares a multistage flow table approach to path analysis. He does this in the interpretation of occupational changes from Blau and Duncan's (1967) sample of 20,000 American men. A stage-state model can be tested through the flow table model, which gives the advantage of being able to model particular routes rather than only the interval-level regression coefficients between states. Runyan, in his interpretation, suggests the probabilities associated with particular routes could be compared to "common knowledge" or the implicit theories of life course. The only problem with this idea is that the original survey respondents are likely to have influenced their retrospections through their own implicit theories.

Other Approaches to Life Stories

Dailey (1959, 1971) proposes a theory of graphs that he uses as an interpretative system for narrative accounts of human behaviour. Episodes, actors, and themes are connected by the lines of a directed graph. Dailey proposes a scheme for sampling the population of life story episodes, but the episodes are stratified within significant environments (work, home, school, and leisure) and for significant persons. This is similar in format to a life story grid. He summarizes career histories as career lines, which have a similar form to occupational trajectories. However, Dailey's main use of graph theory is as a tool in training sessions for clinicians, rather than as a interpretative tool for research using life stories.

Herbst (1970) suggests a system for autobiographical data intermediate between text and life story grids. Sentences about particular events in a relationship history (meeting, dating, engagemet, and wedding) are coded as to the amount of each partner's initiation, feelings of "we," giving up of other friendship, and affective state. Affect trajectories and other graphs are drawn. Herbst takes a particular psychological theory (Kurt Lewin's, 1951, topometric model) and applies it successfully to the interpretation of retrospective life account data. This approach integrates the elicitation and interpretation of longitudinal accounts with a particular theoretical approach. Its application to life story data would require extensions of the model to deal with transformations attributable to the respondent's construct system.

Ninoska de Marina (1981), a postgraduate student at Brunel University, investigates retrospective accounts of the process of therapy; she can be thought to be looking for themes underlying sets of events. It is an investigation both of the patient's concepts of self and significant others at particular time-slices and, more importantly, concepts of change processes.

The aim is to develop procedures to give a clear view of the client's understanding of the changes involved in therapy. A special development of the MAUD (MultiAttribute Utility Decomposition) program (Humphreys and Wishuda, 1981) is used to involve the clients in the location, reduction, and clarification of a large number of constructs elicited relevant to particular periods and particular areas of the individual's life. The MAUD program can investigate, interactively with the client, constructs and related degrees of satisfaction with different stages of life. These are elicited both in informal discussion and by methods of elaboration.

Each elicited attribute has an ideal point elicited, and the MAUD program uses forced choices (Humphreys, 1980) to produce a utility model that can indicate relative importances of the constructs and an overall ranking of the time points from each particular perspective.

This is then done for various other areas of importance to the subject. The way the MAUDs are done ensures both that the person's own view of parts of the changing self are produced, and that the person's evaluations of various aspects of the process are elicited. The distinctions extracted can be seen to be dynamic conceptions. Dynamic categories are formed through groupings of these constructs at different periods of time, which are then linked to the attributes elicited in the MAUD system.

The statements from the interviews and other methods of elicitation are statements of feeling, thoughts, and experience; or, more generally, views of the social world and of the self. The categories into which these are linked are scaled by a variety of own-categories procedures on two-dimensional "maps." The groupings are typically unnamed, but often material elicited during the interview is used to establish the basis for the relations between the grouping displayed. Each map is constructed for each client at each particular time point of importance to him or her. In one sense it is static as each map shows a "time-specific" perspective.

The MAUD program, on the other hand, is used dynamically, but this means that the attributes elicited in each MAUD session with the client span all time periods. Hence, multidimensional unfolding techniques are also used to locate each MAUD-elicited attribute from each structural map in order to understand how the signification of the attributes changes through time. The multidimensional unfolding techniques require the construction of what is, in effect, a three-way grid (Tagg, 1974, 1980), exploring the structural and dynamic dimensions of the therapeutic process. The respondent rates himself or herself at each time period as to how near the groups of attributes they felt in terms of awareness, importance, and affect. The respondent is encouraged, when generating attributes, to produce statements of feelings, thoughts, experiences, and perspectives on self and the world.

Then trajectories on groupings for each type of involvement are tested against the client's experience to elicit dynamic explanations based on the client's experience. This elicitation concentrates on key events, acute changes, and important groups. The study shows a systematic approach to life story interviewing at the single-case level.

The most important aspect of such developments in life story interviewing is the exploitation of the relationship between the role of informant and the joint roles of researcher, interviewer, and interpreter. They are designed to ensure that the researcher's or clinician's interpretations of these conceptions are in agreement with the informant. De Marina's project provides a procedure for negotiation towards that agreement; it aims for a model of the patients' view of his or her past, rather than a study of past events and their timing, almost incidentally mediated through the respondent's retrospections. However, this thorough exploration of retrospection requires many long sessions.

In a similar way, Runyan (1978) describes life courses as sequences of person–situation interactions, implying a desire for the recovery of person by situation grids (Endler and Magnusson, 1974) on a series of key themes of the life course. Although this conception may be relevant to the theory of life course, the influence of the informants' current construct system is likely to make appropriate retrospective data difficult to produce. A state needs to be recorded for a series of behaviours in a series of situations for each of a series of time slices. This process could then be repeated for informants. This would give a four-way matrix of the style suggested by Runyan's model. It is possible that through multiway scaling (Carroll and Chang, 1970) an initial model could be constructed of individual differences in memories of the life course.

The Reliability of Life Stories

This section summarizes many of the points in this chapter, by addressing factors that should be taken into account before using life story methods. These factors are indicated by the concept of reliability. Levy (1981) suggests that statistical measures of reliability should not be substituted for substantive factors that a researcher should take into account when choosing a method. Unless the statistical measure of reliability is interpreted as only one measure of resilience against sources of error, as in generalizability theory terms (Cronbach et al. 1972), there is a danger that the concise scientism of a statistic will preclude proper considerations. In other words, research methods should be subservient to theories and research problems, not vice versa. One of the important points made in the section on interviewing was the importance of research orientation in shaping the content of the interview. There is a danger when choosing life story interviews that the method will become the first criterion for research procedure decisions.

What Levy suggests is that, in making choices about methods, researchers should ask questions in terms relevant to the substantive problem. Researchers should not be concerned about the reliability of life story methods in abstract but rather should ask what the plausable rival explanations are, for example, forgetting or retrospective reconstruction, and what defenses are possible against such interpretative competition. He stresses the point of producing an unambiguous and communicable research product. This major criterion for interpretability has four subcriteria of relevence to life story interviewing. The first criterion is validity. Do life stories have meaning? In textual form they do have an immediate, practically publishable validity. The second criterion is objectivity. Are the ways in which life stories are communicated and compared the only possible basis for interpretation? The third criterion is generalizability, or truth. First, would the informant on reinterview produce material giving rise to the same interpretations? Second, do individuals who cannot be distinguished in interpretation produce indistinguishable products on reinterview? The fourth criterion is proof, which is the criterion of plausability. Does the method lead to interpretations that resist alternative explanations?

It is rare in the use of life story methods that one can feel certain of fulfilling all four criteria. Sometimes it is possible to get some assurance against retrospective bias. Cornfield and Haenszel (1960) summarize an investigation of smoking and lung cancer, where fortuitously one group of those diagnosed as having lung cancer turned out not to have it. As their reported smoking habits were more similar to those without lung cancer, it confirmed there was no appreciable tendency to overreport smoking by those who thought they had cancer, or whose interviewers thought they had lung cancer. Such fortunate occurrences are the exception that point to the rule that retrospections tend to be a reconstruction of the past to make sense for the respondent. Also the more the respondents feel they have to explain themselves, the more distorted the reconstructions are likely to be. However, this chapter is less concerned with single retrospective questions, which can lead to errors because they are overdemanding, than it is concerned with the more extensive life story interview. Although particular items may be subject to a series of sources of error, the combination of items that are interpreted are more difficult to fabricate.

Because of the nature of life story research, there are few studies of the reliability of textual life stories. In most cases where there is corroborative material, incompatibilities are resolved before methodological research writing is done. Incompatibilities are resolved with the respondent as another method of elaborating the life story product. This strategy is presumably based on the idea that, although the remembered sequence of similar events is recalled at best only in a loose, partial order, the cross-referencing between classes of events can often locate the time patterns more exactly if chronological accuracy is important in a particular study. Whether such a detailed process is undergone to answer closed retrospective survey question is doubtful; precise chronological judgements are therefore open to some doubt.

Goldstein (1979) expresses a cautious attitude towards retrospective data. This attitude is also shown in Moss and Goldstein (1979), which contains several papers that highlight the problems associated with retrospective questions in surveys. As it is likely that all the sources of misinterpretations applicable in such data are present in life story texts, these papers are summarized below.

Baddeley (1979) reports psychological investigations of relevence to retrospective recall errors; he asked members of an experimental psychology panel to remember when they had previously attended and what had happened. The extent of forgetting was dramatic. Baddeley concludes "forgetting will be maximal when asking for details of one out of many similar incidents" and suggests "the time interval between the event and the survey should be minimized" (p. 25). He also suggests that the reconstructive bias of retrospection leads subjects to "try to make sense of given incidents" (p. 25). Baddeley suggests that leading questions that encourage such reconsttructions should be avoided. Such advice should be tempered by an observation that the passive role of a psychological panel member, and the frequently confusing nature of experiments, is hardly likely to encourage encoding of similar permanence to that of an individual who, for example, chooses to attend a parent's funeral.

The extent of reconstructive bias may also depend on the value given to the role of informant. If the research is only using the informant as a relatively cheap recording medium, it is obvious that reconstructive bias is one of the major sources of error; studies that encourage individuals to remember events that had little importance to them will be most at risk. Administrative records would be more effective. However, in studies where interpretation of past events are more central, reconstruction is less of a source of bias and more of an object of study.

Cherry and Rodgers (1979) were able to compare retrospections with longitudinal data. They concentrated on asking whether and at what time children had diseases. They concluded that if an experience was slight or ambiguous, retrospective reports are likely to be hearsay, guesswork, or grossly inaccurate. This emphasizes that one is unlikely to recall things that were not important enough to be memorized originally. Cherry and Rodgers also suggest that if the potentially disruptive effect of intervening similar events is acknowledged, "retrospective innaccuracies are not simply (if at all) a function of time, but also of the experiences of the respondent during the period" (p. 40). This suggests that allowances for forgetting should be made on the number of intervening events rather than on time.

Cherry and Rodgers further suggest that retrospections of attitudes are particularly liable to distortion. They also note that question design and informant motivation may explain some of the differences between retrospective and longitudinal studies. They also appreciate that "official" corroborative records are not clear of biases and that many steps are required in the generation of a date in retrospection. As a consequence, perhaps the best one should hope for in retrospection is an ordering of events recalled, rather than an accurate objective time judgement.

Why might life story methods be considered as a possible research method with all the problems described in this and previous sections? When the informants are being used purely for their memory, it will be because the costs of using administrative records is too high, or because the concepts under research are not recorded in such records. In this way, the retrospecctive bias itself may be something of interest; only if this is the case will the retrospective method be the best! There are many areas where life story methods will have some value as a source of restrospective information, if used with due caution. For example, one use would be for the elaboration of administrative material. The classes of contamination for which researchers should be prepared are listed in Figure 5.

Three main sources of error are identified in Figure 5. There are effects from memory, interviewing, and reconstruction. These are not necessarily independent. For example, changes in interviewing practices are the best

I. Memory
   A. Salience and encoding
   B. Intervening similar events
II. Interviewing
   A. Demand characteristics
   B. Lines of questioning
   C. Methods of recording
III. Reconstruction
   A. Narrative style
   B. Cognitive load
   C. Present construct and value system

Figure 5 Sources of error in life story studies.

way to control reconstruction bias. Each subheading in Figure 5 can be seen as a source of error that could be addressed in a hypothetical generalizability study. In lieu of such an ideal, this section suggests a series of strategies that can control such sources of error both within the life story method and by using external corroborative material.

Memory as a source of error summarizes the findings of Baddely (1979) and Cherry and Rodgers (1979). These suggest that, if retrospective questions are asked about events which were not at the time sufficiently salient for encoding, replies are likely to be wildly inaccurate. It is possible that accuracy requirements for individual recall are not so stringent as those for research purposes. Mothers could be remembering timings of children's diseases in sufficient detail for her own criteria. Perhaps by making clear, with questioning or a monthly event grid, the requirements for accuracy, respondents can be encouraged to use cross-referencing to improve the accuracy of their reconstructions. Of course, it is possible that the details are forgotten, but some control of the error should be gained by interviewing strategy.

Encoding and salience denote the source of error most obviously subject to improvement by the use of other methods of enquiry. Although official records are likely to be subject to some sources of error, these are likely to be independent from the sources of error in encoding. Whether the records that survive into archives are representative is only one of the sources of error. The process of encoding suggests a strategy for disengaging some reconstructive bias. It can be argued that the intensity of encoding is an indicator of values and attitudes held at that time; it is possible that if attitudes have changed, memories should be available that are less explicable to the respondent's reconstructions. Although this may require recall under hypnosis or Freudian free association, encouraging respondents to recall inexplicable memories might be a way to indicate past attitudes.

The second memory-related source of error is that of intervening similar events. Respondents find it difficult to distinguish particular occurrences of event types; they will attribute features of one event to another. It is probable that a conglomerate typical event is recalled rather than a specific event. It is possible that some control on this could come from interviewing strategy, not only by using cross-referencing but also searching out varieties in remembered events. With both styles of memory effects, it is only with external corroborative sources of information that appreciable reductions of error will be forthcoming. All types of life story retrospection will be, to unknown extents, subject to both sources of error.

There is a definitional problem with control of error in retrospection. What are the limits to what is to be seen as part of an event? Particular salient events, like marriages, may be remembered; but what degree of detail is associated with that memory? Further, the effect of rehearsal on such memories is probably to produce a continually changing narrative, which may be contrasted with less-rehearsed memories. One possible strategy to overcome the effect of intervening similar events is to concentrate on unique or salient events. These should be less susceptible to memory effects. This then poses the question of what is similar; all events have some overlap, which could lead to confusion. It is possible to see rehearsals as similar intervening events, in that they reactivate and reconstrue memories?

Sources of error primarily due to interviewing fall under three headings, each in an area where strategies are available to control error in a life story investigation. There is a strong influence of both the interviewer and the respondent's understanding of what are the demand characteristics of the task. Internal improvements in error control should come from developments of interviewer behaviour-shaping along the lines suggested by Cannell et al. (1981), coupled with increased use of tools, like the life story grid, that make accuracy requirements explicit.

A life story grid increases control by helping to draw together memories. On their own, memories are not able to provide the strict time judgement often demanded by survey retrospective questions, unless several orderings from different lines of questioning can be combined. The life story grid provides a tool for such convergence.

The understanding of the situation by both participants requires explicit planning and monitoring to increase control of the life story interview method. Brenner (1979) points out the paradox whereby interviewers are both seen as the source of error and also as the instigator of the relationship with the respondent. The interview as a social process is controllable by a skilled interviewer; awareness of the patterns of control could lead to a combination of control of error and increased rapport that would contradict the traditional paradox.

The use of corroborative material in combination with a life story interview will help to reduce the demands on accuracy, and enable the thrust of interviewing to be turned towards the illustrative insights that respondents can give. If the interview is used to give interpretation of other materials, it can be less demanding and more effective.

Lines of questioning can be a source of error in terms of directiveness. At low levels of directiveness, respondents may either be uncertain what is required or may construct fanciful elaborations. At higher levels of directiveness, questioning may produce guessing because of the desire of the respondent to produce an acceptable reply. Cannell et al. (1981) suggest that the former is more of a problem in retrospective reporting; however, these behaviour-shaping strategies are less applicable to the more diffuse retrospections of life story interviews. It is to be expected, nevertheless, that control of directiveness will effect levels of error; the relationship is likely to be a single-peaked function with an optimum at an intermediary level of directiveness.

The stages of recording are each a source of error. For textual information there can be both transcription and coding bias. There are routine ways of controlling such errors. Disentangling the bias of researcher on text coding is a little more difficult. This is possible if context-dependent parsing and coding systems can be made explicit and reproducible across research teams. The development of automatic coding systems may be the eventual way of achieving this explicit approach. The advantages of the researcher–interviewer doing "hot transcription" is that the ambiguities of retrospections in their recorded version become apparent in time for resolution in future sessions.

The final sources of error are those associated with the reconstructive aspects of retrospections. The first, narrative style, is specific to textual life stories. This is the way the respondent tends to tell the stories of his or her past. Some of these narratives will be influenced by previous retrospections on the same events, but even when the story is being told for the first time there will be differences due to the types of story scripts and themes (Schank and Abelson, 1977) held by the particular respondent.

Cognitive load is an allied problem; the task of retrospection, especially the estimation of dates, requires considerable effort. Without help, this cognitive load will produce errors; respondents will just not manage to get all their diffuse memories together in a satisfactory time to answer apparently simple retrospective questions. The use of recall aids like life story grids gives a controlled structure that could lessen the stress, although it may conversely increase stress by making requirements more explicit. Certainly the cognitive load can also be reduced by changing the life story product requirements so that precise dates are not required.

One method of controlling reconstructive bias may be to use story structure analysis procedures. In that story telling is a present activity, it might be possible to gauge the influence of present-day constructs and ideologies on reconstruction and make some alowance for them. The allowances would probably take two forms: first, trying to construe what original events might have been by controlling for the effects of constructs and values; and second, to make an allowance for the better recall on the cognitively organised and salient items.

As life story interviews are a qualitative method exposed to many sources of error, all possible controls should be used to increase the reliability of the data. Although some of the internal procedures may give some improvement, it is through external corroborative material, when available, that the full value of the method can be developed.

CONCLUSIONS

This review of life story interview interpretation concludes with several lines of development that may enable the method to become a more valuable research tool.

The array of methods for monitoring and controlling retrospective bias mentioned in the last section require detailed investigation. If research can estimate the effects of various aspects of the structuring process, strategies for allowing for such effects can be based on a firmer footing. A model of the memory for life cycle events, for example, the details of the processes involved in the retrospection of these events, would provide evidence that could be used to increase the quantitiative modelling available to monitor substantive differences in life stories.

Many disengagement procedures aim to change the emphasis in the applications of the construct system used on the past. Some of these strategies can be seen as similar to therapeutic procedures in personal construct theory. For example, the procedure whereby the respondent is asked to retell an episode, ignoring some previously regnant construct or theme, has many similarities to fixed role therapy. Generally, if one can learn about the retrospective construct system in general application, one may be able to allow for its effects in interpreting retrospections of particular events.

A second area where developments would be valuable is in the advice given as to how to use data analysis packages to process life story grids. It is possible, with varying degrees of difficulty, to use packages to construct the cross-sectional derivatives for each individual, transition matrices, and also moving variables; these were the type of operations Balan et al. (1969) found so difficult. However, methods of coding and the procedures for aggregation are specific for a particular application and package and are given below only in outline. These suggestions assume a file of changes has been created, where each record is a change in value of a particular variable for an individual at a position in time.

The operations for the extraction of cross-sections are done through sorting. The changes file needs sorting on individual and time; a subset is made of change records before or at the required time point. Then a cross-section is the last value for each variable for each individual. Transition matrices can be extracted from a sorted file of changes through lagged variable construction followed by tabulation. Moving variables, such as the number of children under 5, can be derived from a changes file by transformation and aggregation operations. Recent versions of packages such as SPSS (SPSS, 1983) and SAS (SAS Institute, 1982) have facilities for such complex file operations, but further developments are required before such procedures can be described as convenient.

The third line of development is in the application of interpretative systems of multidimensional scaling. The multifaceted nature of life story data requires an interpretative technique that can be used for an integrated representation of the substantive keys of the information. Association matrices can be derived from separate time orderings in differing areas to produce independent scalings of time. Such time scalings could also be produced from paired comparison judgements. These could be interpreted as maps of one-dimensional time in two or three dimensions. It may be possible to derive a technique that could constrain the positions of those points that are in common between these areas of life so that the spaces may be compared. The techniques for scaling can also be used to develop the understanding by the respondent of the past, as in de Marina's (1981) work. These attempt to make explicit reconstructive structures and also to recreate the structures apppropriate at particular points in time.

Finally, there is the possibility of computerized life story taking. Medical developments (see, e.g., Card and Lucas, 1981) suggest that history taking of the checklist type can easily be conducted by computer. It may be possible to envisage a system that requires a respondent that can type, in the same way as MAUD, but elicits structured life story text of a restricted type. This would elicit events, prompt for actors and settings, and seek out precursors of events in story structure style. If individuals and computers can share and use a common story structure, however limited, this could be used to prompt for the same kind of explanations, causes, and details that a human interviewer might request. However, in that such a system begins to demand machine understanding, it is hardly conceivable until the problems of computational semantics begin to be solved. It thus remains likely that comparative life story studies will continue to remain an arduous task for many years.

REFERENCES

Agar, M. (1980). Stories, background knowledge and themes: Problems in the analysis of life history narrative. *American Ethnologist, 7,* 223–239.

Baddeley, A. (1979). The limitations of Human Memory: Implications for the design of retrospective surveys. In Moss and Goldstein, *The Recall Method in Social Surveys.* London Institute of Education Studies No. 9.

Balan, J., Browning, H. L., and Jelin, E. (1973). *Men in a developing society: Geographic and social mobility in Monterey, Mexico.* Austin: University of Texas Press.

Balan, J., Browning, H. L., Jelin, E., and Litzler, L. (1969). A computerized approach to the processing and analysis of life histories obtained in sample surveys. *Behavioral Science, 14,* 105–120.

Balan, J., and Jelin, E. (1980). La structure sociale dans la biographie personal. *Cahiers internationaux de Sociologie, 69,* 264–284.

Barker, R. G. (1968). *Ecological Psychology Concepts and methods for studying the Environment of Human Behavior.* Stanford, CA: Stanford University Press.

Barnett, V. (ed.) (1981). *Interpreting multivariate data.* Chichester: Wiley.

Becker, H. S. (1970). The life history method. In N. K. Denzin (Ed.), *Sociological methods: A sourcebook.* London: Butterworths.

Bertaux, D. (1980). l'approche biographique. Sa validite methodologique, ses potentialities. *Cahiers Internationaux de Sociologie, 69,* 197–226.

Bertaux, D., and Bertaux-Wiame, I. (1981). Life stories in the bakers' trade. In D. Bertaud (Ed.), *Biography and Society.* London: Sage.

Bertaux, D. (Ed.) (1981). *Biography and society: The life history approach in the social sciences.* Sage Studies International Sociology 23.

Blau, P. M., and Duncan, O. D. (1967). *The American Occupational Structure.* New York: Wiley.

Boden, M. (1977). *Artificial intelligence and natural man.* Hassocks, Sussex: Harvester Press.

Bogdan, R., and Taylor, S. J. (1975). *Introduction to qualitative research methods: A phenomenologic approach to the social science.* New York: Wiley Interscience.

Breaux, J. J. (1977). Analysis of complex data: The description and analysis of dynamic behaviour in fire situations. Fire Research Unit. Univ of Surrey, presented BPS Ann Conf Exeter, April.

Brenner, M. (1979). Interviewing: Towards a sociology of a research instrument. Paper prepared for BSA/SSRC conference on Methodology and the Technique of Sociology, University of Lancaster, January.

Brenner, M. (1981). *Social method and social life.* London: Academic Press.

Bromley, D. B. (1977). *Personality description in ordinary language.* New York: Wiley.

Brown, J. M., and Sime, J. D. (1981). A methodology for accounts. In M. Brenner (Ed.), *Social method and social life.* London: Academic Press.

Cannell, C. F., Miler, P. V., and Oskenberg, L. (1981). Research on interviewing techniques. In K. F. Schnessler (Ed.), *Sociological methodology.* San Francisco: Jossey-Bass.

Card, W. L., and Lucas, R. W. (1981). Computer interrogation in medical practice. *International Journal of Man–Machine Studies, 14,* 49–57.

Carr-Hill, R. A., and MacDonald, K. I. (1973). Problems in the analysis of life histories. *Sociological Review Monograph, 19,* 57–95.

Carroll, J. D., and Chang, J. J. (1970). Analysis of individual differences in multidimensional scaling via an N-Way generalization of "Eckart-Young" decomposition. *Psychometrika, 35*(3), 283–319.

Casey, R. L., and Masuda, M., and Holmes, T. H. (1967). Quantitative study of recall of life events. *Journal of Psychosomatic Research, 11,* 239–247.

Catini, M. (1981). Social-life history as ritualized oral exchange. In D. Bertaux (Ed.), *Biography and Society*. London: Sage.

Chalasinski, J. (1981). The life records of the young generation of Polish peasants as a manifestation of contemporary culture. In D. Bertaux (Ed.), *Biography and society*. London: Sage.

Cherry, N., and Rodgers, B. (1979). Using Longitudinal study to assess the quality of retrospective data. In Moss and Goldstein (Eds.), *The recall method in social surveys*. London Inst. of Education Studies No. 9.

Cornfield, J., and Haenszel, W. (1960). Some aspects of retrospective studies. *Journal of Chronic Disease, 11,* 523–534.

Cronbach, L. J., Gleser, G. C., Nanda, H., and Rajaratnam, N. (1972). *The dependability of behavioral measurements: Theory of generalizability for scores and profiles.* New York: John Wiley.

Dailey, C. A. (1959). Graph theory in the analysis of personal documents. *Human Relations, 12*(1), 65–74.

Dailey, C. A. (1971). *Assessment of lives: Personality evaluation in a bureaucratic society.* San Francisco: Jossey-Bass.

De Marina, N. (1981). Personal Communication. Department of Psychology, Brunel University.

Denzin, N. K. (1981). The interactionist study of social organization: A note on method. In D. Bertaux (Ed.), *Biography and society.* London: Sage.

Elder, G. H. (1978). Family history and the life course. In T. Haraven (Ed.), *Transitions.* New York: Academic Press.

Endler, N. S., and Magnusson, D. (1974). Interactionism, trait psychology, psychodynamics, and situationi'sm. Psychological Laboratories, University of Stockholm, Sweden.

Farraday, A., and Plummer, K. (1979). Doing life histories. *The Sociological Review, 27*(4), 773–798.

Featherman, D. L. (1982). The life-span perspective in social science research. Forthcoming in five-year outlook on Science and Technology National Science Foundation, Washington, DC.

Ferrarotti, F. (1981). On the autonomy of the biographical method. In D. Bertaux (Ed.), *Biography and Society.* London: Sage.

Gilbert, G. N. (1980). Being interviewed: A role analysis. *Social Science Information, 19*(2), 227–236.

Gittins, D. (1979). Oral history, reliability and recollection. In Moss and Goldstein (Eds.), *The recall method in social surveys.* London Institute of Education Studies No. 9.

Goldstein, H. (1979). *The design and analysis of longitudinal studies.* London: Academic Press.

Goldthorpe, J. H. (1980). *Social mobility and class structure in modern Britain.* Oxford: Clarendon Press.

Goodnight, J. (1980). S.A.S. Presentation at Compstat 1980 Edinburgh, August.

Gottschalk, L., Kluckhorn, C., and Angell, R. (1945). *The use of personal documents in history, anthropology and sociology.* New York: Social Science Research Council.

Hedges, B. M. (1981). Investigating personal leisure histories. *Survey Methods Newsletter,* Autum, 3–4.

Herbst, P. G. (1970). *Behavioural worlds: The study of single cases.* London: Tavistock Publications.

Hindley, C. (1979). Problems of interviewing in obtaining retrospective information. In Moss and Goldstein (Eds.), *The recall method in social surveys.* London Institute of Education Studies No. 9.

Hockey, S., and Marriott, I. (1980). *Oxford concordance program: Users manual.* Oxford University Computing Service.

Humphreys, P. C. (1980). Decision aids: Aiding decisions. In L. Sjoeberg, T. Tyszka, and I. A. Wise (Eds.), *Decison analysis and decision processes.* Lund, Sweden: Doxa.

Humphreys, P. C., and Wishuda, A. (1981). Multi-Attribute Utility Decomposition MAUD. Brunel University, Deighton Analysis Unit: Technical report 79–9/2 Second Edition, April 1980.

Karweit, N. (1973). Storage and retrieval of life history data. *Social Science Research, 2,* 41–50.

Kelly, G. A. (1956). *The psychology of personal constructs.* New York: Norton.

Kohli, M. (1981). Biography: Account, text, method. In D. Bertaux (Ed.), *Biography and Society.* London: Sage.

Levy, P. (1981). On the relation between method and substance in psychology. *Bulletin of the BPS, 34,* 265–270.

Lewin, K. (1951). *Field theory in social science.* New York: Harper & Row.

MacIntyre, S. (1979). Some issues in the study of pregnancy careers. *Sociological Review, 27*(4), 755–771.

Mandler, J. M., and Johnson, N. S. (1977). Remembrance of things parsed: Story structure and recall. *Cognitive Psychology, 9,* 111–151.

Moss, L., and Goldstein, H. (Eds.). (1979). *The recall method in social surveys.* London: Institute of Education Studies No. 9

Newcombe, R. D., and Rutler, D. R. (1982). Ten reasons why attribution theory fails to account for ordinary explanations of behaviour. Unpublished paper, Social Psychology Research Unit, University of Kent at Canterbury.

Nicole, G. (1980). Données Autobiographiques et Praxis Culturelle. *Cahiers Internationaux de Sociologie, 69,* 291–304.

Pelto, P. J. (1970). *Anthropological research: The structure of inquiry.* New York: Harper & Row.

Perlman, J. (1974). Methodological notes on complex survey research involving life history data. Monograph 18. Institute of Urban and Regional Development University of California., Berkeley.

Poivier, J. P., and Clapier-Valladon. (1980). Le concept d'ethnobiographie et les recits de vie croises. *Cahiers Internationaux de Sociologie, 69,* 351–368.

Pool, IdeS, McIntosh, S., and Griffel, D. (1969). On the design of computer-based information systems. *Social Science Information, 8,* 69–118.

Read, M. W. (1980). Ethnographic field-notes and interview transcripts: Some preliminary observations on the computer management of text. University College Cardiff, Sociological Research Unit, Working Paper No. 8.

Richardson, H. P. (1977). Non-multidimensional scaling as an aid in the analysis of open-ended interview data. ABS Housing Research Unit, presented BPS Ann Conference, Exeter, April.

Rumelhart, D. E. (1975). Notes on a schema for stories. In D. G. Bobrow and A. Collins, (Eds.), *Representation and understanding: Studies in cognitive science.* New York: Academic Press.

Runyan, W. M. (1978). The life course as a theoretical orientation: Sequences of person–situation interaction. *Journal of Personality, 46,* 569–593.

Runyan, W. M. (1980). A stage–state analysis of the life course. *Journal of Personality and Social Psychology, 38*(6), 951–962.

Runyan, W. M. (1981). Why did Van Gogh cut off his ear? The problem of alternative explanations in Psychobiograph. *Journal of Personality and Social Psychology, 40*(6), 1070–1077.

SAS Institute. (1982). *SAS user's guide: Basics.* Cary, North Carolina: SAS Institute.

Schank, R. C., and Abelson, R. P. (1977). *Scripts, plans, goals and understanding: An inquiry into human knowledge structures.* Hillsdale, NJ: Lawrence Erlbaum/Halsted/Wiley.

SPSS. (1983). *SPSSx User's Guide.* New York: McGraw-Hill.

Stone, P. J., Dunphy, D. C., Smith, M: S., and Ogilvie, D. M. (1966). *The general inquirer: A computer approach to content analysis.* Cambridge, MA: MIT Press.

Synge, J. (1981). Cohort analysis in the planning and interpretation of research using life histories. In D. Bertaux (Ed.), *Biography and society.* London: Sage.

Tagg, S. K. (1974). The subjective meaning of rooms: Some analyses and investigations. In D. V. Canter and T. Lee (Eds.), *Psychology and the built environment.* London: Architectural Press.

Tagg, S. K. (1980). The analysis of repertory grids using the MDS(X) program series. Mimeo from PLU University of Edinburgh.

Tagg, S. K. (1981). The user interface of the data analysis package: Some lines of development. *International Journal Man-Machine Studies, 14,* 247–316.

Thomas, W. I., and Zaniecki, I. (1958). *The Polish peasant in Europe and America* (first published 1919–1921). New York: Dover.

Thompson, P. (1978). *The voice of the past: Oral history.* Oxford University Press.

Thorndyke, P. W. (1977). Cognitive structures in comprehension and memory of narrative discourse. *Cognitive Psychology, 9,* 77–110.

Visvalingam, M., and Rhind, D. W. (1976). Compaction of the 1971 UK Census Data. *Computer Applications in Geography,* 3(3–4), 499–511.

Wall, W. D., and Williams, H. L. (1970). *Longitudinal studies and the social sciences.* Social Science Research Council Review. London: Heinemann.

Zarpati, Z. (1981). The methodological use of the life history approach in a Hungarian survey on mobility and urbanization. In D. Bertaux (Ed.), *Biography and Society.* London: Sage.

9

Inferring from Verbal Reports to Cognitive Processes

LISANNE BAINBRIDGE

INTRODUCTION

"Think aloud" verbal reports are frequently used to obtain information about cognitive processes during complex behaviour. This chapter, which is primarily methodological, describes techniques that are available to analyse these data. The first task is to develop the verbal material into a form for further analysis by inferring referents and connecting material. Because verbal data are too rich in detail for complete analysis, the next stage is to develop reliable categories for describing the material, relative to a particular empirical question. A description of the material in terms of these categories can be made from frequency counts of the categories. It is more complex to identify sequences of occurrence of statement types, which hopefully describe the programmes/routines underlying a particular cognitive process or the decisions determining the sequence of behaviour.

What can verbal reports tell us about how speakers think and the knowledge they have? This is obviously a very broad question, and the brief discussion here will concentrate on methodology. The examples are oriented to the analysis of data from operators in an industrial process control plant.

Recent commentators, particularly Nisbett and Wilson (1977), have shown that verbal reports may not be a valid description of mental processes. Indeed, there is no way in which the validity of a report of mental processes can be checked independently. There have been several types of reaction to Nisbett and Wilson's paper (including some discussion by Brown and Canters, Chapter 10 in this volume). White (1980) has criticised them on both theoretical and methodological grounds. Other writers, such as Smith and Miller (1978) and Bainbridge (1979), have emphasised that, as

ISBN 0-12-131580-0

verbal reports give interesting data, it is important to try to find the circumstances in which their validity is high. Problems with the validity of reports may arise because the underlying thought processes are not available to conscious access or are not verbal in form, so that the thoughts are distorted in translating from one medium to another. Ericsson and Simon (1980) have discussed the different types of verbal report that are required in different experiments and the types of data that may be available for verbal report. They suggest a general model for the way in which verbal reports may be generated and review the available data.

This chapter hurdles over the validity issues and instead concentrates on how verbal material can be analysed. At a minimum such an analysis will lead to hypotheses that can be investigated further by other methods. The assumption will be that verbal reports provide "strong" data that can be analysed in detail, although the full possibilities will not be explored here.

The question of what the speaker thinks and knows is obviously a broad one. The coverage must be very brief here. The methods so far available are still inadequate and incomplete; more detailed discussion is available in Bainbridge (1979). The methods used follow from those developed by Newell and Simon (reported in, e.g., 1972). They used the approach of asking someone to "think aloud" while doing a task. This gives verbal material that differs in syntax and type of content from the material obtained in interviews. This is illustrated in the following report fragments:

1. I shall have to cut (furnace) E off, it was the last to come on, what is it making by the way? E make stainless, oh that's a bit dicey, I shall not have to interfere with E then.
2. If a furnace is making stainless, it's in the reducing period, obviously it's silly, when the metal temperature and the furnace itself is at peak temperature, it's silly to cut that furnace off.

These two examples come from the same furnace operator, the first while he was doing the task, and the second during a lull in activity a few minutes later, which he filled by talking about his general control strategy to the investigator. Further data on this difference in verbal behaviour in different verbalizing tasks has been found by, e.g., Benjafield (1969). One infers that in an interview situation the verbal reports give better information on the content and interrelations in the speaker's knowledge, rather than on how this knowledge is used in a particular task, while verbal protocols collected from someone who is actually doing a task give information about the dynamics of the use of knowledge, but not about its full range. For further speculations on this see Bainbridge (1979, Tables 2 and 3).

As will be seen, natural language understanding and obtaining agreement between judges are the basic tools used in the data analysis. I have been fortunate to study industrial process control situations, in which the things that the speaker might be talking about are more or less constrained to the process plant and product, so that identifying the range of the speaker's referents is relatively simple. In an investigative interview with more wide-ranging referents, the problems of analysis are much greater. This problem is at its most intense in trying to understand schizophrenic language, which is well known to be difficult to interpret (see, e.g., Salzinger et al., 1970).

PREPARING THE MATERIAL

The first stage is to segment the verbal report into the basic analysable units. This can be done at two levels: dividing the material into a sequence of separate phrases and into groups of phrases. One then infers the referents in the phrases, the interconnections between them, and any missing material where possible.

Phrases

The continuous text is divided into phrases, using the analyst's natural language understanding. The following piece of report will be used in the examples. (The dots indicate pauses in the tape-recording.)

> C is on oxidation now that's something you can make an estimate for it's a quality so I must leave it alone . . . oxidation average length is one hour 30 minutes for C and started at time zero no it didn't it started at time 33 minutes how confusing of it so it's got nearly one and a half hours to run . . . I'd better check that oxidation for C one hour 30 minutes started 50 minutes ago so it's got 37 minutes to go . . .

Separated into phrases this text becomes:

1. C is on oxidation
2. now that's something you can make an estimate for
3. it's a quality
4. so I must leave it alone
5. oxidation average length is one hour 30 minutes on C
6. and started at time zero
7. no it didn't
8. it started at time 33 minutes
9. how confusing of it
10. so it's got nearly one and a half hours to run

11. I'd better check that
12. oxidation for C one hour 30 minutes
13. started 50 minutes ago
14. so it's got 37 minutes to go

Notes: in this section of protocol the controller is talking about a furnace called "C." Phrases 1–4 talk about general properties of the "oxidation" stage through which the furnace is going; and phrases 5–14 make an estimate of the time at which C will finish oxidising. Figure 1 shows graphically how these phrases are interrelated. The average length is given in a job aid booklet, and the time the stage started on the controller's display panel.

The division of the text into phrases (which might loosely be described as minimum grammatical units, though the language in such reports is often not at all well formed) is done by natural language understanding of judges. This can often be done by people who have no knowledge of the specialist content of the material. Because these judges are using unobservable processes to make the analysis, it is necessary to use several judges working independently and to measure the agreement between them, either by counting the percentage of occasions when they agree or by using a statistical technique to measure the concordance.

Combining Phrases into Groups

Two methods can be used for combining phrases into groups; both make use of the semantic content. The first approach is to identify the pronominal referents, as these indicate cross-references between phrases.

There are three ways of identifying pronominal referents. The most reliable can be used for identifying pronominal referents in a description of an ongoing task. It requires an independent record of the states of the environment during the task, from which the referents of such phrases as "it's at 35 now" can be identified. Another method involves going through the report afterwards with the speaker to check on the meaning (this can only be done if the verbal report is recorded in short segments and transcribed immediately). This may raise some problems as it allows an additional opportunity for the speaker to rationalise what he or she was doing, perhaps adding after-the-event material that the speaker was not thinking about at the time. The third method is to use judges' semantic knowledge of the task.

After the links between phrases provided by pronominal referents have been made, further groupings can be identified on the basis of judges' knowledge of what items go together in the task. The result of doing this for the material above is given in Figure 1. Because one judge is using his or her own semantic knowledge to make this analysis, many people trying

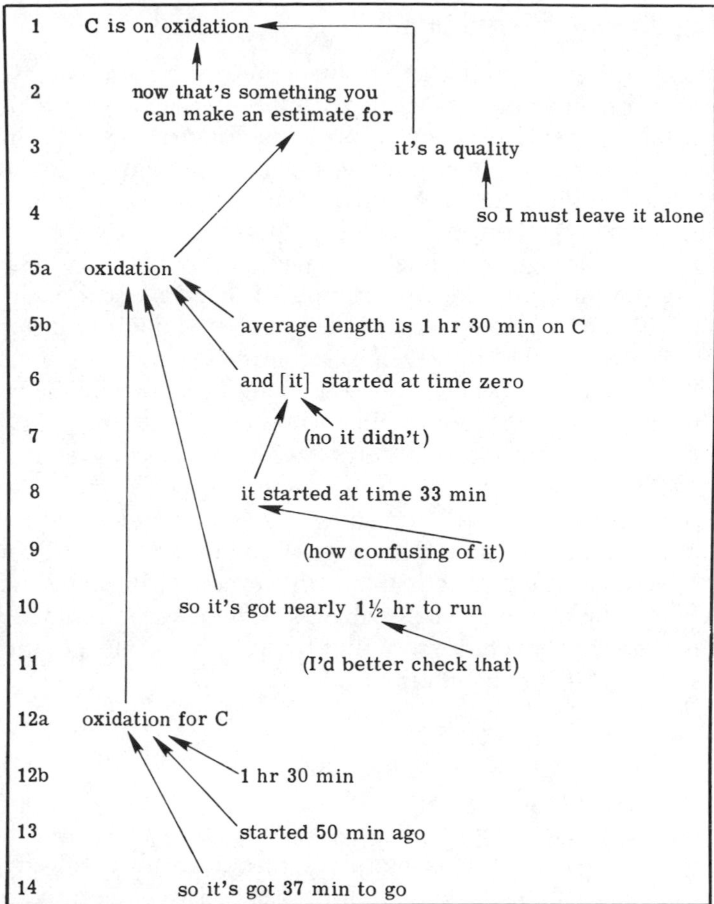

Figure 1 Graphic representation of the interrelationships of phrases 1–14.

this for the first time think that all they are managing to do is to attribute their own knowledge to the speaker. This is in fact unavoidable as it is how all language understanding is done. However, the method can at least be given reliability if this grouping is done by several judges and a concordance obtained.

One can also take advantage of this necessity by making an explicit record of one's own knowledge used in the analysis and using this as a record of the knowledge one is attributing to the speaker. For example, in Figure 1, lines 1–4 list properties of C furnace and lines 5–14 recount a method of calculation. These points, as shown in the notes above, are also what one has to mention to a person unfamiliar with the task before he or she can understand the report.

Inferring Connecting Material

As mentioned in the introduction, there are many reasons why verbal reports may be incomplete. One is that the speaker may not mention things that he or she thinks are obvious to the listener. These are inferred, both in natural language understanding and in the present type of analysis, by a knowledgeable receiver. Another reason for incompleteness is that thought is often faster than speech. It is not possible to reconstruct material that has passed through someone's mind so quickly that no clue about it has been given in the report. An example of this type of thought is the possibilities that may be reviewed and rejected very rapidly while problem solving. It can be possible, however, to reconstruct some types of intervening material when the speaker says something that must be the result of some thinking that he or she has not mentioned. For example, in lines 10 and 14 of the above example, the controller states the result of a calculation, so he must have made this calculation in some way. The report does not necessarily indicate how the intervening processes were carried out, only that they must have been done. However, in some tasks in which the same situation recurs frequently, as happens, for example, in many industrial process control tasks, it may be possible to combine what is said on different occasions to obtain a fuller account of what is happening. In the above example, lines 5–10 can be interpreted as

5	read STAGE LENGTH
6/8	read STAGE START TIME
10	TIME TO GO = X

(Lowercase indicates operations that are inferred, uppercase items that are explictly mentioned. This interpretation has already involved considerable inference about underlying processes; this will be discussed further below.)

When these lines are combined with lines 12–14, a complete picture of the processes between line 8 and line 10 can be inferred:

(5)	12	read STAGE LENGTH
(6/8)		read STAGE START TIME
		read time now
	13	TIME SO FAR = time now − start time = Y
(10)	14	TIME TO GO = stage length − time so far = X

Together with the results from the identification and grouping of phrases, these inferences give the material that is used in further analyses.

CONTENT ANALYSIS

There are many styles of analysis called content analysis. These typically involve counting frequencies of occurrence for categories of material. There are standard computer programmes that count word frequencies, which have been used in many studies (see, e.g., Hays, 1967; Dolezel and Bailey, 1969; also Tagg, Chapter 8 in this volume). This section will give brief examples of analyses using frequency counts on categories of material that are more complex than words.

Having prepared the material as described in the previous section, one can analyse the frequency of occurrence of particular categories: phrases, groups of phrases, or within phrases. These categories, their instances, and the frequency counts can be used as the origin for further analyses of category members or of the contexts in which they occur.

One of the main problems is to develop the categories to use, because they must be both relevant to the investigation and reliably usable by the judges who assign the material to them. Rasmussen and Jensen (1974) describe the iterative method that must be used in developing the categories. First, several judges independently develop a set of categories. Then they attempt to use each other's categorisation schemes. This both pools the inferences the judges have made about the important distinctions to make in analysing the material, and also tests whether different people can repeatably make the same allocation of material to the categories. If not, then an analysis using these categories cannot give reliable data, and the categories must be revised, again with the judges working independently during development, and coming together for assessment.

The categories developed, to be useful, must be ones that encourage further inferences about the material. For example, the distribution of frequencies may suggest emphases in the way the speaker thinks about the topic; or the categories can be used simply as a preliminary sort before further analyses. For example, the analyst could look further at all instances of the phrases that have been categorised as "comment on own behaviour" to see if the phrases have any common properties. If the categories are based on semantic or syntactic aspects of the reports, one might wish to count only the occurrence of overall concepts (e.g., birds) or to count the frequency of individual instances (e.g., robins vs. blackbirds). Different aspects of syntactic structure could be differentiated. For example, one might wish to distinguish between active and passive voice as reflecting different emphases by the speaker. Or one could differentiate between different types of conditional statements, for example, comparing "A therefore B" with "B because A." Whether one can do this depends not only on whether one is interested in this level of analysis but also on whether the concepts at this level occur with sufficient frequency to make a frequency count something more informative than a simple listing of categories used. The categories may also imply inferences about the types of cognitive process underlying them; for example, "statement of fact" and "comment on own behaviour" may imply different types of underlying cognitive activity. The categories are therefore always a function of particular empirical questions. If there is a set of categories that can be applied in many different circumstances, the categories are likely to be so general that the results of using them will not be very rich.

To give further examples of the categorising approach, we can look at the task of identifying characteristic structures within the phrases of reports made during an industrial process control task. We will look at categories at two levels: the types of referent words that it is useful to identify within the phrases, and the characteristic patterns in which these occur. For example, the phrase

the temperature is 45°

can be interpreted as a statement of the form

VARiable has VALue

(Capital letters indicate categories within phrases.) The phrase

the steam pressure is 101

can then be categorised as a statement of the same form. Having identified all statements of this type, one can then look at the categories further, e.g., finding out how many different instances of "VARiable" occur, and with what frequency, or concentrating on the "VALue" instances and seeing how accurately they are specified. One has to consider whether to categorise "there's steam temperature—it's rising" as a statement of the same type, or whether this would loose some of the information in the report, so this statement should be interpreted as

VARiable has CATEGorised VALue

This statement also gives an example of the way in which categorising retains information considered important for a particular analysis but loses other aspects; this phrase is also syntactially different from the previous instances, but it has been assumed that this is not relevant to the question of how VARiable VALues are processed by the speaker. The syntactic change rather than the semantic one might, of course, be the emphasis of an analysis being made for other purposes.

This simple statement type also occurs as a component in more complex ones, e.g.,

I'll try to run the temperature down to about 400°

ACTion gives VARiable has VALue

The statements of this type in the report give a sample of the speaker's knowledge of how changes in the outside world can be effected. Again, the way in which this is expressed may give useful information. The speaker can also give information about his or her knowledge of the conditions under which certain effects occur, which indicate his or her knowledge of wider interactions in the plant behaviour:

We have to have 50° superheat before we can run it up

This could be described as

When VARiable has VALue then ACTion gives VARiable has VALue

or more simply, if one is not interested in distinguishing between different ways of expressing conditional knowledge, (e.g., to test whether they typically occur in different task contexts) as

ACTion given VARiable.

A collection of condition statements made by the speaker also gives a sample of his knowledge. In the process control task, it is interesting to ask what other event sequences in the plant the speaker might be able to think about by following through sequences of the knowledge of conditions on events that he has expressed. Unfortunately, there are two problems with this type of data. One is that, in the situation of thinking aloud while doing the task, one will only obtain a limited sample of the controller's knowledge, relative to the particular situations in the test period; so this corpus of the speaker's knowledge will be very incomplete. A fuller corpus may be obtained from interviews (see, e.g., Cuny, 1979). However, there is also a problem with this. Cooke (1965) found that a controller may be able to express some knowledge about a process, but his or her control actions may not reflect this knowledge. In other words, the speaker may make a statement about knowledge that is solely at an "intellectual" level, and also vice versa. Anyone analysing verbal reports must always keep this sort of proviso in mind.

These examples have been from the identification of categories of material within phrases. Similar methods can be used for studying categories of phrases, or of groups of phrases, though the categories are necessarily more general and therefore more care may be needed to ensure that they are unambiguous to judges. As an example, the phrases in Figure 1 might be categorised as follows (these categories are just given as an example and have not been properly tested for reliability as described above):

1. fact
2. strategy
3. fact
4. strategy
5. fact
6. fact
7. comment
8. fact
9. comment
10. prediction
11. strategy
12. fact
13. fact
14. prediction

Again, it may be useful to distinguish subcategories, depending on the questions one is interested in and the amount of data available. It might, e.g., be useful to distinguish between statements of fact about past and present, or between comments expressing general strategy compared with rules for behaviour at this particular time.

The categories used in describing groups of phrases have to be even more general, i.e., there may be an even more distant relationship between the actual material in the report and the way in which it is described. As an example, the explanatory notes given for the main example in this chapter are equivalent to a categorisation of types of activity in that piece of report. Rasmussen and Jensen (1974) and Umbers (1981) give examples of this type of analysis in maintenance and process control tasks.

SEQUENCES IN THE CONTENT

Rasmussen and Jensen (1974) use their analysis of groups of phrases into categories as a basis for studying sequences of activity to identify the speaker's general strategies. This can also be done at the level of sequences of individual phrases. The level of categorisation at which sequences in the material can be sought depends on the range of referents in the material. For example, in the fairly small "world" of controlling a simple process plant, the frequency of occurrence of very similar statements is sufficient to allow one to analyse the sequence of activity, phrase by phrase. Rasmussen and Jensen studied maintenance technicians. In each report the speaker was working on a different piece of equipment each time, and each time maintenance activities differed. Consequently, in this type of task the behaviour is not repeated at the level of individual phrases; to search for common properties of the behavior in these different situations, one must look at a more global level.

The most frequently used, fully specified, rigorous procedure for analysing sequences is to make a Markovian analysis, i.e., to find the probability of transition from one item to another. Unfortunately, this method gives a very limited description of the properties of a sequence. For example, one can make a Markovian analysis of the tune of "Three Blind Mice," obtaining a table of the probability of a note at one pitch being followed by a note at each of the other pitches in the tune. This is not, however, a very helpful description of the tune because "Three Blind Mice" is not a probabilistic sequence. It is exactly the same every time, and this important feature has completely disappeared in the analysis. Markovian analysis can be a useful preliminary technique to determine which transitions are most frequent and therefore are most likely to be rewarding to study further. However, if one prefers to assume that the people producing verbal reports are not acting in a random way, and that their reports reflect activity that is at least to some extent structured and repeatable (one may even wish to infer the goals that underlie this structure), then one would like to use techniques that increase the possibility of finding more determinate sequences in the behaviour. The techniques that will be described are also applicable to the analysis of sequences in nonverbal behaviour.

Sequences of Phrases

The sequence in which individual items are mentioned in the report can indicate the standard "routines" or "programmes" with which the speaker thinks about a particular topic. One can only reach any strong conclusions about this, however, if one has several examples of each type of behaviour. The reports are always incomplete at some level, and one may have several hypotheses about the processes intervening between two phrases. Unless one has other examples of the same behaviour, which constrain the number of hypotheses that can be used to account for them, such an analysis remains very speculative and unwieldy. For example, in the main example as analysed in the section on combining phrases into groups, it would be possible for phrases 8 and 10 to be linked by the following calculation:

stage end time = stage start time + stage lengh

time to go = stage end time − time now

The actual method that was used is indicated by phrase 13, which appears in another occurrence of the same behaviour. That example also makes it clear that in this sequence analysis one is working with "categorised" phrases, which have been identified as representing a particular type of general activity, rather than with the individual details of the language in which these activities were expressed.

The frequently occurring sequences identified in this way might be considered as cognitive programmes, and this is the main technique of workers who use verbal protocols as data when developing simulations for cognitive processes. There is a fairly extensive literature on this type of theory development, of which Newell and Simon (1972) is a classic example.

Sequences of Groups of Phrases

Identifying the sequence of groups of phrases is more difficult because one wants to infer what influences the speaker to move from one topic to another. One cannot take the speaker's word for it, for as Nisbett and Wilson (1977) have shown, speakers do not necessarily have good access to this type of information about their behaviour.

To do this analysis one therefore needs a record of the earlier verbal report because previous items discussed (if taken as reflecting the speaker's thoughts) can affect the choice of later behaviour. A record of the environment is also needed because changes in this may influence what is the most appropriate item for the speaker to consider next. Again, making a record of the environment and its changes is relatively simple in a small "world" such as a simple process control task, which may be monitored in full during the time period that the controller is thinking aloud. It may be much more difficult, or impossible, in interview situations with a wide range of possible referents, and so analyses of this type of material must be much more speculative.

To do this analysis one identifies the instances of transitions from one type of behaviour to others, e.g., behaviour A may be followed by behaviour B or by behaviour C. This can be identified from the Markov analysis. One then looks at the whole context of the speaker's behaviour and the environment to see whether any dimension consistently has one value when A is followed by B and another when A is followed by C. If so, then one infers that the value of this dimension determines the behaviour sequence at this point.

The example given here again comes from a process control task. The speaker frequently made remarks such as "it's above now," "it's below," and the problem was to identify what dimension of the process he was using to make this judgement, i.e., on what dimension did the values determine whether he used behaviour X (judge "below") or behaviour Y (judge "above"). There were two main candidates for the basis of his judgements: a display that showed the total power being used at the time, and a display showing the discrepancy between present power usage and target power usage. Table 1 shows the distribution of judgements at different levels of the total power display; Table 2 shows the distribution of judgements at different levels of the discrepancy meter. It is clear that the use of the judgements correlates with the discrepancy meter reading and

Table 1
FREQUENCY OF ASSESSMENT AT DIFFERENT TOTAL POWER VALUES

Total power	Above	Alright	Below	
31–40		1	3	
41–50	2	2	2	
				comparison value
51–60	2	3	1	
61–70	2			
71–80			1	

not with the total power display, so the speaker is assumed to be using the discrepancy meter reading in making his judgements.

Note that this example does not come from the analysis of sequences of groups of phrases, but here the technique has been used to identify pronominal referents. This illustrates clearly that most of the techniques used in analysing verbal reports can be used to study any level in the organisation of the material.

Methods of identifying the sequence of sections of the verbal report can be used in a specific way to identify the speaker's decision determinants and make inferences about his working memory (see, e.g., Bainbridge, 1975), or in a more general way to identify the speaker's overall strategy (see, e.g., Rasmussen and Jensen, 1974).

Table 2
FREQUENCY OF ASSESSMENTS AND DISCREPANCY METER READINGS

Discrepancy	Above	Alright	Below
41–50			1
31–40			
21–30			
11–20			3
6–10		3	2
1–5		2	
1–5	1	1	
6–10	1		
11–20	2		
21–30			
31–40	1		
41–50	1		

CONCLUSION

Papers that discuss the difficulties of collecting verbal reports and the distortions they may contain have been referred to in the Introduction. This methodological review takes an optimistic approach, even though analysing verbal reports is not easy, nor are there many time-saving techniques that can be applied.

The choice of complex behaviour is influenced not only by immediate circumstances but also by planning in relation to the predicted future or by reference to similar past events. It is difficult or impossible to get sufficient evidence from observed nonverbal behaviour to suggest or constrain hypotheses about such cognitive activities. As a consequence, we know very little about the processes underlying complex behaviour. Verbal report analysis is currently one of the richest ways of investigating the nature of behaviour that is a function of either past or future. The methods described here make explicit the flexible analytic techniques that can be used.

REFERENCES

Bainbridge, L. (1975). The representation of working storage and its use in the organisation of behaviour. In W. T. Singleton and P. Spurgeon (Eds.), *Measurement of Human Resources.* London: Taylor & Francis.

Bainbridge, L. (1979). Verbal reports as evidence of the process operator's knowledge. *International Journal Man–Machine Studies, 11,* 411–436. Reprinted in E. H. Mamdani and B. R. Gaines, *Fuzzy Reasoning and its Applications.* Academic Press, London, 1981.

Benjafield, J. (1969). Evidence that 'thinking aloud' constitutes an externalisation of inner speech. *Psychonometric Science, 15,* 83–84.

Cooke, J. E. (1965). Human decisions in the control of a slow response system. Unpublished doctorate in philosophy thesis. University of Oxford.

Cuny, X. (1979). Different levels of analysing process control tasks. *Ergonomics, 22,* 415–425.

Dolezel, L., and Bailey, R. W. (Eds.). (1969). *Statistics and Style.* Elsevier, New York.

Ericsson, K. A., and Simon, H. A. (1980). Verbal reports as data. *Psychological Review, 87,* 215–251.

Hays, D. G. (1967). *Introduction to Computational Linguistics.* Elsevier, New York.

Newell, A., and Simon H. A. (1972). *Human Problem Solving.* Prentice-Hall, Englewood Cliffs, N.J.

Nisbett, R. E., and Wilson, T. D. (1977). Telling more than we can know: Verbal reports on mental processes. *Psychological Review, 84,* 231–259.

Rasmussen, J., and Jensen, Aa. (1974). Mental procedures in real-life tasks: A case study of electronic trouble shooting. *Ergonomics, 17,* 293–307.

Salzinger, K., Portnoy, S., Pisoni, D. B., and Feldman, R. S. (1970). The immediacy hypothesis and response produced stimuli in schizophrenic speech. *Journal of Abnormal Psychology, 76,* 258–264.

Smith, E. R., and Miller, F. D. (1978). Limits on perception of cognitive processes: A reply to Nisbett and Wilson. *Psychological Review, 85,* 355–362.

Umbers, I. G. (1981). A study of control skills in an industrial task, and in a simulation, using the verbal protocol technique. *Ergonomics, 24,* 275–293.

White, P. (1980). Limitations on verbal reports of internal events: A refutation of Nisbett and Wilson and of Bem. *Psychological Review, 87,* 105–112.

10

The Uses of Explanation in the Research Interview

JENNIFER BROWN AND DAVID CANTER*

REASONS FOR USING EXPLANATIONS AS EMPIRICAL DATA

In order to make daily life comprehensible, people give explanations to one another. They will describe, for example, how things work, what justifies a particular action, who influenced a specific event, or why certain incidents occurred. Explanations are invoked to make something more intelligible. Thus, the objectives of the explanations people give are similar to those of the researcher. There would, therefore, appear to be value in a collaborative effort between social scientists and the subjects of research in attempting to gain a better understanding of human activities and experience. This chapter, then, examines the rationale for using explanations as the *data base* in the investigation of psychological phenomena.

There are both conceptual and methodological implications of adopting explanations as a primary data base. In order to facilitate an appreciation of these implications, the chapter outlines the purposes of explanations, discusses the mediating influences of the eliciting circumstance, examines the role of the explainer, and charts the goals of the research investigator. We then illustrate the uses of explanations from empirical examples of data collected for two research projects dealing with the study people's behaviour when buying a house or being involved in a fire.

In defining a context for the rendering, authentication, and interpretative power of explanations, a framework is offered (in the main, following Bromley 1977) that draws upon a legal model of inquiry. It is argued that

*We are grateful to Professor Bromley for his helpful comments on an earlier version of this chapter.

ISBN 0-12-131580-0

psychology and the law have a common interest in explanations, and the former can benefit from the methods and ruminations of the latter. Such a "quasi-judicial" model accommodates the collection, veracity, and interpretation of ordinary explanations better than the more orthodox model based on the laboratory experimental tradition.

The choice of methods for collecting and analysing data depend not only on the topic but also goals of the research and the scale of the investigation. These choices themselves are influenced by the orientation of the investigators. In Chapter 5 this volume, Canter, Brown, and Groat make reference to the constraints placed on research investigations by the adoption of particular methods. In some instances the choices of methods are made for the ease of the researcher and to enable him or her to use ready-made statistical packages for analysis.

We are advocating an intensive research design that focuses on the experiences of the primary participants. This requires procedures such as the multiple sorting task (described in Chapter 5), which help the respondent to convey her or his story. As outlined, the multiple sorting procedure enables modes of categorization and conceptual differentiations to be examined. The present chapter elaborates the broader context, in which a sorting task may well figure as a component part, that of eliciting explanations of a person's actions in a particular way.

If we turn to the various research studies that make use of the explanations given by people of their lives and experiences, a recurring theme is the desire by the researchers to provide a full and elaborate account of the particular events they are investigating. This is mirrored by the sense of dissatisfaction with the impoverished view that more traditional methods of research provide of human experiences.

More specifically, six different research goals can be discerned from the range of studies adopting explanations as their primary data base: each goal is now considered.

Building Theory

In their longitudinal study of child-rearing practices, the Newsons (1976) wanted to adopt a hypothesis-generating strategy since they were sceptical about drawing conclusions from laboratory studies, given the richness of their experiences encountering mothers in their own homes. They wished their study to develop within an ecological framework (cf. Barker, 1968) and believed that fashioning an interview in which respondents could "bring out the detail and variety, the reservations and ambiguities, the principles and the expedient exceptions to principles which they believed to be implicit to the process of child-readring" (p. 31) was the only viable way to achieve their aims. They looked to the explanations of the mothers themselves as a basis for fashioning their own theory of childrearing.

Another example of a study in which the participants gave reasons for their actions that were used as the basis for a theory explaining those actions is a study of members of the National Front (Fielding, 1982). The research aim was to *understand* why National Front members believed what they do and to examine the fit between political beliefs and their actions as an extreme right-wing nationalist party. In particular, the research aimed to outline National Front ideology as expounded by the leaders, show how these are interpreted by members and then enacted. Again, an evolutionary strategy was employed by developing a relationship between the investigator and his or her primary contacts, which enabled the latter to provide contemporary, anticipatory, as well as retrospective accounts of and justifications for action.

Making Policy

A second objective for the use of naturally occurring explanations is to shape and influence policy- and decision-making. Three ways can be identified in which the explanations of ordinary people can be policy oriented.

A first example is drawn from the Newsons' study. They indicated that if high credence is placed on the respondents' comments, then it becomes difficult to dismiss particular instances because they do not conform to what is generally acceptable. If the explanation makes sense to the respondent, then relevant actions must take their comments into account. In effect, the explanations people give extend the range of the researchers' frame of reference.

Second, the researcher may become, directly, an agent for change because she or he has a special relationship to the issues under study. For example, Toch (1972) prefaced his book *Violent Men,* which is an insightful account of violent offenders, by stating "we hoped that we could supply diagnostic information that would ultimately lead to better management and more effective treatment of these prisoners in state penitentiaries" (p. 9). In a further example, Rhona and Robert Rapoport (1971), in a detailed account of the experiences of five dual-career families, hoped to create a public awareness for this particular social structure and the trials and tribulations as well as successes of having a nontraditional family structure.

Third, the emphasis that people use can comment in an insightful way on their experiences and may act as a loudspeaker to make professionals more aware of their clients as people with valid opinions. Thus, Oakley (1980) solicited accounts from the inmates of Salvation Army hostels and found that there were discrepancies between the institution's understanding of why the men were in those hostels and the reasons the men themselves gave. The research was able to have an input into both the policy of the Salvation Army regarding long- and short-stay accommodations and into the architectural design brief for the building of new hostels.

Amplifying Understanding

Typically, a structured questionnaire is used to establish what people have experienced, then the investigator attempts to explain the relationships found in the questionnaire responses. As the history of the social sciences shows, this may often be a powerful research procedure. However, enabling the respondent to provide his or her own account of why events occurred may often bring to light aspects that may remain invisible when looked at in a traditional way, as Marsh et al. (1978) illustrate, for instance, when studying football hooliganism.

An example of the comparisons of response to a self-completion questionnaire and an open-ended interview is given from a study of participant's perceptions of the papal visit to Great Britain in May–June 1982.[1] The research strategy called upon both face-to-face interviews and self-completion questionnaires. It was evident that people were able to expand their explanations of why they had come and of their religious beliefs in the interview but felt severely restricted by the particular questionnaire used. Out of 120 respondents, 46 (40%) made specific reference to the problem of answering the questions and to being circumscribed by the questionnaire format, emphasising that matters of religious faith and belief are particularly susceptible to explanation and qualification. While the questionnaire was able to collect some important background data, the open-ended interview greatly facilitated the task of explaining the sometimes opaque feeling about religious faith.

Providing a Multidimensional Perspective

Some topic areas are so involved, and a full and valid account of why certain things occur within them is so complex, that they can only be readily explored by allowing the people who have direct experience of them to explain them in their own terms. Pahl and Pahl (1971) illustrate this in their study of managers and their wives.

They conducted informal interviews with managers and their wives,

[1]This study, funded by the Nuffield Foundation and the University of Surrey, was undertaken by Michael Hornsby Smith, Jennifer Brown, Betsy Cordingley, Joan O'Bryne, and Anne Scurfield.

which enabled them to explore many themes crossing traditional social science boundaries. They concluded by remarking that their informants were not only highly articulate, highly intelligent, and enjoyed thinking about their situations, but also they were able to comment on many more topics and in greater detail about the relationship between those topics as a consequence of the open-ended, face-to-face interview technique than might have been the case with a more constrained research procedure.

A related point has been expressed by Kaplan (1964) and also by Bromley (1977) who argue that examination of sequences of related events provides insights that may not be evident from scrutiny of single episodes. Kaplan describes it thus: "Each element of what is being described shines as it were with light reflected from all the other elements—it is because they come to a common focus that together they throw light on what is being explained" (p. 329).

Dealing with Innovatory Subject Matter and Target Populations

In the spirit of taking people's explanations seriously, the topics for investigation tend to be more realistic, specific, or sensitive than the more general issues explored through questionnaire surveys or structured interviews. Thus, there have been a number of detailed studies of prisoners providing accounts of their experiences (Cohen and Taylor, 1972; Toch, 1972; Tutt, 1976). In addition, by concentrating on the explanations a person has to give, often in a face-to-face setting, disadvantaged respondent groups may be helped to articulate their views—as with the Salvation Army Hostel users in Oakley's (1980) study.

Coping with the Failure of Traditional Procedures

Another reason for making recourse to the method of intensive interviews to elicit explanations may be the failure of other procedures. For example, Bromley (1977) aimed to develop a rational and objective method for the analysis of complex adult personality descriptions. He argues that the positivist tradition has clearly failed to give an adequate description and explanation of personality, which is why he embarked "on the difficult and uncertain enterprise of investigating personality descriptions in ordinary language" (p. 45).

The message from all these examples is the recognition that people who volunteer as informants in research investigations have more to offer than the researcher may sometimes care to admit or be able to accommodate within their research procedures.

ERROR AND BIAS

Recognising and desiring to release the wealth of understanding locked in the informant's head requires a commitment of time and resources in collecting, analysing, and interpreting fascinating, revealing, but often unwieldy, data. Repertory grid and multiple sorting procedures represent one kind of compromise that allows the respondent some flexibility in conveying his or her set of personal meanings. Carefully prepared questionnaires (structured or open-ended) may also, in some circumstances, be appropriate. Collecting explanations is another.

The assumptions underlying this commitment to the use of the respondent's own explanations are twofold. First, the respondent is in the best position to provide an accurate account of the events under investigation, and second, the respondent's own account provides one of the best explanations of those events. But this raises the question of the acceptability of the explanation, its authenticity, and possible sources of bias and error in both its giving and receipt—in other words, methodological considerations of data collection and analysis, reliability, and validity.

Criticisms that are levelled at the use of people's own accounts suggest that they fail to render authentic accounts through lack of knowledge of what they are doing (Shotter, 1977); by providing the most plausible explanation for their behaviour when it is demonstrably false (Nisbett and Wilson, 1977); by lack awareness of subtle nonverbal behaviours (Argyle, 1978); or by the biases that appear to be endemic in judgements under uncertainty (Kahneman et al., 1982).

In a discussion of some of these claims, Bowers (1981) marshalls evidence to show that Nisbett and Wilson are mistaken when they say that if people are right it is more often by good luck than good judgement and that they have no introspective access to the determinents of their behaviour. Indeed, Marsh et al. (1976) go further and claim "everything we can do can be redone in talk" (p. 21). Certainly, investigators do not have privileged access to people's feelings, motives, or intentions without first listening to their personal disclosures. Armistead (1974) makes the point that investigators are even less likely to find the content of these feelings, motives, or intentions by using more orthodox procedures such as questionnaires or experiments. Certainly by the use of explanations, events may be reconstructed to answer questions that informants may not have conscious awareness of, or provide an overview of an experience beyond the knowledge of any one participant. This will be illustrated by reference to two empirical studies with which we have been involved.

By using explanations as a data source, it is not essential that they be taken as the only valid account of why something has occurred. Neither is it essential that the explanations be taken completely at face value. There may be "unintentional" explanations within an account a person gives, or the account itself may suggest an explanation to the researcher that can be corrobroated in other ways.

Clearly, such challenges to authenticity must be taken seriously and the interview procedure developed so as to minimise them. There are certainly a number of psychologists who question the power of these challenges.

Some light is thrown on one approach to corroboration by Lloyd-Bostock (1979, 1982). She discusses the problems of error and bias in attributions of responsibility and the practical as well as theoretical implications this has for the area of tort law. She suggests that adequate explanation arises from both its *context* and *purpose.* In law, she argues, responsibility judgements are made within an elaborate framework of definition that not only influence the level of response but are tied to consequence. Consequently, legal rules sometimes prescribe the response level so that classification according to contextual level leads automatically to a responsibility judgement (e.g. manslaughter, murder or justifiable homicide).

Thus, the context in which an explanation is given is an important basis for evaluating the authenticity of that exploration. If the explanation seems inappropriate to the context, as when self-defense is used to justify an attack in a situation that did not appear to be threatening, then the validity of the explanation may be questioned. But this implies, further, that the context for the explanation and the role of the person given the explanation have some particular properties to them, which carry direct consequences for the explanations given.

ROLE AND CONTEXT

Gergen and Gergen (1982) argue that reasons for choice of one type of explanation over another are usually given in terms of preference, parsimony, internal coherence, aesthetics, or intelligibility, but they do not find these reasons very helpful or convincing. It is more fruitful to recognise that competing explanations may be accounted for by reference to mediating (contextual and personal) infleuences. These influences may be defined in psychological terms as the role of the explainer, role of the investigator, and style of interaction.

Role of Explainer

It has been pointed out that if people are asked for an explanation of their actions, they may and probably will provide different versions when

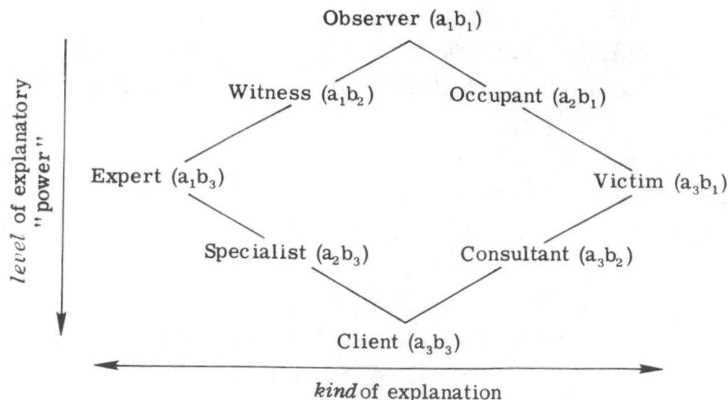

Figure 1 Eight types of explainer. The pairs of letters with subscripts refer to the relationship to the phenomena being explained.

a. Degree of involvement
1. Incidental
2. Social
3. Personal

b. Amount of expertise
1. Publicly available
2. Special to situation
3. Special to role

(Taken from Canter and Brown, 1982.)

giving that account to policemen, journalists, or confessors. (Canter and Brown, 1981; Bromley, 1977).

Rather than a weakness, this can be a strength in that a taxonomy of explanatory roles can be developed and harnessed to particular research issues. Canter and Brown (1981) define eight types of explainer by two axes (as shown in Figure 1)—level of explanatory power and kind of explanation—and further define the types by degree of involvement and amount of expertise. It was argued that a person fulfilling one of these roles was likely to call upon a particular class of explanation because she or he has different degrees of involvement with the event (e.g., as a participant or observer) and expertise available to bring to bear on his or her observations. Accordingly, in collecting explanations, differing roles of the informant vis à vis the particular events would be expected to provide a multi-perspective set of accounts. The task for the research is to place these into a coherent explanatory framework.

Role of Investigator

The role of the scientific investigator seeking the explanation might also be expected to exert some mediatory influence. If we fit her or his role into the framework presented above, then the same dimensions that characterise the role of the ordinary explainer can also be used for the scientific explainer. The equivalent social science mode of ordinary explainer (labelled "victim" in Figure 1) would be participant-observer, while a laboratory-based investigation is equivalent to the role of "expert." The most comfortable role for the psychologist depends on the aims of the research. For those seeking to elicit ordinary explanations, the degree of involvement we advocate is social involvement special to the situation (termed "engaged spectator" by Harre and Secord, 1972). This enables a dialogue to take place between investigator and informant without the distance of an experimental approach or blurring of distinctions in participant observation.

Interactive Style

The manner in which the explanations are elicted might also be expected to affect the kind of information given. A typology of interview styles has been proposed by Massarik (1981) in which he specifies a set of dimensions: (1) style of exchange (mutuality–inequality, trust–distrust, acceptance–hostility, closeness–distance) and (2) level of information (specific–general, shared–exclusive). In an interview characterized by mutual hostility, such as between an unco-operative suspect and a detective, there may be attempts by the former to withhold information. On the other hand, the depth interview (equivalent to investigator as engaged spectator) is characterised by an elevated level of rapport, with the interviewer genuinely concerned with the interviewee as a person, while the interviewee reciprocates in terms of seeking clarification of the purposes of the interview and active participation in the process of gaining understanding. This constitutes a co-opting of the respondent in creatively contributing to the research, a style reiterated by researchers adopting the explanatory approach.

Ideally, then, for the purposes of the research interview the informant should have as much involvement and knowledge as possible, the investigator should adopt an intermediate level of involvement and degree of knowledge, and the interactive style should be that characterised by the depth interview. However, other permutations are possible, depending on the needs of the particular research investigation as other chapters in this book reveal.

A QUASI-JUDICIAL MODEL

A description of particular methods by which explanations are collected are beyond the scope of this chapter (the Rapoports, 1971, describe their method of dual interviewing; Toch, 1972, peer interviewing; Brown and

Sime, 1981, account interviewing; Bromley, 1977, case study methods; Fielding, 1981, participant observational techniques). Rather here it is intended to draw attention to the framework within which such methods can be assessed. Evidence is collected, selected, and presented according to rules, analogous to jurisprudence. The propositions and inferences are supported with corroborative testimony, and conclusions include reservations. As Bromley (1977) emphasises, what emerges is a basis for the equivalent of case law. As he states:

> A psychological "case-study" is a scientific account, in ordinary language, of an individual person in normal or problematical circumstances. These circumstances form a substantial episode (or group of related episodes) in that person's life. A psychological "life-history," by contrast is a comprehensive account of the person's tendencies and characteristics revealed through an analysis of the principal episodes making up that person's life (p. 162).

(Life histories are discussed by Tagg, Chapter 8 in this volume). Case studies are a reconstruction and interpretation based on the best available evidence—how and why a person did what he or she did at a particular time and circumstance.

Our main *assumptions* are that such accounts not only can be reconstructed from a person's own insights as well as other people's testimonies and additional corroborative evidence, but furthermore, by collecting explanations, they often contain more than the person may be consciously aware of. Information may be gleaned from them by the investigator, as Jonathan Sime (1980) did in estimating distances people travelled through a building on fire. This may well represent the most effective data base from which to derive the best possible account of the particular phenomena under investigation.

Bromley (1977) adopts the term "quasi-judicial" for a methodology based on legal rather than natural science principles. He outlines six requirements for such a method. We have developed this in Table 1 to suggest some legal equivalents.

These rules have to do with the design and conduct of the investigation (data collection) achievement of research goals (data analysis) and representation of the results (research reports). The methods of judicial inquiry may be drawn upon at all these stages.

The police, e.g., are required to obtain explanations from people about their whereabouts, actions, and motives. When questioning witnesses, they are subject to judges' rules (Williams, 1976). The officers must only put questions "as may be needed to make the statement coherent, intelligible and relevant to the material matters: he shall not prompt him" (p. 72). Further, a police witness statement should reflect the person's own words and not be translated into official vocabulary that "may give a misleading

Table 1
RULES FOR THE QUASI-JUDICIAL METHOD

Bromley's six rules	Legal equivalent
1. Investigator reports results truthfully	Testimony under oath
2. Aims and objectives of the investigation are stated explicitly	Formal charges are laid
3. Assessment of the achievement of aims and objectives	Presentation of evidence in court
4. Investigator is properly trained	Legal qualifications required to play formal role in court
5. The person is placed in his or her ecological (physical, cultural, social, symbolic) context	Extenuating/mitigating circumstances are considered
6. The account is written in good plain English	Case law/understandable to jury/as viewed by a reasonable person

impression of the genuiness of the statement" (p. 74). The role of the informant as witness may be expected to colour the conduct of the police interview, which would be rather different if the informant was suspected of a crime. Furthermore, when charging a suspect, if the formal procedure is not adopted, then the case is dismissed in court. Again, the various testimonies that are presented in court are subject to examination and have to be supported by corroborative evidence such as forensic or eye-witness accounts. For example, even a confession of guilt may not be accepted without corroboration.

A series of corroborative checks can be used to authenticate explanatory accounts in the manner of legal evidence. These have been developed in another paper (Brown and Sime, 1981). These checks were divided into those that dealt with the internal consistency of the explanatory account and with external corroboration of its validity. Underlying these checks are the stringency with which they are applied and the degree to which the explanations must mirror an external objective reality or subjective perceived reality. Trankell (1972) has described a formal procedure for analysing witness statements (termed "statement reality analysis"), which differentiates between subjective and objective reality. This is an analytical nonquantitative approach akin to the corroborative checks outlined in Table 2.

Once a set of explanations has been collected and corroborated, the task of providing a coherent account of them remains. This is often accomplished within a theoretical framework such as the role-rule models of Harré and Secord (1972) or Canter (1983) and presented to the scientific community. Levine (1974) likens the acceptance or rejection of a research

Table 2
CHECKS ON THE AUTHENTICITY OF AN ACCOUNT[a]

Criteria of objective/ subjective reality	Degree to which an account mirrors the objective reality or reflects the perceived reality
Criteria of internal consistency	Degree to which the account giver contradicts, corrects, or gives apparently logically inconsistent or paradoxical information
	Check through negotiation of information *during* the account gathering
	Check in terms of "logically adequate criteria" *after* account has been collected
Criteria of external corroboration	Degree to which the account may be matched against information relative to the event outside the immediate accounting situation
	Physical corroboration Similar to silent corroboration in forensic science; e.g., includes injury incurred in rape or, injury and damage to building, layout, and furnishings of house in a fire
	Comparative corroboration Secondary evidence used to check against independent accounts of some event or other sources; examples are artefacts, records (used in anthropological and historical research), estate agent circulars, press reports, coroner's report, official statistics
	Concordance corroboration Multiperspective analysis (as of fire) that determines degree of concordance between separate accounts by participants in the same event
	Expert corroboration Checks against expert opinion, e.g., when there is incomplete information; examples are estate agents, firemen, police, forensic scientists

[a]Adapted from Brown and Sime (1977).

investigation to the adversarial process of cross-examination, which is characteristic of the British and American legal systems. Accounts of ordinary explanations may be rejected if the sort of checks we advocate are not adhered to. For example, Angell (1945) rejected an account of the personality development of black youth in the urban South of America. Because no excerpts from personal documents were given, the interviewers' results were so intermixed with the authors' interpretations that no judgements could be made with respect to the validity of the interpretations.

VARIETIES OF EXPLANATION

Although there are many discussions in the literature on the nature of explanations and the varieties of them that exist (see, e.g., Antaki, 1981), for the purposes of illustration in relation to the research interview three kinds of explanations can be identified, describing an experience, ascribing agency, and attributing morality. The actual form an explanation takes varies, e.g., it may be an account of an accident or a habit, or a reference to norms. Underlying these is the notion of increasing complexity. Thus, descriptive explanations referred to by Kaplan (1964) as semantic are those that make the meanings of events or experiences clear in a simple and straight-forward sense. They are most likely to be factual accounts or provide background information (describing, e.g., the physical setting) from which clear inferences can be drawn.

Ascriptive explanations are identified by Antaki and Fielding (1981) as serving to ascribe *agency* to sequences of actions—define who is present or why events happen. Bromley (1977) makes a distinction between mentalistic and dispositional explanations. Mentalistic explanations refer to experiences of wants, needs, and feelings; dispositional explanations refer to regular or consistent patterns of behaviour, such as habits. These defintions overlaps to some extent with Gergen and Gergen's (1982) differentiation of empowered or enabling explanations, both having to do with the agency of action. They give the example of a neighbour running past your house early one morning. To explain this by reference to a habit is an empowered explanation, i.e., the neighbour's habit of daily running for the past 10 years empowers the action. If, on the other hand, the neighbour's running was a whim, it does not demand the action of running but merely facilitates or enables the action to occur. In other words, surrounding circumstances must be taken into account when providing an explanation.

The most complex forms of explanation are those called upon to justify action. These are explanations that typically seek mitigation or excuse, and they often involve the attribution of blame to self or others or the surrounding circumstances (Brewin, 1982). Morality explanations defend the propriety of behaviour; e.g., accidents are defined by Sutherland (1959) as unintended actions. Tedeschi and Reiss (1981) say these types of explanation are typically used in justification or excuse. Accidents occur when unforeseen circumstances or events happen to disrupt a person's behaviour, and accident explanations are often given in mitigation to try and nullify some consequence. Accidents may also be used as description, e.g., as in the coroner's verdict of accidental death.

Actions that may be impulse reaction to emotion or mood states are also used by way of excuse (Tedeschi and Reiss, 1981). Intense powerful emotions may be associated with strong reactions resulting in untoward outcomes that normally would not have taken place, e.g., fear resulting in manslaughter.

Tedeschi and Reiss (1981) reserve appeals to norms and rules as explanations to justify actions, e.g., using a stereotype to warrant racist or sexist behaviour, although Mixon (1974) shows they can be used descriptively to describe games, e.g., cricket (or in Mixon's example, baseball) is described by reference to its rules.

Mixon also refers to the Milgram obedience experiments and shows how reference to the norms and rules of conducting psychological research in laboratories can be used to explain (justify) the conforming subjects' apparent administration of lethal electric shocks.

Forms of explanation, then—be they habits, accidents or rules—may be used variously as description or justification.

SOME EMPIRICAL EXAMPLES

Describing an experience, ascribing agency, and attributing morality differ in their level of complexity and explanatory power and the same form of explanation, e.g., habit, accident, or whatever may be used in all of any of the three modes. In terms of a research design, the types of explanation sought obviously depend on the issue the researcher wishes to make intelligible.

By drawing upon the research we have been associated with, we will demonstrate the effectiveness of using people's own explanations of their experiences when buying a house or being involved in a fire.

It is perhaps worth emphasising a number of points that become clear when considering these empirical examples.

1. The experiences are not precipitated by research. That is, they exist independently of whether or not they are the subject of research, and people are merely recounting their feelings, actions, and behaviour. They often have to articulate these experiences in a series of exchanges with professionals, e.g., firemen, solicitors, the police, and estate agents. The informants to the research are not being asked anything new but rather are being placed in a special situation in which to recount their particular drama.

2. In seeking explanations of these behaviours, the research aim is not only to represent actions but understand them from the perspective of the primary participants, i.e., the person herself or himself. Such a research strategy reveals information and insights that probably would not be dis-

covered using different procedures; moreover, this type of research has the potential to integrate the explanations to yield a more complete picture than perhaps is available to any one particular participant.

3. Although the eliciting situation is one that aims to help the respondent give an account in his or her own words, there are clearly stated research objectives that provide an agenda for the information that is sought.

Descriptive Explanations

Our first detailed example is drawn from a series a related studies of people's behaviour during fires.[2] Sime (1980) identified the need to have an accurate indication of how people moved through a building when it is on fire. This is a question of some importance to the building regulations dealing with the time it should take to evacuate a building. It is central to knowing why some people manage to escape from buildings on fire and others, who do not, are found dead some distance from where they were last known to have been. Hitherto, the main criteria for building guidelines has been the time it takes people to move through exits of various widths.

Sime makes the point that not only do people find it difficult to estimate distances moved, but also previous research fails to take into account the physical layout of the building. Research by Pauls (1980) also had established discrepancies between estimated and actual times to evacuate buildings. However, most estimates are based on experimental simulations, and there have been few attempts to conduct research on people who have actually experienced a fire. The research problem, then, is to give a more accurate account of the distances over which people moved and the rate of movement, with a view towards potential applications to the framing of fire regulations. Since people find it difficult to give accurate distance estimates, the information was constructed from accounts of fire victims' explanations of their behaviour.

Accordingly, Sime analysed 33 police witness statements of the survivors of a hotel fire that took place in Brighton on January 6th, 1976. Since there were five fatalities in the fire and arson was suspected, the witness statements were released to the research team after the court case. They were subject to corroborative checks and legal cross-examination. At the time the fire broke out 38 people were present in the hotel, and it was estimated by the fire brigade that it took only 6 minutes after the fire had been discovered for the flames to have enveloped the central staircase. By

[2]Study sponsored by the Fire Research Station and undertaken by David Canter, John Breaux and, Jonathon Sime.

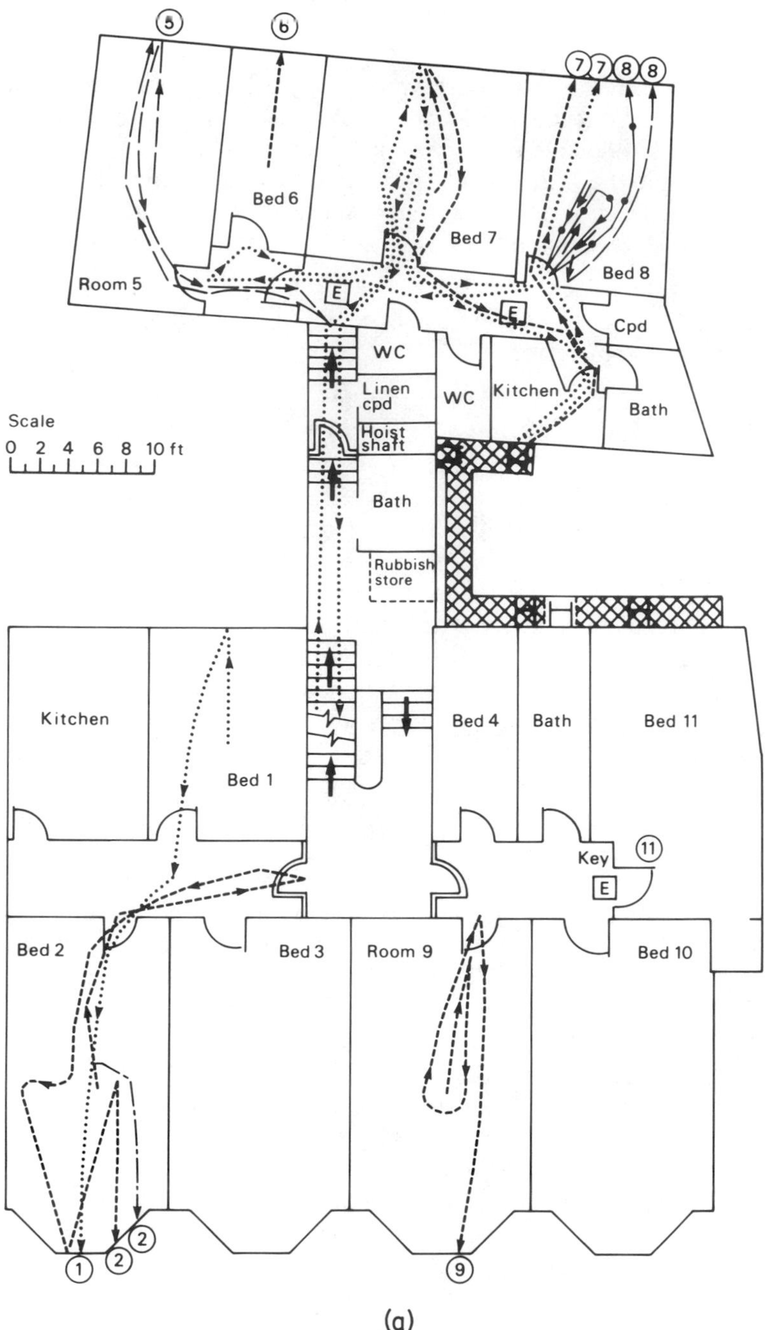

Figure 2 Floor plans of the hotel in Brighton, showing the movements of the residents as they try to escape the fire on (a) the first floor, (b) the second floor, (c) the third floor, and (d) the fourth floor.

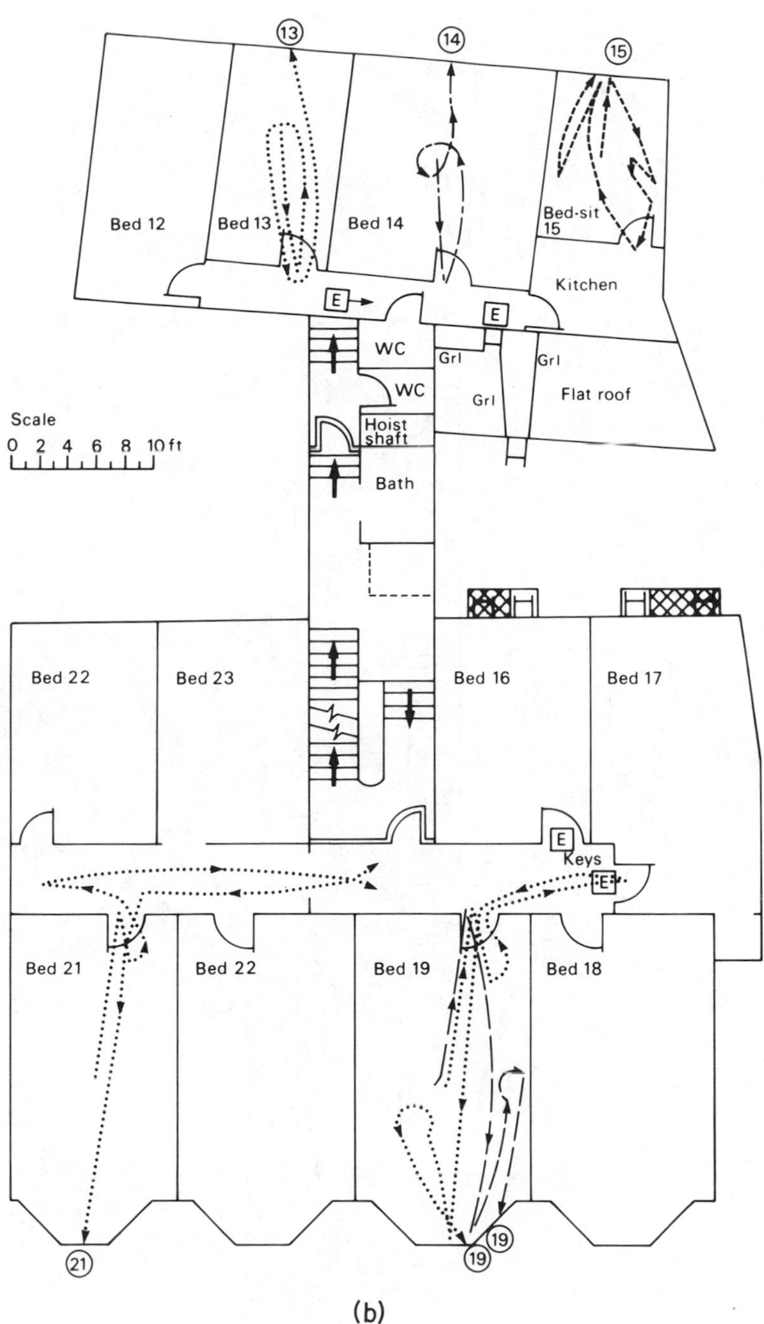

13
14
15
Bed 12
Bed 13
Bed 14
Bed-sit 15
Kitchen
E
E
WC
WC
Grl
Grl
Grl
Flat roof
Hoist shaft
Bath
Scale
0 2 4 6 8 10 ft
Bed 22
Bed 23
Bed 16
Bed 17
E
Keys
E
Bed 21
Bed 22
Bed 19
Bed 18
21
19
19

(b)

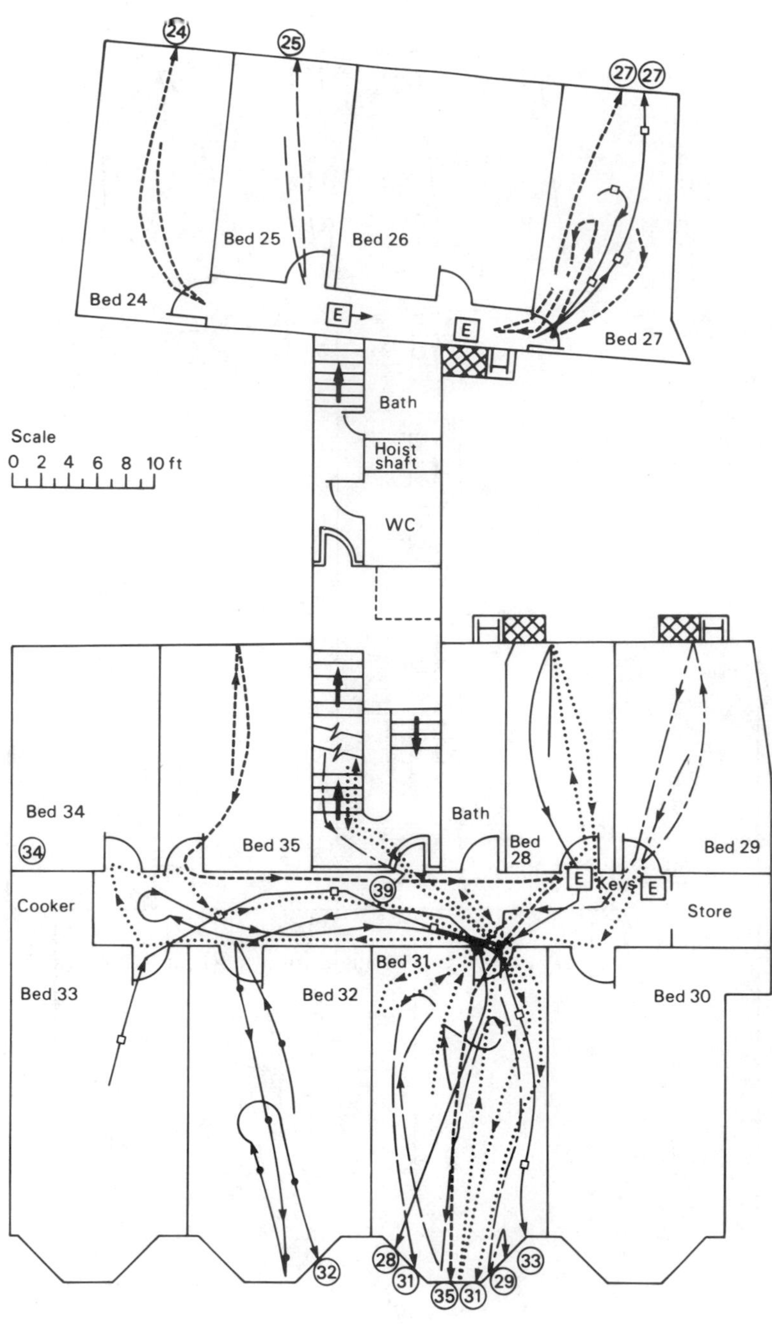

24
25
27
27
Bed 25
Bed 26
Bed 24
E
E
Bed 27
Bath
Scale
0 2 4 6 8 10 ft
Hoist shaft
WC
Bed 34
34
Bed 35
Bath
Bed 28
Bed 29
Cooker
39
E
Keys
E
Store
Bed 31
Bed 33
Bed 32
Bed 30
32
28
31
35
31
29
33

(c)

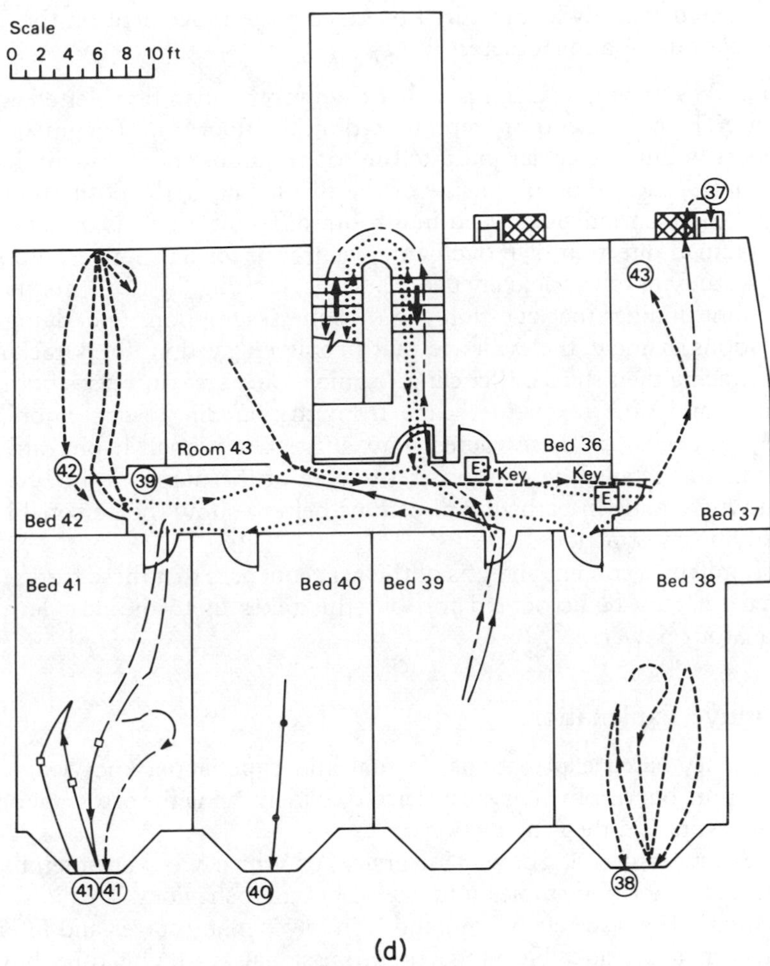

(d)

the time most of the residents became aware of the fire, about 2 A.M., it was spreading rapidly through the central core of the building. Sime adopted the following procedure to estimate the distance people moved to escape safely from the hotel; the information was obtained from the police witness statements.

1. A record was made for each individual's action sequences relative to the location from his or her room to the point of escape.
2. The movement was traced onto a scale plan of the building (⅛ inch to the foot).

3. The distance was measured by tracing the movement on the scale plan using a mapometer.

Each of 33 survivors was in his or her own room when first alerted about the fire. The movements are represented on the floor plans (Figure 2). The numbers within the circles indicate the room number of a resident, his or her point of escape, or in the case of the five fatalities, the position of the body. Where an individual died in a room different from his or her own, the assumed direction of movement was traced for illustrative purposes.

This study of routes actually taken and distance highlighted a number of important findings that question some of the assumptions underlying fire regulations, namely, the evidence that people engaged in "backtracking," i.e., retracing their steps or "circling," which, of course, increases both the distance and time taken to escape from the building. Furthermore, although the plan of these routes may suggest irrational, haphazard behaviour, the detailed descriptions by people of the purposes they had in mind when going in particular directions help to show the personal logic underlying most actions.

It is only by a content analysis of the act sequences that these features of movement may be accounted for, but this takes us to the next level of explanatory power.

Ascriptive Explanation

In agency-based explanations, factual and experiential knowledge are called upon, but commentary is restricted to identifying the actors involved in the events and their interactions.

A research group at Surrey University, of which we were members,[3] conducted a series of studies into house-buying behaviour. This is an activity that takes place every day, and it involves many stages and interactions with a considerable range of professionals and would-be buyers and/or sellers.

An early task for the research team was to identify the role figures involved in a house-buying transaction and the stream of actions and interactions that result in a successful purchase. This was achieved by eliciting explanations from estate agents, solicitors, surveyors, mortgage brokers, buyers, and sellers about their own actions and where they intersect with those of others. Once the individual sequences had been drawn out, the research team reconstructed the house-buying episode by providing a plan of all the sequences. This was then taken back to the original respondents who commented upon the accuracy of the representation of

[3]Study sponsored by the Fire Research Station and undertaken by David Canter, John Breaux, and Jonathon Sime.

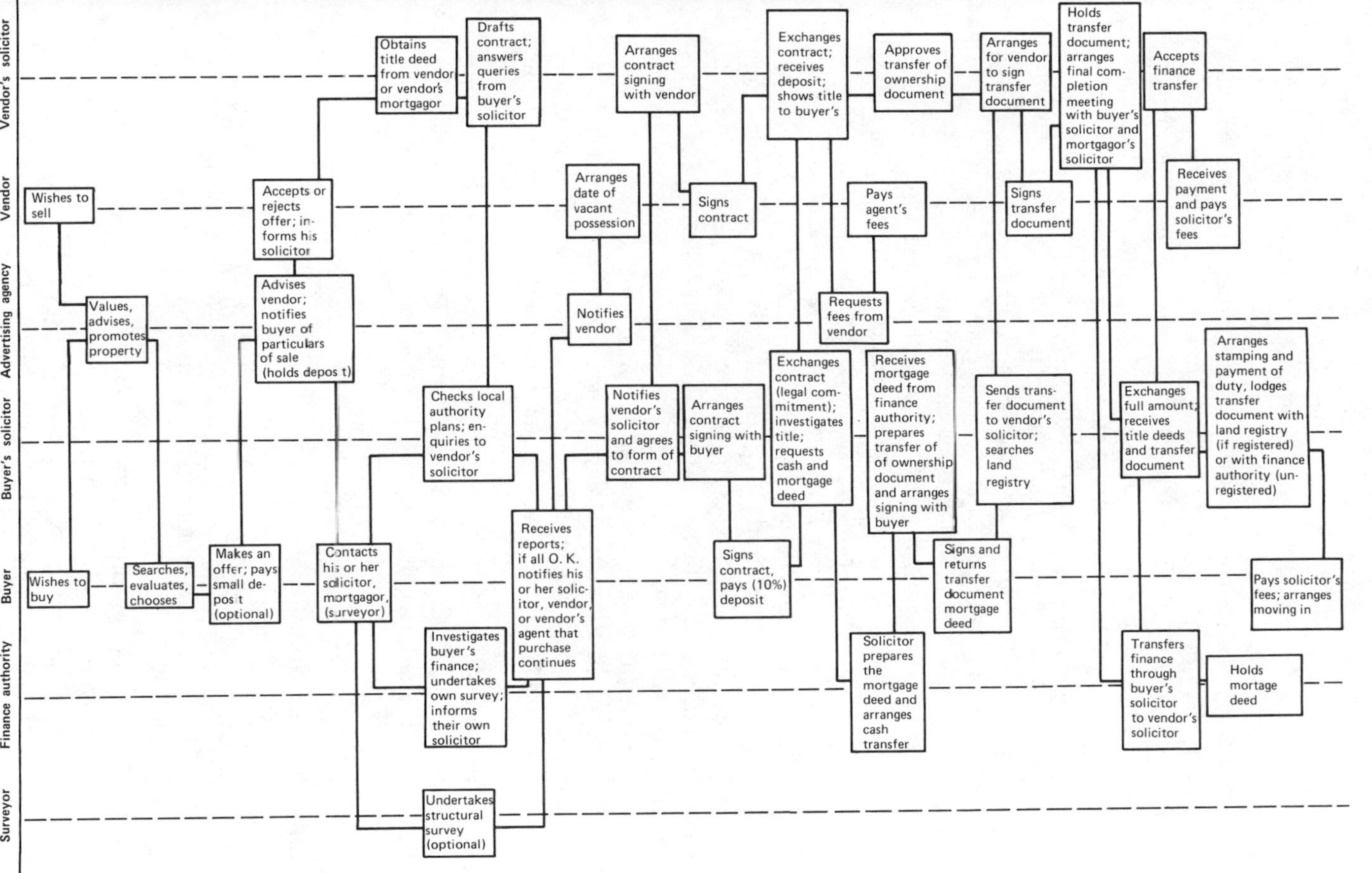

Figure 3 Summary diagram of the process of buying a house. (Taken from an internal report, entitled "A Study of House Buying," of the Housing Research Unit.)

their particular involvement in the transaction. The diagram went through a number of such "iterations."

Some two dozen participants assisted the research team in constructing this summary diagram of the house-buying process. Once drawn up, the team had the opportunity to present it to a group of building society managers and another group of estate agents. Some further refinements were made in the light of comments that were received.

The summary diagram is presented in Figure 3. A number of observations may be drawn from the diagram. First, the researchers were able to provide an overview of a sequence of events beyond the expertise of any one participant because the participant is concerned with her or his own and intersecting interactions rather than tangential interactions. Second, over 40 different major events are recorded. As the purchaser proceeds she or he is less involved, and a successful purchase lies more and more in the hands of the professionals. Finally, as an activity that ordinary people engage in, they have to have a fair degree of verbal fluency and understanding as they negotiate their way through this sequence. The researchers were tapping directly the understanding of the primary participants. In addition, because of the potential complexity of the task, it would be difficult to imagine how the data might have been collected other than having the participants not only elaborate their experiences but also have a chance to comment upon the completed summary diagram.

A fuller account of the methodological considerations is available in Brown and Sime (1981). However, one point worth making here is the general lack of formal procedures to train researchers to interview. The members of the research team in this study (also the fire research and the study of Salvation Army Hostel users) did undergo an interview training programme. This involved videotaping mock interviews and analysing the reactions of both interviewer and interviewee and critical reviewing of the interviewing technique.

Morality Explanations

In seeking to explain the propriety of actions, people place valuation on them by employing justifications, excuses, praise, or blame. This type of "moral" explanation can be illustrated by another example from the house-buying studies.

About 10% of the population move and buy houses annually (Weinstein, 1975). Many of these sales involve the building up of chains of buyers and sellers. People buying houses may also be selling one at the same time, but the person they sell to may also be selling their own house as well. Prospective purchasers have to juggle the timing of the two transactions so that they can exchange contracts simultaneously, otherwise there

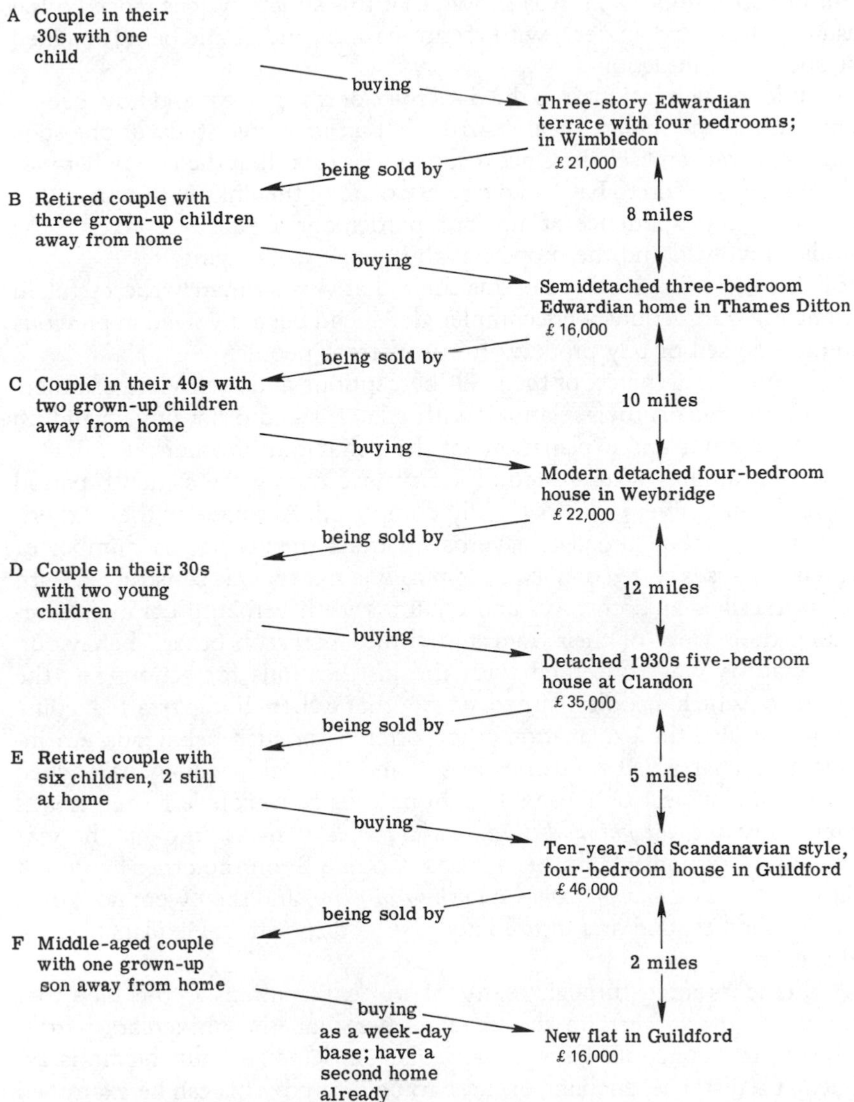

Figure 4 Diagram of the transactions for six families of buying and selling homes, showing the interrelations between families and homes.

are extra costs involved as well as other inconveniences. Thus, connected sets of transactions may build up with a series of buyers/sellers forming a "chain" in which all the transactions indicated in Figure 3 must be co-ordinated. This is clearly a potential cause of great stress.

From a questionnaire study (Alliance Building Society, Housing Research

Unit Report number 2), it was shown that this situation does indeed often result in stress and anxiety, with recriminations and blame being assigned for abortive transactions.

In order to gain insight into the dynamics of this process and how people cope with it, the research team carried out an intensive study of one such chain of buyers and sellers. Once again, it was clear that the researcher was in a unique position to have an overview of all of the links in the chain that is beyond the experience of any one participant. Figure 4 represents the families involved and the properties they were exchanging.

Six families were involved in this chain that was ultimately successful, in that all the transactions were completed. All had been involved in previous attempts to sell or buy property from different people.

By compiling a matrix of their self-perceptions and their view of others we can observe (1) their relations with adjacent and other buyers and (2) self-justifications and explanations of the behaviour of others.

The six families were visited at least twice during the 5-month period before the deals were all successfully completed. Accounts of their experiences were tape-recorded and verbatim transcripts made. A number of content anlayses were conducted. Typically a matrix was constructed with the six families as both rows and columns with verbatim comments reflecting their view of their own and commentary on others' behaviour. One analysis was concerned with the justifications for action, i.e., the degree to which people blamed each other when things started going wrong but also the explanations they offered for such behaviour. An interesting exchange is between buyers A and B. A felt generally harangued and was the subject of abusive telephone calls from couple B, but, it was stated, only *after the husband B had had a couple of drinks,* implying he was not entirely responsible for his actions. Couple B, on the other hand, felt that Mrs A was a *a tough cookie, a pushy American,* and they were not going to be pushed around and intimidated, i.e., a dispositional explanation for behaviour.

A theme running through many of the explanations is the idea that pressure from *elsewhere* in the chain rather than the immediate parties involved, forces actions from a particular participant. Thus, blame is assigned at a distance, enabling excuses to be offered. This can be examined by reference to particular extracts from the buyers explanations.

> *Mr. E:* We had been patient for over 6 months and liking the people who were buying our house. Once I've agreed a thing as far as I'm concerned it sticks. But after 6 months the pressure was building up, winter was coming up, and we didn't want to move in winter. Now was the time to apply a bit of pressure. We had had two or three weeks of the solicitor phoning mine saying, "Yes, we can complete next week." By the third week I said, "Let's do something about this."

What is interesting is the attempt to neutralise taking a tough line—liking the couple, sticking to one's word, not wanting to move during the bad weather. However, the effect on their buyers was fairly dramatic.

> *Mrs. D:* Then Mr E gave us an ultimatum. It was the Thursday after Easter. Our solicitor rang up and said Mr E's solicitor has said either exchange today or forget it. So there was absolute panic all round.

Thereafter, the reverberations were felt right through the successive links in the chain. Mrs D indicated this as follows:

> It's all very well to give us an ultimatum in the middle of the day, but we can't contact everybody . . . we just kept our fingers crossed and did what we could. Actually the only hold-up was the last link in the chain (couple A). Their mortgage company wouldn't give them a formal offer of a mortgage.

However, despite the pressure there were attempts to maintain cordial relations with the adjacent links by blaming people in transactions further away; e.g., Mrs D had no direct contact at all with couple A yet had a clear view of what their situation was and suggested the delays were largely their fault.

Others in the transaction also tried to mitigate the difficulties of their adjacent link as shown in the following:

> *Mrs. C:* The Ds were a super couple and were very proper in their dealings, but they did pressure us at the end, but they themselves were being pushed.
>
> *Mrs. B:* Mrs D rang us twice a week for about a month. She did this as a kind of exercise. She felt that if she didn't keep on at people they would fall by the wayside. Then the bombshell dropped at Easter, and she was on that phone haranguing us.
>
> I don't think the Es were quite aware of the urgency. The Cs had been frustrated in various ways. Their vendor (i.e., couple D) was breathing down their necks. The As had trouble with their mortgage. We were under the impression that they were cash buyers, but they weren't and didn't seem to realise how long it would take to get a mortgage.
>
> *Mrs A:* Mrs D was neurotic and histrionic. She thought we were cash buyers which we were not. They kept ringing us up and pushing us to get our mortgage. It was C's fault, who were dithering and holding up the chain.

The comment from an estate agent involved in two of the transactions help shed real light on the various views of what was happenings.

Estate agent: I think what should have happened was that the Ds shouldn't have held onto their original buyer (couple C). They should have looked for a new one rather than waiting for a situation which was totally out of their control. D's buyer's property was the bottom of the problem. But they had got themselves morally committed. Morality is a word which we feel ought not to be used in such a transaction; it's really a business.

Further detailed analysis revealed the counterbalancing of blame, excuses, and mitigating circumstances that the people in this series of transactions invoked in order to feel a sense of personal justification but also maintain the personal relationships with their buyers in order to accomplish their goal. This is characterised by Brewin (1982) who makes a distinction between causal responsibility and culpability and the excuses offered.

Causal responsibility refers to the extent to which an individual's actions have resulted in an outcome, while culpability is the degree to which the individual deserves to be blamed. In his study of the coping strategies of work accident victims, there was some evidence that responsibility and culpability were indeed distinguished. Interestingly, subjects (his term) who reported feeling culpable (i.e., deserved to be blamed) returned to work earlier than those who did not. Brewin concludes that what is important in coping is the individual's perception of causes of the accident (whether or not this coincides with a consensual assessment).

In our house-buying chain, blame was attributed to others (rather than self) but to people in transactions not immediately adjacent to the respondents' own. To do so presumably would be maladaptive as it would jeopardise the relationships between buyer and seller; instead, mitigating excuses are offered.

The accounts in this analysis were subject to the corroborative checks outlined in Table 1 in terms of the internal consistency of the accounts and the tracing out of the sequences of events (more detail is given in Brown and Sime, 1981).

SUMMARY AND CONCLUSION

Recourse to ordinary explanations of experiences is often made with the admission that people have a rich and elaborate conceptual understanding of what, and why, they do what they do. Moreover, it is the admission of the failure of more traditional procedures to elicit this rich vein of understanding that has lead researchers (Toch, Cohen and Taylor, Newsons, Pahls, Rapports) to focus on research methodologies designed to mine this resource and provide accounts of these explanations.

The two developments of the research interview we are advocating, then, is, first, the recognition of the status of ordinary explanations as respectable data, and second, the proposal that the open interview offers an effective way to elicit explanations. These developments presume a desire to understand and explain rather than predict behaviour. We have tried to formulate a framework that provides for the systematic collection of explanations by adopting a quasi-judicial method. The law is intimately concerned with accounts and consequences of action. There is a mutual advantage to both lawyers and psychologists in developing links between the two disciplines. Bridges can be built at various points, e.g., conceptual analysis such as Lloyd-Bostocks' (1979) discussion on legal definitions of responsibility and implications for attribution theorists; data collection such as Loftus and Zanni (1975) on the acceptability of eyewitness testimony; presentation and acceptance of research findings such as Levines' (1974) scientific adversaral process. A legal model of inquiry also offers a powerful set of conceptual tools for examining the reliability and validity of explanations.

We have provided examples of three broad classes of explanation that increase in their level of complexity: describing the experience, ascribing agency," and attributing morality. These represent an unfolding of forms of explanation, such as habits, excuses, and social norms, that help to make some event or behaviour intelligible. In addition, there is a recognition that an understanding of the role of the explainer and the eliciting situation is relevant to understanding the content and detail of the story. The central aim is to make the respondent *hero* or his or her own drama by providing a context—the research interview—in which the individual's story may be told. In addition, there is a recognition that the role of the explainer and the eliciting situation affect the content and detail of the story. The researcher's task is to construct a multiperspective account of the particular event he or she is investigating, drawn from the explanations given by the primary participants. In this way insights are frequently revealed, and a total picture emerges that is beyond the experience of any one of the participating individuals.

REFERENCES

Alliance Building Society Housing Research Unit (1978). *House Buying Chains.* Guildford: University of Surrey.

Allport, G. W. (1942). *The Use of Personal Documents in Psychological Science.* New York: Social Sciences Research Council.

Angell, R. (1945). A critical review of the development of the personal document method in sociology 1920–1940. In *The Uses of Personal Documents in History Anthropology and Sociology* (Social Science Research Council), pp. 177–232. New York: Social Science Research Council.

Antaki, C., and Fielding, G. (1981). Research on ordinary explanations. In *The Psychology of Ordinary Explanations of Social Behaviour* (C. Antaki, Ed.), pp. 27–56. London: Academic Press.

Argyle, M. (1978). Discussion chapter: An appraisal of the new approach to the study of social behaviour. In *The Social Context of Method* (M. Brenner, P. Marsh, and M. Brenner, Eds.), pp. 237–255. New York: St. Martin's.

Armistead, N. (1974). *Reconstructing Social Psychology.* Harmondsworth: Penguin.

Barker, R. G. (1968). *Ecological Psychology.* Stanford, CA: Stanford University Press.

Bowers, K. S. (1981). Knowing more than we can say leads to saying more than we can know. In *Towards a Psychology of Situations* (D. Magnusson, Ed.), pp. 179–194. Hillside: Erlbaum.

Brewin, C. (1982). Adaptive aspects of self blame in coping with accidental injury. In *Attributions and Psychological Change* (C. Antaki and C. Brewin, Eds.), pp. 119–134. London: Academic Press.

Bromley, D. (1977). *Personality Description in Ordinary Language.* Chichester: Wiley.

Brown, J., and Sime, J. D. (1977). Accounts as a general methodology. Paper presented to the British Psychological Society's Annual Conference, Exeter, March 31st–April 4th.

Brown, J., and Sime, J. D. (1981). A methodology for accounts. In *Social Method and Social Life* (M. Brenner, Ed.), pp. 159–188. London: Academic Press.

Canter, D. (1983). Putting situations in their place: Foundtions for a bridge between social and environmental psychology. In *Social Behaviour in Context* (R. Furnham, Ed.). London: Allyn and Bacon.

Canter, D., and Brown, J. (1981). Explanatory roles. In *The Psychology of Ordinary Explanations of Social Behaviour* (C. Antaki, Ed.), pp. 221–242. London: Academic Press.

Cohen, S., and Taylor, L. (1972). *Psychological Survival.* Harmondsworth: Penguin.

Fielding, N. (1981). *The National Front.* London: Routledge and Kegan Paul.

Fielding, N. (1982). Observational research on the National Front. In *Ethics of Social Research* (M. Bulmer, Ed.), pp. 80–104. London: Macmillan.

Gergen, K. J., and Gergen, M. M. (1982). Explaining human conduct: Form and function, In *Explaining Human Behavior* (P. Secord, Ed.), pp. 127–154. Beverly Hills, CA: Sage.

Harré, R. (1981). Psychological dimensions. In *Explaining Human Behaviour* (P. F. Secord, Ed.), pp. 93–126. Beverly Hills, CA: Sage.

Harré, R., and Secord, P. F. (1972). *The Explanation of Social Behaviour.* Oxford: Blackwell.

Haward, L. (1981). *Forensic Psychology.* London: Batsford.

Kahneman, D., Slovic, P., and Tversky, A. (1982) (Eds.). *Judgement under Uncertainty: Heuristics and Biases.* London: Cambridge University Press.

Kaplan, A. (1964). *The Conduct of Inquiry.* Scranton, PA: Chandler.

Kelly, G. (1955). *The Psychology of Personal Constructs.* New York: Norton.

Levine, M. (1974). Scientific method and the adversary model. *American Psychology, 29,* 661–677.

Lloyd-Bostock, S. (1979). The ordinary man and the psychology of attributing causes and responsibility. *Modern Law Review, 42,* 143–168.

Lloyd-Bostock, S. (1982). Attributions of cause and responsibility as social phenomena. In *Attribution Theory and Research, conceptual Developmental and Social Dimensions* (J. Jaspars, F. Finchman, M. Hewstone, Eds). London: Academic Press.

Loftus, E., and Zanni, G. (1975). Eyewitness testimony: The influence of the wording of a question. *Bulletin of Psychonomic Sociology, 5,* 86–88.

McCall, G. J., and Simmons, J. L. (1978). *Identities and Interactions.* New York/London: Free Press/Collier-MacMillan.

Marsh, P., Rosser, E., and Harré, R. (1978). *The Rules of Disorder.* London: Routledge and Kegan Paul.

Massarik, F. (1981). The interviewing process re-examined. In *Human Inquiry; a Source book of New Paradigm Research* (P. Reason and J. Rowan Eds.), pp. 201–206. Chichester: Wiley.

Mixon, D. (1974). If you won't deceive, what can you do? In *Reconstructing Social Psychology* (N. Armistead, Ed.), pp. 72–85. Harmondsworth: Penguin.

Newson, J., and Newson, E. (1976). Parental roles and social context. In *The Organisation and Impact of Social Research* (M. Shipman, Ed), pp. 22–48. London: Routledge and Kegan Paul.

Nisbett, R. E., and Wilson T. D. (1977). Telling more than we can know: Verbal reports on mental processess. *Psychological Review, 84,* 231–259.

Oakley, R. (1980). Profiles and Perspectives of Hostel Residents. M.Sc. Thesis, University of Surrey, Guildford.

Pahl, J. M., and Pahl, R. E. (1971). *Managers and Their Wives.* London: Allen Lane.

Pauls, J. (1980). Building evacuation, research findings and recommendations. In *Fires and Human Behaviour* (D. Canter Ed.), pp. 251–275. Chichester: Wiley.

Rapoport, R., and Rapoport, R. (1971). *Dual Career Families.* Harmondsworth: Penguin.

Shotter, J. (1977). Agency and Accounting. In Criticism of Harre and Secords 'open souls' Doctrine. Paper presented to the British Psychological Society Social Psychology Section Annual Conference, University of Durham, September.

Sime, J. D. (1980). Measuring people's movement in a fire. Paper presented to the Third International Seminar on Human Behaviour in Fire. University of Edinburgh, September.

Sutherland, N. S. (1959). Motives as explanations. *Mind, 68,* 145–159.

Tedeschi, J., and Reiss, M. (1981). Verbal strategies in impression management. In *The Psychology of Ordinary Explanations of Social Behaviour* (C. Antaki Ed.), pp. 271–309 London: Academic Press.

Toch, Hans (1972). *Violent Men.* Harmondsworth: Penguin.

Trankell, A. (1972). *Reliability of Evidence.* Beckmans.

Tutt, N. (1976). *Violence.* London: Her Majesty's Stationery Office.

Weinstein, E. T. A. (1975). The movements of owner occupier households between regions. *Regional Studies, 9,* 137–145.

Williams, Sir W. J. (1976). *Moriarity's police law.* 23rd ed. London: Butterworths.

11

Scientists' Interview Talk: Interviews as a Technique for Revealing Participants' Interpretative Practices

JONATHAN POTTER AND MICHAEL MULKAY

INTRODUCTION: INTERVIEWS AND SOCIAL STUDIES OF SCIENCE

There has been a long tradition of interviewing in social studies of science. The seminal work of Merton and his students was based partly on data collected in interviews (e.g., Merton et al., 1956; Zuckerman, 1972). And, despite numerous analyses based on naturally occurring quantitative data, such as citations, some of the most important work of the 1960s and 1970s was founded upon interviews (e.g., Hagstrom, 1965; Mitroff, 1974). In the past decade, social studies of science have been strongly influenced by the early work of Thomas Kuhn. This work implied the possibility of a social psychology of science that connected scientific progress to the perceptions, values, and group membership of scientists. These phenomena could not be easily assessed by means of the formal scientific literature; only by examining scientists' informal commentary did it seem that a true picture of scientists' actions and beliefs could be formulated (see references in Mulkay 1979, 1980). Interviews seemed perfectly suited to this kind of research.

For the most part interviews are used as a technique for obtaining information that will enable the analyst to describe, explain, and/or predict social actions that occur outside the interview, although as Bainbridge in Chapter 9 of this volume discusses, it is possible to obtain ongoing commentaries from informants during some actual activity. Investigators usually attempt to extract from participants' verbal responses in interviews an accurate formalised version of the latter's actions, motives, interests, and so

ISBN 0-12-131580-0

on, which can be used to describe and explain what is going on in some naturally occurring area of social life. When interviews are employed in this way, it is assumed that, as long as the investigator makes proper allowance for participants' inevitable partiality and makes stringent checks on the reliability of the data, she will be able to compose something approaching an accurate, literal account of the aspects of the interview in which she is interested.[1] We wish to emphasise in the present chapter that this approach to interviews, both in science and other areas of social life, makes the analyst's conclusions heavily dependent on the interpretations of social action carried out by participants. We also wish to suggest that participants' interpretations are much more variable and inconsistent than is normally recognised, and to show that a radical revision is therefore required in our use of interview material. Instead of attempting to produce definitive versions of participants' actions and beliefs, we will argue that interview data should be used to reveal the interpretative practices through which participants come to construct versions of their social world. Our argument will be illustrated by referring to some of our own data that deals with the actions of research scientists in social psychology and biochemistry.

In the relatively unstructured interviews typical in social studies of science, the investigator has in mind certain topics that seem to be important in the light of previous research, but which are too complex to be defined in detail in advance. For instance, in our studies of research scientists, we were interested in such complex themes as theory choice, scientific consensus, and familiarity with and use of philosophical conceptions. Attempts were made to ensure that these topics were covered in every interview, but in a way that allowed respondents to talk freely and at length and that make it possible for these topics to occur naturally, as each respondent talked about the development of his scientific career and about the evolution of his area of research. Consequently, interviewees were able to describe in detail at least some of the complexities of their own and their colleagues' social actions.

Assuming that open-ended interviews have been recorded and each transcribed in full, the next task in the analysis of such data is usually to extract and collect together all passages dealing with specific topics. This is followed by the crucial step of making consistent sense of each collection of data. It is at this point that something akin to triangulation begins; that is, each specific passage is compared with each other passage in relation to a given topic in order to eliminate certain responses as unreliable, to furnish reinterpretations of problematic responses, and to judge what is the best

[1]To clarify potentially confusing constructions we will refer to all analysts as 'she' and to all scientist participants as 'he.'

overall interpretation. The process can then be extended by comparing the data from different topic headings and, once again, by modifying one's interpretations so as to produce overall analytical consistency. In due course, it is hoped, a coherent, composite account will emerge of, say, the social actions whereby a particular network of researchers adopted and became committed to a particular theory. The aim in any particular case study, whether or not interviews are used, is to build up "an overall reconstruction of what went on" (Mackenzie and Barnes, 1979). It is assumed that, in the long run, it will be possible to bring together the conclusions of a number of such case studies to formulate a provisional, yet empirically based, social theory of scientific knowledge-production or to test and improve upon existing conjectures about this broad area of social action.

We have tried above to summarise briefly how open-ended interviews have been used within an overall strategy designed to describe and explain complex sequences of social action that occur outside the interview. One feature of this investigatory procedure to which we wish to draw particular attention is that the analytical work of the investigator follows from and is necessarily derivative from the interpretative work of participants. In other words, the investigator's access to the events in which she is interested, insofar as she relies on the research interview, is mediated by the interpretations of events, actions, attitudes, and so forth, which are made by participants during the interview. Of course, interviewers can try to minimise their own active engagement in the interview; they can learn to be relatively nondirective, and so on (see, e.g., Brenner, Chapter 2 in this volume). Moreover they can, as we have noted, try to use systematic comparison to eliminate or reinterpret "problemantic" responses in order to distill a reasonably impartial or literal account of those actions occurring outside the interview, which are the main subject of study. We wish to suggest, however, that respondents' accounts of social actions are so variable and so dependent on detailed changes in interpretative context occurring in the interview that the task of extracting a single, coherent analyst's version from the data cannot be satisfactorily accomplished. If this is so, it has important implications for our use of interview data. We will explore some of these implications after we have illustrated some of the difficulties of the traditional analytic approach to interviews.

THE PROBLEM OF VARIABILITY

Variability from the Traditional Perspective

Methodologists and researchers have, of course, long been aware of the problems arising from the variability of participants' responses. Two basic difficulties have been recognised: that of variability from one participant to another and that of variability among the responses of particular individuals. Consider the way in which these problems are handled in a standard sociological work on research methods (Bogdan and Taylor, 1975).

> Truth then emerges not as one objective view but rather as the composite picture of how people think about the institution and each other. Truth comprises the perspectives of [the various kinds of participants involved]. (p. 11)

> While the interviewer does not search for "truth" in his or her subject's words she or he should be alert to purposeful distortions of facts and events. . . . If you do indeed find contradictions in your subject's story, gently confront him or her with the evidence. . . . Suspected lies often turn out to be misunderstandings or honest changes in a subject's perspective. (pp. 116–117)

Both these methodological problems are treated here as manageable technical problems. It is assumed that, although each partcipant's views change over time, at any specific juncture, he will "think about the institution" and about other participants in a particular way. Apparent inconsistencies in a participant's responss are to be identified and then explained away, if possible, by means of further interaction between investigator and respondent, and by means of further interpretative work by both parties. Once the coherent "view" of each actor has been built up out of his talk, the task of the analyst is taken to be that of putting together a "composite picture" that not only reconciles and makes sense of these divergent individual perspectives, but does so in a way that furnishes explanations of recurrent social actions.

We wish to suggest however, that the kinds of inconsistencies in respondents' accounts mentioned above can be seen to be so pervasive, when one examines interview data in fine detail, that they cannot be treated as a marginal technical problem. We cannot show clearly in one short chapter just how pervasive they are, but we can illustrate the kind of analytical difficulties that they pose. Further documentation of our claims can be found in the various papers we will refer to in the course of our argument.

Variability in Interview Data

The following illustrative passage is taken from an interview with a biochemist we have called Fasham, who is giving an account of why he rejected the theory proposed by a colleague called Watson. This theory deals with the functioning of a complex enzyme termed the ATPase. Technical biochemical issues are mentioned only passing and do not need to be fully understood by the reader.

A. (1) I would not say Watson's mechanism is incorrect. (2) I think it is "optimistic" at this point. (3) I guess I am much more conservative by nature than he is. (4) And I am looking for something simpler to explain things than the mechanism he is using. (5) This type of flip-flop mechanism, it may be right. (6) You can't say it is wrong. (7) But on the other hand, you can't say it's right by any means. (8) Now that mechanism has been proposed for simpler enzyme systems and in all the cases where that's really been looked at very closely in similar systems it is proven to be not the case. (9) He certainly has experiments that are constent with this hypothesis, but to my mind it is far from proven. (10) I would like to see it a little simpler. (Fasham, 9)

Three considerations or criteria of theory choice are advanced here by Fasham as guiding his action of not accepting Watson's theory: that Watson's mechanism is not simple enough (sentences A4 and A10), that the type of mechanism he proposes has not been found to operate in enzymes that are simpler than the ATPase (sentence A8), and that, although there is some evidence in its favour, it has not yet been proven to be correct (A5–7, A8, and, particularly, A9).

The speaker does not seem to claim that his criteria are widely accepted by other scientists. Indeed, he seems to propose in sentences A3–4 that his choice of the criterion of simplicity, or perhaps his interpretation of that criterion, is conditioned by his conservative personality. On the other hand, his references to proof, to consistency with the evidence, and to what has been shown to be the case in simpler systems all seem to imply the existence of some standards that are shared. His own use of criteria is not presented as if it were totally idiosyncratic. Thus, in this passage Fasham provides an account of his action in which his action of choosing between theories appears to follow necessarily from his commitment to a coherent combination of objective and subjective, or shared and individual, criteria.

However, as we look more closely at this scientist's talk about theory choice, it becomes increasingly difficult to sustain the view that he applies his criteria in a single, uniform fashion because, subsequently in the interview, each of his criteria was discussed again in different contexts and interpreted quite differently. As a result, his account of theory choice given in passage A becomes difficult to accept at face value. Let us consider here only the criterion of simplicity. In the next excerpt, which follows quotation A a short time later, the same scientist discusses the virtues of alternative mechanisms and sketches the outline of his own working hypothesis.

B. (1) I think the other main contender for a mechanism is some sort of complex regulation, and it is pretty clear that *some* complex regulation

> is going on. (2) It could be some combination of the two, because you know you have more nucleotide-binding sites than you have catalytic sites. (3) There is no doubt about that. (4) So, I look for some variant of those two mechanisms. (5) That would be my working hypothesis right now. (Fasham, 11)

Having dismissed Watson's hypothesis partly on the grounds that some simpler mechanism is required in extract A, in this later passage the speaker advances as his alternative an hypothesis that combines Watons's mechanism with "some sort of complex regulation" (B1–2). It is difficult to see how this notion could be simpler than, and therefore preferable to, that of Watson. Whereas complexity is presented as a major defect of Watson's theory (A4–10), it becomes a strong point in favour of Fasham's own conception. Thus, an apparent criterion of theory choice is applied selectively and its significance altered in a way that lends support to the speaker's own scientific judgments. The speaker does not seem to be assessing the various hypotheses against the invariant criterion of simplicity. Rather, having used one interpretation of this criterion to "show" that Watson's ideas are unacceptable, the speaker appears subsequently to reverse its implications when formulating his own alternative hypothesis.

Can this inconsistency be treated in the way that the methodologists quoted above have in mind? Is there, for example, evidence of "purposeful" distortion? It might be argued that criteria are merely being used opportunistically to denigrate a rival theory in extract A, and that the speaker's own research practice as depicted in extract B shows that he does not "really" take this criterion seriously. Yet, it is equally plausible to argue that the criterion is seriously held and applied by the speaker and that it is his particular research practice that is opportunistic. There seems to be no grounds provided in either of these extracts for deciding that one interpretation of the criterion is a purposeful distortion while the other is a straightforward and literal description, in other words, that one account is reliable and the other is unreliable. There is no firm basis for carrying out such categorisations. Furthermore, it has been shown elsewhere, not only that all three of the criteria of theory choice identified by Fasham above are subsequently undermined in his interview but that this is typical of participants' responses on this and other topics in disciplines as different as biochemistry and social psychology (Mulkay and Gilbert, 1985; and see later references).

If one insists on treating this problem as a mere technical difficulty, rather than a product of a misconception of the nature of interview data, it is possible to try, as was proposed in the first quotation above, to eliminate inconsistencies through further interaction. It is doubtless the case that when interviewers attempt in this way to elucidate apparent inconsistencies, they will be able to elicit from respondents various kinds of reinterpretations that are often adequate as far as the interviewer can judge. But given the interpretative flexibility of the resources that respondents use to give accounts of their actions, as displayed in passages A and B above, this is hardly surprising. It is difficult to accept, therefore, that interactionally effective reinterpretation by respondents is sufficient to allow the investigator to treat the interpretative outcome as analytically unproblematic. Furthermore, additional requests for clarification by the interviewer will often generate further apparent contradictions instead of reducing them, as can be seen in the next passage.

C. *Interviewer.* (1) Did Lewis fully understand the chemiosmotic theory?
Respondent. (2) Not when I got there, no. (3) Though Lewis is a very clever guy. . . . (4) He was certainly absolutely objective and well capable of recognising the force of any other theory. (5) And I'm sure by the time I left he was in favour. . . .
Interviewer. (6) I'm not very clear about Lewis. (7) Is there a point at which Lewis comes to accept the chemiosmotic theory?
Respondent. (8) I couldn't tell you that. (9) You'd have to ask him that. (10) I left in 1971 or so. (Rollins, 14)

Just before passage C occurs in the interview transcript, Rollins, who was a student of Lewis, explains why Lewis did not accept a particular biochemical theory. The interviewer then asks whether, in the respondent's view, Lewis understood that theory (C1). Rollins replies that Lewis did not understand it at first. He then proceeds to identify various redeeming features of Lewis as a scientist, only two of which are given here (C3–4); and he concludes that, by the time he left Lewis's lab, the latter was in favour of the theory in question.

There then follows eight sentences, not reproduced above, in which Rollins refers to other work in Lewis's lab that was "very beautiful" and "tremendously helpful." At this point, the interviewer returns to the question of Lewis's acceptance of the chemiosmotic theory. Despite Rollins's prior statement that Lewis was in favour of this theory by the time Rollins left the lab, the interviewer professes uncertainty. Presumably he was aware of potentially discrepant information on Lewis from other sources and was not prepared to accept Rollins's account of his own opinion without further specification. In other words, he can be seen as checking an apparent inconsistency. He does not succeed, however, in thereby reducing his interpretative problems. For Rollins now asserts without reservation that he is unable to furnish any estimate at all of Lewis's views with respect to this theory (C8–10). Thus the result of the interviewer's intervention is to make problematic all of Rollins's statements about Lewis's scientific views. Furthermore, because Rollins's statements on this topic were closely linked with his general account of social activity in Lewis's lab, extended passages of Rollins's testimony suddently become suspect.

The investigator's attempt to reconcile inconsistency by means of social interaction in the interview has merely served to generate additional contradictions. Nevertheless, although this exchange did not help the analyst to "build up a coherent reconstruction," it is helpful to us as methodologists. For it suggests that particular statements, such as C2 and C8–10, are so socially contingent, so heavily dependent on interactional and interpretative work going on in the interview, that they cannot be used as components in an analysts' account of what is actually happening in this research network; and it suggests that some appropriate methodological response is required.

Variability in Noninterview Data

One reasonable response to the difficulties we have been identifying is to treat interviews as no more than a supplementary technique and to take from them only what is compatible with conclusions established by means of data more directly derived from the actions in which we are interested. Alternatively, one might abandon interviews altogether and seek to rely entirely on more direct records. We suggest, however, that even such direct records will be the outcome of practicipant's context-dependent interpretive practices.[2]

We will illustrate this point by examing some noninterview material taken from a group of European social psychologists. Specifically, this is data derived from formal research papers produced for publication and from transcripts from semiformal conference discussion of those papers. This sort of data can be considered to be naturalistic in that it is not produced specifically for the researcher. Instead, it documents participants' commonplace verbal and written interaction. It is, then, a direct record of certain important features of scientific life. Let us closely examine one example of this sort.

The following passage is taken from the conclusion of a paper presented by Biggs at a workshop on application attended by social psychologists. It

[2]In some cases analysts have tried to produce purely objective quantitative measures of scientific activity. For example, they have used measures such as the frequency of citation of certain research papers as indicators of quality, recognition, or influence. We have argued in detail elsewhere that this putatively objective data is also parasitic upon participants' interpretative formulations (Mulkay et al., 1983; see also Edge, 1979; Potter, 1981).

concerns the applicability of his research into the effects of television violence on viewers. Our interest will not be directly with technical issues to do with the research, but with the way that the usefulness of research findings is depicted.

D. (1) We are not applied social psychologists; rather we consider ourselves as experimental social psychologists who choose to investigate empirically and theoretically problems having implications for the society; with the hope that such knowledge will be some day applied by others than ourselves.[1]
Footnote 1. (2) Fortunately, this happens sometimes in the area of mass-media and violence in Europe. (3) For instance, the BBC television recently circulated a new guidance policy booklet which clearly takes into account the results of most recent research. (4) The Swiss television also devoted one of its most favourite programmes to the problem of filmed violence and to our approach to this topic. (Biggs, unedited manuscript, p. 15)

Biggs writes, in sentence D1, that he does not regard himself as directly engaged in applied social pscyhology, but as producing knowledge that can be applied by others. This knowledge is applicable because it concerns social problems that have particular implications for society. He presents his empirical and theoretical work as having been undertaken with application in mind and his results as being applicable in principle to the solution of social problems. In the footnote, two examples illustrating the application of such knowledge are given (sentences D3–4). These examples are presented as showing that the findings of empirical and theoretical research are sometimes actually applied. They inform us that television companies have taken notice of such research in the past; in one case incorporating it into a policy booklet and in the other basing a programme around the author's theoretical approach. These examples thus provide a warrant for thc applicability of the reported research and justify its inclusion in this particular conference.

Following this presentation, the first discussant took up the issue of the influence of Biggs's research in practical contexts.

E. (1) . . . your work [is a good example] of really the way to look at a topic in a slightly more discriminating way than, certainly in the aggression research, was typical in the 60s. (2) But I think this presents a great problem for researchers who actually want to convince officialdom. (3) Because it is bad enough trying to get people to understand what a main effect means, but once you start trying to describe what an interaction is, and perhaps even a second-order interaction, then officials say "well, you are obviously not very confident about it." (4) If a programme on television doesn't necessarily lead people to be aggressive, but it goes through a peer group, or it only affects some children, or it may have a delayed response, I mean; you have obviously done poor research or there isn't really a phenomenon there, and you are just some woolly-minded liberal standing on a soap box and we hear one of those every other day. (5) And so they can discard it. (Aldridge, transcript, B10–11)

This speaker suggests a practical difficulty for the application of Biggs's research (E2). The problem he identifies is that the sorts of results that Biggs has obtained, because they require some degree of statistical skill to understand them, will not be persuasive to officials who make policy decisions (E3). In sentence E4 the speaker parodies the image that these (unspecified) officials will have of the social researcher. He describes the ways in which the results will be interpreted as erroneous ("there isn't really a phenomenon there") or as a product of political interests ("just some woolly-minded liberal standing on a soap box"), and can thus be discarded (E5). Thus, the discussant tends to undermine Biggs's application claim, suggesting that the relevant officials will ignore his research.

When the discussant has finished speaking Biggs takes issue with his point.

F. (1) I am not so sure about your intuition, or your conviction, let's say, that the officials would be less touched, that this kind of research with interactions, no main effects, would have less impact. (2) Er, I am not convinced, but at least I have some . . . evidence that they don't like, that people in the TV, for example, would like that once there is violence on TV it is bad. (3) They don't like that, and they are not naive enough to think that it has no influence. (4) So, in some sense they are very glad that someone says that, you know, it can have effects, but not for everybody, not in all circumstances. (5) Maybe they will say that so they have nothing to do. (6) That could very well be. (7) But at least in one recent journal that position was, you know, advances, that position was appreciated, and on the Swiss TV also. (8) But maybe it is in order so that they have every justification not to do anything. (9) That can be. (10) But if you say violence on TV is bad I think it, you block them also. (11) Well, that would be my reaction. (12) I am not sure that would have less impact. (Biggs, transcript, B15)

Biggs suggests, contrary to the discussant, that the "TV people" dislike claims that violence is bad per se (F2), and that they are also experienced enough to know that violence has some effect on viewers (F3). These officials are thus "glad" of interactional effects that support neither extreme (F4). In sentence F7 Biggs repeats, in support of this claim, the two examples that appear in the paper (sentences D3–4). However, in sentences F5 and 8 Biggs provides a further, and significantly different, argument against the discussant's point. He suggests that the officials may use research that recognises the presence of complex interactions to legitimate their inactivity. Whereas in the written text and in the oral presentation of the paper the response of the media is depicted as a clear instance of research leading to changes in everyday social action, in the conference setting these same actions are depicted as, quite possibly, actually a way of avoiding change. Biggs is implying here that officials may well respond to social psychological research in accordance with their interests and that they may use its findings merely to justify policies that they would have implemented anyway and that have their "real origins" elsewhere. This conception of the practical impact of social psychology seems far removed from Biggs's initial formulation concerning the genuine utility of his work.

The first point that we want to draw from these three extracts is that the problem of variability does not disappear when we concentrate on more direct records of scientific activity; variability should not be viewed as a special product of the interview situation. In the above example we can see that Biggs's written version of how his research is utilised is very different from the version he produced in response to questioning in the discussion. Furthermore, in varying his account of the practical impact of his research, Biggs is not simply giving alternative versions of the actions of the television agencies, but also providing different accounts of the nature of his research and of his own professional actions. This example is, of course, only an illustration. But significant and theoretically interesting variability has been a recurrent finding in those of our studies that have been based on scientific records of this kind. It seems, therefore, that variability must be considered as a general feature of scientists' accounts of social action.

What are we to make of this variability? We suggest that instead of treating it as a methodological problem it can be used as an analytic resource. If we look again at Biggs's speech in extract F, paying particular attention to what he is trying to *do* in this speech, we can start to make more sense of it. As Biggs interacts with his critic, the notion of "impact" (F12) that he has been using is subtly attenuated. By the end of the extract, "impact" may mean that results are put into some sort of practice; but equally it may mean quite the opposite, that the results "lead to" *inactivity.* Biggs has fashioned an account of the (potential) impact of his work specifically to repudiate the discussant's suggestion that it will have little impact. In doing so, he has introduced an interpretation that was not used in his paper. This interpretation is, however, particularly suited to the specific interactional task of undermining the discussant's central criticism, in that it enables the speaker to maintain some kind of utility claim even in a situation where his research may have no ostensible outcome. Thus, Biggs's account in extract F can be seen as specifically constructed to deal with two central tasks: to reply to the point that such work would be ignored because of its complexity and to maintain the view of the research as having significant applications.

This example, in addition, illustrates the *flexibility* of this kind of account. Although two very different versions of the utilisation of the research are given, both were subsumed under a single model of application, or a "standard utility account" (Potter and Mulkay, 1982; see also Potter, 1982). This standard utility account is employed both in instances where officials are depicted as using the research to guide policy and to educate the public about the problems of television violence, but also where officials use the research as a rhetorical justification for doing nothing. The notion of application it embodies is so open-ended that the speaker is able to draw the two contradictory accounts of action together as documents of the utility of his research. Variability of this kind is not random, but directed towards maintaining a standard interpretative model of application. Thus, it seems that there may be orderly interpretative practices underlying the variability in accounting.

Our response, then, to this kind of material is to treat the two versions of action provided by the participant as equally viable and to try to understand how such versions are generated in the course of social interaction. As we have indicated, the more traditional response to the problems raised by this kind of analysis might be to eliminate one of these versions as mistaken or as purely rhetorical. Again the problem is, which one? We have illustrated the way in which Biggs's spoken reply (F) is fashioned to suit the specific social context, and it could be argued that this should be taken as rhetorical while the written account is taken as embodying a correct and literal description of the utilisation of Biggs's research. However, there are some good reasons for not making this move. First, and specifically related to this example, we can look at the extract from the paper as also being directed at social functions above and beyond mere "description." For example, we can treat the "standard utility account" in this extract as a legitimating device. For in our society it is difficult to discredit any action that can be successfully depicted as facilitating control over the physical or social worlds. By characterising research in terms of the standard utility account, research scientists fashion a potent legitimation for the acquisition of funds and other social resources (Potter and Mulkay, 1982).

Second, and more generally, there is a growing body of work that has examined the social construction and function of scientific and other texts (e.g., Gilbert and Mulkay, 1980; Potter et al., 1984; Smith, 1978; Woolgar, 1980). To mention just one example, Yearley (1981) has examined the procedures used by nineteenth-century geologists for identifying the falsity of opponents' positions and the way these procedures are organised within a scientific text. He notes that such a "refutatory" text cannot be read literally because these procedures are at times inconsistent or even contradictory. However, the particular sequence in which the procedures are presented, and the way presuppositions of the opponent's falsity are drawn upon, stop these inconsistencies and contradictions from becoming easily apparent. The text reads persuasively and coherently; it is only the analytical process of deconstruction through close rereading which makes it problematic.

There are, therefore, good arguments against assuming that statements in scientific papers or utterances scientists make at conferences should be taken as straightforward descriptions of scientific activity or belief. These sorts of materials appear to be the product of scientists' flexible and context-dependent interpretative practices in just the same way as are interviews. There will, then, be no advantage to be gained from rejecting interview data in favour of apparently more direct records, for we will not thereby get any closer to "what is really happening."

ORDER AND INTERPRETATIVE PRACTICES

So far we have concentrated mainly on the range of problems that arise in analysing various kinds of discursive data produced by scientists. We have noted that the accounts embodied in such data are highly variable and that analytic formulations that are based on them appear to be inescapably parasitic on participants' interpretative practices. In this section we wish to look more positively at a particular example of how such data can be fruitfully analysed. We will attempt, with the aid of accounts given in interviews and at scientific conferences, to illustrate a novel approach to the phenomenon of theory choice and show the way in which an understanding of the variability in accounting can be used as a resource for analysis.

Accounting for Theory Choice in Biochemistry

The following extracts are taken from an interview with a biochemist. They contain accounts of the rejection and selection of particular theories. As before, there is no need to grasp the technical details of the extracts for the purposes of our present argument.

G. *Interviewer.* (1) You said earlier that you gradually came to accept the chemiosmotic theory as a general framework.
Respondent. (2) Well, I never rejected it wholeheartedly. (3) I was impressed by the data that indicated that the original version of the Spencer hypothesis could not be correct. (4) That is, if you assume there was a proton gradient that drove the reaction, the energy available from the electron motive force across the mitochondrial membrane was not sufficient to achieve ATP synthesis if only two protons were moved per ATP formed. . . . (5) This was first demonstrated by Howell and Mulhern and later substantiated in a number of laboratories. . . . (6) We had here also, in connection with other studies that we were doing, calcium transport studies, that also indictated that the proton yield was higher than two. . . . (7) I was very early convinced that Spencer was right with respect to the *generation* of protons. (8) I had no doubt that electron transport was resulting in a proton gradient between the interior and the exterior. (9) The very elegant studies that were subsequently made in anion and cation transport fit in beautifully with that aspect of his work. . . . (10) There were a few *key* experiments that convinced me. (11) The Perry and Esberger experiment I think was influential in convincing me. . . . (12) All of this accumulated over a period of years to convince me that Spencer's general concept was correct. . . . (13) I think in a stepwise fashion more and more people are being convinced. (Waters, 3–7)

H. *Respondent.* (1) Many years ago we postulated the mechanism for fatty acid synthesis. . . . (2) It turns out now that fatty acid synthesis is very *much* like we postulated long, long ago, except that there are residues stuck on this enzyme that do this transfer of two carbon units and condensing them into fatty acids. (3) But I don't think our paper inspired anyone to do additional experiments, even though it did turn out to be, in concept, pretty right. (4) This depends on where something is published, how convincing your arguments are, the reputation of the individual who makes the hypotheses, and so on. (5) Biochemistry is a very heterogeneous business. (6) There are all sorts of good things and all sorts of bad things that go to make the whole community of biochemistry, and I don't know what the factors are that predict when things will really click and when they won't. (Waters, 26–27)

In these two extracts the speaker is talking about two quite different theories. In extract G he explains and justifies his partial acceptance of the "chemiosmotic theory" entirely by selecting experimental findings and treating their theoretical implications as unproblematic. Certain *elegant studies* and *key experiments* together convinced the speaker that electron transport produced a proton gradient which was involved in ATP synthesis, as Spencer, the originator of the chemiosmotic theory, had proposed (G9–11). Nevertheless, the *data* (G3) produced in *various laboratories* indicated that the number of protons transported per ATP formed had to be greater than the two predicted by Spencer's theory (G6–7). Thus, the speaker's particular view of chemiosmosis is presented as if it were the only possible one, given the available evidence. In short, he is able to present his choice of theory as necessary by ignoring the possibility that the experimental evidence could allow other theoretical conclusions. In a similar manner, the growing acceptance of the central ideas of chemiosmotic theory by other scientists in the field (G13) is depicted as following in a fairly direct and unproblematic fashion from the gradual accumulation of experimental evidence.

In passage H, the speaker is faced with a quite different interpretative task. Here he has to explain, not why a supposedly correct theory has been accepted, but why a supposedly correct theory was *not* adopted over a long period of time. He does not abandon the notion that there are independent, presumably experimental, procedures for judging whether a theory is correct. Indeed, he implies that it is on such grounds that he now knows that his earlier theory was right all along. Nevertheless, in fashioning his explanation for the long neglect of his theory, he makes the *application* of these experimental procedures socially contingent. It depends, he suggests, on the place of publication of a theory, on the plausibility of one's ideas to other scientists, on the author's reputation, and on those factors implied in the intriguing etcetera clause (H4). Moreover, he continues, this is not an isolated and unrepresentative case (H6); biochemistry as a whole is a thing of shreds and patches (H5–6). The fate of scientific hypotheses is totally unpredictable and the factors that produce success and failure are too complex to be grasped or specified by the speaker (H6).

We can see the speaker in these two passages drawing upon very different general notions of the way theories are chosen. These notions, or "accounting systems," have been shown to be a recurrent feature of biochemists' talk about theory choice (Mulkay and Gilbert, 1983; see also Gilbert and Mulkay, 1982). In the first accounting system, which we will call the empiricist account, the adoption of a theory is described, explained, and justified by reference to experimental results. The production of these results is treated as unproblematic, and their theoretical implications are taken to be fairly unequivocal. Experimental findings or data are presented as *requiring* the speaker to adopt a particular theory. In general, the production of correct belief is taken to be assured as long as scientists are allowed to get on with their work of furnishing reliable experimental results.

In contrast, the second version, which we will term contingent, makes the production of correct belief much less certain and straightforward. It treats experimental results as uncertain accomplishments, with variable theoretical implications, the interpretation of which may often or always be influenced by a range of noncognitive factors. From this perspective, scientists' certified beliefs about the natural or social world may consist of a mélange of the correct and the incorrect, or, more radically, they may simply be those beliefs that groups of specialists have found it expedient to adopt.

We can bring order to these different systems of accounting for theory choice by the same means we used with the social psychologists' accounts of application, that is, we can analyse their specific context of use and function. In the interviews, the empiricist notions of theory choice were predominantly used when the speaker was engaged in explaining, and at the same time legitimating, his own beliefs. The empiricist perspective is particularly effective for this. By using this perspective a speaker displays his beliefs as held because "that is the way the world is." Unless the experimental evidence is itself challenged, no further justification is necessary. Thus, we can see in extract G how the speaker warrants his own version of the chemiosmotic theory as arising unproblematically and necessarily from the evidence.

The contingent perspective on theory choice tends to occur in rather different situations. It is used when the speaker is trying to make sense of persistent disagreements or when talking about a scientist's failure to adopt a correct theory. The use of the empiricist perspective on these occasions would produce severe interpretative difficulties. For if theory selection is directly constrained by experimental evidence, then disagreements ought to be quickly solved or at least lead to acknowledgement that the evidence is equivocal. Likewise, empirical findings ought always to lead to scientists selecting the correct theory. Clearly these expectations are subject to persistent violation. Such interpretative difficulties do not, however, arise when scientists use the contingent accounting repertoire. By means of this repertoire, occurrences such as these can be made easily intelligible and the scientific world depicted in an orderly fasion.

Accounting for Theory Choice in Social Psychology

We can take this analytic approach to theory selection, which sees scientists as employing two different accounting systems in different interpretative contexts, and use it to make sense of variations occurring in social psychologists' accounts of theory selection produced during conference discussions. As with the interview material, individual accounts or extracts from accounts appear to be literal descriptions of theory choice and of the constraining role of formal criteria. Many of the conference accounts we have analysed exemplify the philosophical position that scientific progress is ensured by a combination of empirical evidence and the restricting force of a small number of general criteria (e.g., Kuhn, 1977; Popper, 1959; Quine and Ullian, 1970). However, other accounts embody a very different understanding of the way theories are chosen. In these accounts, social and particularistic events are emphasised. Moreover, they suggest that formal criteria, such as testability, can only be interpreted with difficulty and that their significance for the progress of the discipline has been greatly exaggerated. In short, then, we can document in psychology conference transcripts the same two perspectives on theory choice that we saw in the biochemists' accounts.

In the following extract, the speaker gives rather different descriptions of the role of the criterion of testability in relation to his own theory and a theory proposed by another speaker at the conference.

I. (1) I would like to return to this game of "I am more refutable than you." (2) I said *refutable,* not reputable, although you can be forgiven for misunderstanding that. [laughter] (3) Um, I don't believe that refutability is the only criterion that we should be judging our models by but, and it is particularly difficult to use it very systematically because we actually don't understand the nature of refutation at all well. (4) Nevertheless, I think it is perfectly reasonable that people should have made such a big thing of it earlier on. . . . (5) Um, they all, everyone pretty well has paid lip service to refutation. (6) It is interesting to notice the strat., the different strategies that people, er, have used. (7) Um, since Norton spoke such a lot, it is a pity he is not here. (8) It's, I would like to draw attention to his, which is very clearly to say "leave me alone, I am doing very well in my own small corner"—you know. (9) "Go and die in your own." [laughter] (10) Leave me alone I, although he says that everybody has a duty to be an intellectual imperialist, he is not trying to produce, um, larger, more ambitious models which are, of course, much easier to, to, er, refute, er, than the less ambig., ambitious ones. . . . (11) Now the good guys are the ones who *are* leaving hostages to fortune, who really *are* laying themselves open to being knocked down in all possible ways. (12) The good guys are the people who are putting up the biggest possible theory that they can imagine. (13) And, um, hoping that, um, it won't be knocked down too quickly. . . . (14) Among these people I would put Squire, um, Chester—I apologise if I have missed anybody else out, I can't remember all the things that have happened in the, in this meeting. (15) But I can, of course, remember what I said, and I am one of the good guys. [laughter] (Young, transcript, Tegd2–4)

In this passage the speaker, Young, fashions an account of his own and other scientists' theories in terms of whether they can be tested, presumably by means of empirical evidence. The passage starts by characterising the evaluation of testability as a game in which the goal is to establish that the player's own theory is refutable, and therefore reputable (I1–2). He then claims that some earlier speakers used a variety of strategies to reduce the possibility that their theories will be undermined through testing (I5). In sentence I7 he singles out Norton for particular comment.

Young criticises Norton for using double standards: on the one hand, Norton advocates an intellectual imperialism, yet at the same time he researches a very delimited area of psychology, using small-scale, unambitious theories (I8–10). These sorts of theories are not, Young claims, so open to refutation as more ambitious models (I10). Although Young stresses that Norton is using testability in a strategic fashion (I6–7), and that testability is not well understood (I3), he does not maintain that it is irrelevant as a constraint on social psychologists' acts of theory choice. He states that it is quite reasonable that people should have emphasised it earlier in the conference (I4). This enables him to use the notion of testability himself, later in the passage, to establish that his own and some similar positions are "reputable"; that they are the "good guys" (I11–13) and, by implication, that their professional actions follow from proper conformity to the rules governing scientific theory choice.

If we analyse this speech in terms of the accounting systems it draws upon, we can see that Young characterises his opponent's theory using the contingent repertoire. The criterion of testability in Norton's case is said to be used "strategically" (I6); it is depicted as being inconsistently invoked in support of Norton's theory at the expense of others'. In contrast, Young characterises his own theory using the empiricist repertoire. In this case the criterion is not presented as open to strategic interpretation, but as an effective constraint on the speaker's actions (I12–13). The action of "refutation" in this case is removed from the speaker's sphere of social action; all he can do is "hope" that his theory will not be undermined by the evidence (I13). As a result of Young's interpretative work, the criterion of testability appears to ensure that his theory is a "hostage to fortune" (I11) and that it will be rejected or retained by virtue of the experimental data alone. This kind of asymmetry is a recurrent feature of participants' accounts of theory choice in the conference data (Potter, 1984). It shows that speakers are able to characterise criteria *both* as impersonal constraints on scientific development *and* as socially contingent devices. Which version they use depends on the specific interactional context.

DISCUSSION: VARIABILITY, RELIABILITY, AND INTERVENTION

Before going on to outline some implications for interviewing practice and analysis, we will briefly summarise the points we have made so far. We have suggested that variability in accounting for various kinds of scientific activity is a pervasive and significant feature of scientists' discourse. This variability is such that *when taken together* these accounts cannot be read as a literal depiction of social action or belief in a particular scientific field. Furthermore, it is not possible to deal with this variability as if it were merely a *technical* difficulty for the analyst. For there are no unproblematic means for separating those accounts that are literal descriptions from those that are not.

We illustrated some of the problems that arise with the two standard ways of dealing with the issue of variability: the elimination of inconsistencies through further interactions in the interview and the use of supposedly more direct records of scientific action. In the first case we noted that there is no guarantee that further interaction will resolve inconsistencies. In fact *new* inconsistencies frequently arise when the interviewer uses this strategy. Moreover, even if the interviewer does succeed in producing an apparently unproblematic response, this may be a result of the respondent's flexible use of interpretative resources rather than the achievement of a literal description. With regard to the second technique, we noted that the data obtained from more direct indicators of scientific activity was subject to the same pervasive variability as interview material itself. Again, no satisfactory criterion could be found for separating those accounts that are "honest and literal" from those that are "rhetorical or false."

We proposed that this variability could be made more intelligible by viewing spoken accounts and records as the product of participants' situated interpretative practices. Variability can thus be viewed as a product of the way actions and beliefs are flexibly characterised in terms of different accounting systems in differing interpretative contexts. For instance, we saw how "theory choice" could be flexibly represented in terms of either an empiricist or a contingent system. When participants use the empiricist repertoire, they make adoption of a given theory appear unavoidable and are thereby able to explain or justify their own current theoretical commitments or the commitments of those with whom they agree. But in many interpretative situations, speakers are required to make certain acts of theory choice appear contingent rather than inevitable; for instance, when they are questioning the support for a theory other than their own. This kind of context-dependent flexibility in the way that action may be represented is a characteristic feature of natural language use (Heritage, 1978), but it is particularly evident when actions and beliefs are characterised in terms of such broad, stereotypical accounting systems as those discussed above: namely, the contingent and empiricist repertoires and the standard utility account.

We have placed great emphasis on the "occasioned" nature of scientists' accounts. Whether they occur in interviews, in conferences, or in scientific texts of various kinds, in every case accounts can only be properly understood in relation to the specific interactional and discursive occasion. When accounts are thus analysed in functional terms, as *doing* certain things, as devised in accordance with specific interpretative contexts, rather than just *stating* or *describing*, it is possible to document regularities in the usage of various scientific accounting systems. As we have illustrated above, different repertoires are suitable for different social situations. Analytical confusion and inconsistency arise when the specific contexts and functions of discourse are ignored and when certain of participants' statements are selected as literal accounts of action and belief. Accounts of all kinds must be understood as the products of participants' contextualised interpretative practices. Thus, for analytic purposes we cannot treat any subset of them as unproblematic and transparent windows onto the social or natural world.

This perspective on scientific discourse has some important implications for the conduct and analysis of interviews. Let us look first at the issue of reliability. Although it is, of course, customary to distinguish reliability from validity, for the practical purposes of interview analysis a consistent account derived from one or more interviews is usually taken as strong evidence for the existence of a corresponding set of actions or beliefs. The very coherence of the discourse is taken as a warrant for the social reality that it appears to reveal. It has, therefore, been traditional practice in the social sciences to try to conduct interviews in a way that minimises inconsistencies. However, we view consistency rather differently, that is, as merely indicating that the respondent is drawing on a limited number of incompatible accounting systems in answering questions. Thus, we have come to regard interviews that contain an internally consistent set of responses as uninformative because such interviews tell us little about the full range of interpretative practices that participants use to construct social meanings. For instance, one of us recently witnessed the construction of part of an interview schedule. There was concern over whether the response "sometimes" as well as "yes," "no," and "don't know" should be allowed respondents answering the question "Do you believe in God?" The researchers decided that "yes," "no," and "don't know" were sensible replies, but that "sometimes" should be omitted. The argument used was that the response "I believe in God sometimes, but not always" was inherently inconsistent and not open to systematic analysis. Thus, the consistency of participants' beliefs was presupposed in the research instrument itself. What these researchers treated as a procedure for ensuring correct and interpretable responses appears to us merely to be a way of excluding certain significant parts of interviewees' discourse from the interview.

When variable responses do occur in interview transcripts, we can analyse them in several different ways. We can, for example, look for structural regularities in the organisation of accounts. For instance, it has been observed that there is a recurrent asymmetry in scientists' accounts of "correct scientific belief" as opposed to "false scientific belief" (Mulkay and Gilbert, 1982a). Second, we can seek to distinguish alternative interpretative repertoires, such as the empiricist and contingent repertoires mentioned above. Third, it may be possible to demonstrate that participants give primacy to certain kinds of account in specific contexts or to certain repertoires when accomplishing certain kinds of interpretative outcomes, such as jokes, justifications, or utility accounts. For example, the empiricist repertoire is generally preferred to the contingent in formal contexts such as research papers (Gilbert and Mulkay, 1980, 1984) while the contingent repertoire tends to be primary in scientific jokes (Mulkay and Gilbert, 1982b). Furthermore, those instances where inconsistencies between accounting systems become apparent to participants are analytically very interesting. They allow us to explicate the devices that participants use to resolve inconsistency and reproduce coherent and unproblematic accounts of their social world for particular interactional situations, despite the potential wide variety of such situations and despite the variety of available repertoires and accounting systems (Gilbert and Mulkay, 1984).

In relatively open-ended interviews, the researcher cannot easily constrain participants' responses. However, stability and consistency may also be produced in the analysis of accounts. An analyst expecting consistency, and not looking for significant variability, may simply categorise together theoretically interesting utterances. We would expect that this would be most likely to occur when the analyst is using broad, relatively undiscriminating categories, such as "power" (Kress and Fowler, 1979) or "role" (Gilbert, 1980), which can encompass wide variations in empirical material and thereby obscure important varieties of participant interpretation.

One of the ways in which we have approached this central analytic problem has been to adopt a particularly "fine-grain" approach to analysis. A prerequisite for this is a complete, verbatim transcript of good quality. Features such as hesitations or corrections, which are often edited out as irrelevant noise, are in fact frequently indicative of the structured properties of the discourse. The common practice of only transcribing those utterances that *appear* to be significant to the analyst when she listens to the tape simply to "hear what is said," means that the research conclusions become heavily dependent on the *unacknowledged* interpretative practice of the analyst. With a complete transcript, and by careful rereading of whole collections of participants' statements on given topics, utterances can be seen in their context of occurrence rather than selectively extracted to appear as documents of scientific actions and beliefs beyond the text.

Furthermore, participants frequently move between different accounting systems very quickly, sometimes from one to another and back within the course of a particular sentence, and such important features of discourse are easily missed by broader forms of analysis. Scientists are continually engaged in constructing orderly and unproblematic versions of their own and other's actions in their discourse. Their accounts must be examined in detail to reveal these subtle processes of construction. However, the issue of exactly how detailed such analysis must be has not yet been resolved. The level of analysis is clearly dependent in part upon its specific objectives; nevertheless, we follow Labov and Fanshel (1977) in suggesting that it will be fruitful to attempt considerably more detailed work than has been carried out up to the present time.

A further analytic implication of the present approach to discourse is that it is important to look at the organisation of accounting in a variety of social contexts. As we have mentioned, accounting systems tend to be deployed differentially from one social context to another. For instance, the standard utility account is rarely qualified or undermined in the formal research literature, whereas the contingent repertoire is hardly ever directly used in that literature. Thus, it is important to examine a vairety of discursive products, both formal and informal, in order properly to elucidate the organisation of scientific accounting. Although interviews on their own will not fully elucidate this organisation, they provide a useful supplement to the formal literature of science, with its narrowly constrained procedures for making scientific activity and belief accountable, and to the direct transcription of informal interaction, which for practical reasons is inevitably very incomplete in its coverage of the social life of science.

The crucial feature of our approach, then, is that we are not using interviews, or any other source of data, to build up an accurate picture of the actions and beliefs of participants in specific domains of social life. Rather, we are using interviews as a technique for generating interpretative work on the part of participants, with the aim of identifying the kinds of interpretative repertoires and interpretative methods used by participants and with the goal of understanding how their interpretative practices vary in accordance with changes in interactional context. Although we have abandoned the traditional assumption that we can infer from interview talk what actully happens in the social realm under investigation, we are nevertheless continuing to assume that we can, in a more restricted sense, generalise from interviews to naturally occurring situations. For we are assuming that the interactional and interpretative work occurring in interviews resembles to some degree that which takes place outside interviews.

In principle, we have to accept that this assumption may be quite unfounded or that the resemblance between participants' accounting practices in these two kinds of context may be so slight as to prevent any useful comparison. However, our studies so far suggest that the interview situation is not culturally unique and that there are many parallels and close similarities in participants' accounts obtained from natural and "artificial" situations. In the short run, there is no doubt that naturally occurring data must have analytical precedence. We are, after all, ultimately interested in how scientists, or other actors, construct their own social worlds, rather than how they interact with social psychologists and sociologists. Thus, naturally occurring data must provide the initial touchstone against which to judge the results of the analysis of interview material. But, in the long run, the very artificiality of interviews may be their main advantage and provide their best justification. For once the analyst abandons the traditional objective of using interviews to get at "the truth"; she is freed from the customary procedure of "minimal intervention." Once the analyst has come to use the interview as a way of exploring participants' variable interpretative practices, there is every reason for her to engage actively in the interview so as to extend the range of interpretative work carried out there.

In other words, in the long run, interviews can be seen as providing perhaps the only opportunity available to the analyst for putting her conclusions to the test. This can be done by attempting to create interpretative contexts within the interview in such a way that the connections between participants' accounting practices and variations in interpretative context can be constructively explored. Thus, from the research perspective that we have advocated above, we may expect research interviews within any specific area of analysis to become increasingly interventionist. But this would not be in the traditional sense of greater use of precoded questions and quantification of responses from "representative" samples. Rather, interviews would be used in an informed manner to generate a partly predicted, interpretative diversity in a way that allows for participants' interpretative creativity.

REFERENCES

Bogdan, R., and Taylor, S. J. (1975). *Introduction to Qualitative Research Methods.* New York: Wiley.

Edge, D. (1979). Quantitative measures of communication in science: A critical review. *History of Science, 17,* 102–134.

Gilbert, G. N. (1980). Being interviewed: A role analysis. *Social Science Information, 19,* 227–236.

Gilbert, G. N., and Mulkay, M. (1980). Contexts of scientific discourse: Social accounting in experimental papers. In K. D. Knorr, R. Krohn and R. Whitley (Eds.), *The Social Process of Scientific Investigation.* Dordrecht: Reidel.

Gilbert, G. N., and Mulkay, M. (1982). Warranting scientific belief. *Social Studies of Science, 12,* 283–408.

Gilbert, G. N., and Mulkay, M. (1984). *Opening Pandora's Box: A Sociological Analysis of Scientists' Discourse.* Cambridge: Cambridge University Press.

Hagstrom, W. O. (1965). *The Scientific Community.* New York: Basic Books.

Heritage, J. (1978). Aspects of the flexibilities of natural language use. *Sociology, 12,* 79–105.

Kuhn, T. S. (1977). *The Essential Tension.* Chicago: University of Chicago Press.

Kress, G. and Fowler, R. (1979). Interviews. In R. Fowler, B. Hodge, G. Kress, and T. Trew (Eds.), *Language and Control.* London: Routledge.

Labov, W. and Fanshel, D. (1977). *Therapeutic Discourse: Psychotherapy as Conversation.* London: Academic Press.

Mackenzie, D., and Barnes, B. (1979). Scientific judgment: The biometry-Mendelism controversy. In B. Barnes and S. Shapin (Eds.), *Natural Order.* London and Beverly Hills, Calif.: Sage.

Merton, R. K., Fiske, M. and Kendall, P. L. (1956). *The Focussed Interview: A Manual of Problems and Procedures.* New York: Free Press.

Mitroff, I. I. (1974). *The Subjective Side of Science.* Amsterdam: Elsevier.

Mulkay, M. (1979). *Science and the Sociology of Knowledge.* London: Allen and Unwin.

Mulkay, M. (1980). The sociology of science in the West. *Current Sociology, 28,* 1–184.

Mulkay, M., and Gilbert, G. N. (1982a). Accounting for error. *Sociology, 16,* 165–183.

Mulkay, M., and Gilbert, G. N. (1982b). Joking apart. *Social Studies of Science, 12,* 585–615.

Mulkay, M., and Gilbert, G. N. (1983). Scientists' theory talk. *Canadian Journal of Sociology, 8,* 179–197.

Mulkay, M., and Gilbert, G. N. (1985). Opening Pandora's box: A new approach to the sociological analysis of theory choice. In R. A. Jones and H. Kuklick (Eds.), *Knowledge and Society: Studies in the Sociology of Culture Past and Present* (Vol. 5).

Mulkay, M., Potter, J. and Yearley, S. (1983). Why an analysis of scientific discourse needed. In K. D. Knorr-Cetina and M. Mulkay (Eds.), *Science Observed: Perspectives on the Social Study of Science.* London and Beverly Hills, Calif.: Sage.

Popper, K. (1959). *The Logic of Scientific Discovery.* London: Hutchinson.

Potter, J. (1981). The development of social psychology: Consensus, theory and methodology in the British Journal of Social and Clinical Psychology. *British Journal of Social Psychology, 20,* 249–258.

Potter, J. (1982). Nothing so practical as a good theory: The problematic application of social psychology. In P. Stringer (Ed.), *Confronting Social Issues: Applications of Social Psychology* (Vol. 1). London: Academic Press.

Potter, J. (1984). Testability, Flexibility: Kuhnian values in scientists' discourse concerning theory choice, *Philosophy of the Social Sciences, 14,* 303–330

Potter, J., and Mulkay, M. (1982). Making theory useful: Utility accounting in social psychologists' discourse. *Fundamenta Scientiae, 3/4,* 259–278.

Potter, J., Stringer, P., and Wetherell, M. (1984). *Social Texts and Context: Literature and Social Psychology.* London: Routledge.

Quine, W. V. O., and Ullian, J. S. (1970). *The Web of Belief.* New York: Random House.

Smith, D. (1978). K is mentally ill: The anatomy of a factual account. *Sociology, 12,* 23–55.

Woolgar, S. (1980). Discovery: Logic and sequence in a scientific text. In K. D. Knorr, R. Krohn, and R. Whitley (Eds.), *The Social Process of Scientific Development.* Dordrecht: Reidel.

Yearley, S. (1981). Textual persuasion: The role of social accounting in the construction of scientific arguments. *Philosophy of the Social Sciences, 11,* 409–438.

Zuckerman, H. (1972). Interviewing an ultra-elite. *The Public Opinion Quarterly, 36,* 159–175.

Index